NO-MAN'S LANDS

Also by Scott Huler

Defining the Wind: The Beaufort Scale, and How a Nineteenth-Century Admiral Turned Science into Poetry

On Being Brown: What It Means to Be a Cleveland Browns Fan— Essays and Interviews

A Little Bit Sideways: One Week Inside a NASCAR Winston Cup Race Team

From Worst to First: Behind the Scenes of Continental's Remarkable Comeback (with Gordon Bethune)

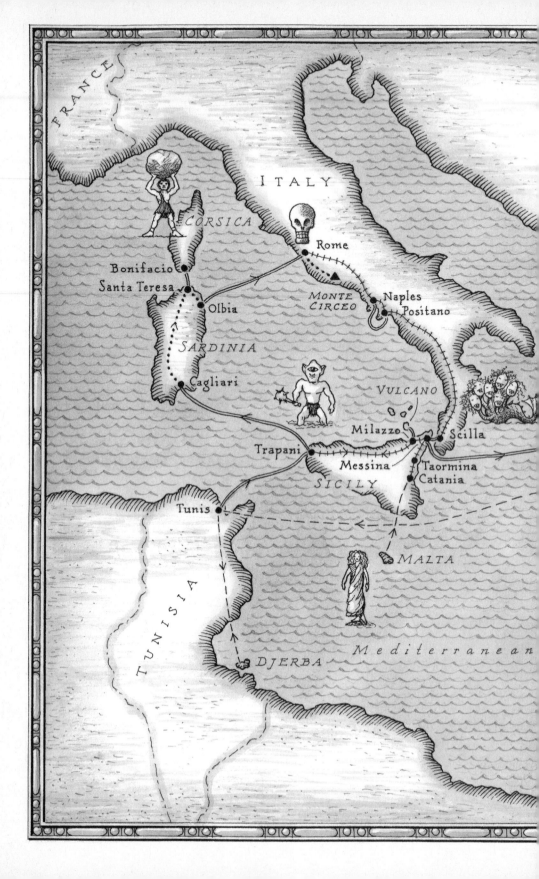

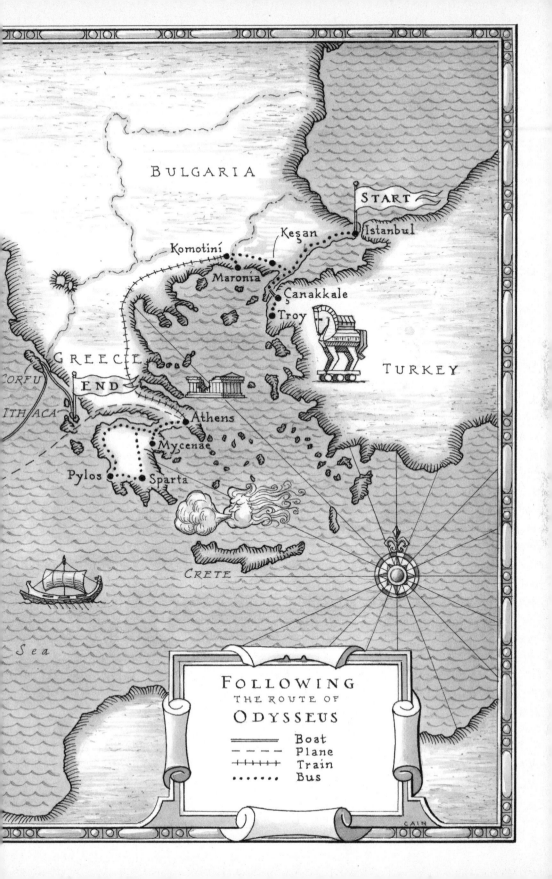

BULGARIA

START

Keşan   Istanbul

Komotiní

Maronia

Çanakkale

Troy

GREECE

END   TURKEY

CORFU

ITHACA

Athens

Mycenae

Pylos   Sparta

CRETE

Sea

FOLLOWING
THE ROUTE OF
ODYSSEUS

———— Boat
– – – Plane
+++++ Train
•••••• Bus

CAIN

One Man's Odyssey Through
THE ODYSSEY

SCOTT HULER

NO-MAN'S LANDS

CROWN PUBLISHERS
NEW YORK

Grateful acknowledgment is made to the following for permission to reprint previously
published material:

W.W. Norton & Company, Inc.: Excerpt from *The Odyssey: A New Verse Translation,*
translated by Albert Cook, copyright © 1967 by Albert Cook. Reprinted by permission of
W.W. Norton & Company, Inc.

Ennis Rees: Excerpts from *The Odyssey of Homer,* translated by Ennis Rees (originally
published by Random House, Inc., 1960). Reprinted by permission of Ennis Rees.

Library of Congress Cataloging-in-Publication Data

Huler, Scott.
  No-man's lands : one man's odyssey through *The Odyssey* / Scott Huler. — 1st ed.
    p. cm.
  Includes bibliographical references.
  1. Homer. Odyssey.   2. Odysseus (Greek mythology)—Travel.   3. Literary
landmarks—Mediterranean Region.   4. Literary landmarks—Greece.
5. Mediterranean Region—Description and travel.   6. Greece—Description
and travel.   I. Title.

  PA4167.A2H85 2007
  883'.01—dc22

2007033202

ISBN 978-1-4000-8282-7

Printed in the United States of America

Images on pages vi and vii, and map of Raleigh, North Carolina, on page 252, are used
courtesy of the author.

DESIGN BY ELINA D. NUDELMAN
MAP BY DAVID CAIN

10 9 8 7 6 5 4 3 2 1

First Edition

For my mother, Rachel

The grand object of traveling is to see the shores of the Mediterranean. . . . All our religion, almost all our law, almost all our arts, almost all that sets us above savages, has come to us from the shores of the Mediterranean.

—Samuel Johnson

Everyone gets everything he wants. I wanted a mission. And for my sins they gave me one.

—Captain Willard, *Apocalypse Now*

Contents

CONTENTS

NO-MAN'S LANDS

Introduction

A Long Story

Of that versatile man, O Muse, tell me the story, how he wandered both long and far after sacking the city of holy Troy. Many were the towns he saw and many the men whose minds he knew, and many were the woes his stout heart suffered at sea as he fought to return alive with living comrades. Them he could not save, though much he longed to, for through their own thoughtless greed they died—blind fools who slaughtered the Sun's own cattle, Hyperion's herd, for food, and so by him were kept from returning. Of all these things, O goddess, daughter of Zeus, beginning wherever you wish, tell even us.

—*The Odyssey*, Book I

THINGS GO WRONG, plans fail, fate makes sport of our best intentions. We say one thing and do another; nothing turns out as we expect. It's an unpredictable life, and we comfort ourselves by blaming greater powers: "If you want to make God laugh," we say, "tell him your plans," and most modern Westerners can be grateful to at least have only the one God whose laughter concerns us. Think, though, of the ancient Greeks. The Greeks had an entire pantheon of gods; the Greeks had gods like we have siblings, cousins, in-laws—and just as busy, just as nosy, too. So the ancient Greeks knew their plans could elicit laughter—and expect trouble—from not just one source but a dozen. That was the gods' favorite thing, interfering with people's plans. Or more accurately, helping people interfere with their own.

It still is, I think. So not long ago, when I briefly took to making plans, I should have been listening for that laughter. You could say I went looking for it. It began, after all, with a public promise—which the gods made sure I broke, almost instantly. Afterward came a headlong journey, filled with discovery, wonder, and adventure, which seems like their kind of joke, too—at least, they've been using it for a while. In the end, of course, it's a long story. You can start almost anywhere.

So start with James Joyce.

ON JUNE 15, 2001, I swore, out loud and on the radio, that I would never, ever read *Ulysses*.

Joyce's *Ulysses* is regularly crowned the most important novel of the twentieth century. Nearly eight hundred pages long, filled with thousand-word stream-of-consciousness run-on sentences, classical references, and asides in various languages, *Ulysses* (the Romanized name, of course, of the Greek hero Odysseus) is considered the birth of modern literature. A modern retelling of the ten years of adventure described in *The Odyssey* of Homer, *Ulysses* takes place all on one day—June 16, 1904, in Dublin. Advertising salesman Leopold Bloom stands in for Odysseus, and the book's episodes have their origins in Homer: There's a Cyclops episode and a Sirens episode and much more, all complex and modern and hard to follow. Friends and experts had been pressing *Ulysses* on me for decades, but despite countless frustrating attempts I had never been able to get very far in it.

Then came the early summer of 2001, which seemed to bring an *Odyssey* onslaught. The movie *O Brother, Where Art Thou?* the Coen Brothers' free retelling of the *Odyssey* story, came out on DVD. *Cold Mountain,* the Charles Frazier novel of a reluctant soldier making his adventurous way home from a horrific war, sat on every night table and was in development as a film. When my oldest friend asked me to read something at his wedding, I was almost unsurprised when another friend recommended "Ithaca," a lovely reconsideration of the wanderings of Odysseus by poet Constantine Cavafy.

And, most especially, Bloomsday approached. Among its devotees *Ulysses* has become less a book than something of a cult, and the feast day for that cult is June 16, Bloomsday. All over the world on that day people read *Ulysses* aloud, celebrate it in drama and song, and, above all, get drunk. In Dublin, Mecca for *Ulysses* cultists, thousands of people gather to enact scenes from the book, engage in panel discussions about the book's opacities, and actually retrace the steps of the book's characters. This outpouring of obsession toward a book I found unreadable drove me mad. After all, I'm a writer—I'm a literary guy. And I believe this obsession makes literary guys look like pseudointellectual nitwits. I wanted to distance myself from those nitwits. So in June 2001 I read a brief essay on the radio announcing that after decades of attempts I was officially declaring Joyce's book not worth the trouble: I was using that year's Bloomsday celebration to forever renounce *Ulysses*. The book ends with Molly Bloom's forever-quoted benedictory, "yes I said yes I will Yes." So on the day its adherents worshipfully followed the footsteps of its fictional characters, I pledged to finally consign the book to my shelf unread, echoing its conclusion: "no I said no I won't No."

I CAN'T SWEAR it was the work of the gods, but I was a liar inside a month.

Someone who heard my essay convinced Matthew, a bookstore manager well read in Joyciana, to lead a *Ulysses* reading group. And because I had written the scornful essay that got the group started, they invited me to join. I had just publicly sworn never to read *Ulysses* as long as I lived; doing exactly the opposite made for a pleasing irony. I joined up. Matthew led us through complex schema and thickets of commentary, and over four months alternated between coaxing and dragging us through *Ulysses*. Occasionally, with Matthew's help, I was thrilled by a pun in two languages, a sly classical reference; more often I complained. Challenged and interested, I still rarely doubted the good sense of my original inclination to give the book up.

And for me, most important was that the farther we moved along, the less Joyce commanded my attention. Instead, I thought more and more about the Homeric tales behind it all. I grew interested in *The Odyssey* itself.

I couldn't help thinking: What gives? Everywhere you turn, *The Odyssey*—and it's not like it's something new. For three thousand years, we've been telling each other the same story. Whether it's Joyce's book or Tennyson's poems, a symphony by Max Bruch or heavy metal by Symphony X, pictures by Matisse or Chagall, we're still finding new ways to tell each other the episodes from that old story. I wondered why.

These are some of the best-known episodes in the world: Odysseus defeats the Cyclops; Odysseus agonizes over the terrible decision between Scylla and Charybdis; Odysseus escapes the Sirens, who lured unwary sailors onto the rocks. I noticed, though, that I couldn't quite remember, for example, how the Sirens lured those unwary sailors. In fact, I couldn't remember a lot. I knew Odysseus poked out the eye of the Cyclops, but I couldn't say how that fit into the larger picture. Scylla and Charybdis was a hard choice, but between what, and regarding why, I was in the dark. I hadn't read *The Odyssey* for years, but even so I seemed to have forgotten a great deal.

My wife noticed my increasing interest in the story, and she one day saw at a flea market a little book with a jacket all of blue: a simply drawn sea, and on it, alone, a tiny yellow boat. *The Odyssey of Homer,* in a 1960 translation by one Ennis Rees, in a nice handbook size. It found a place on my night table, and once our reading group was done with *Ulysses,* I opened *The Odyssey* to reread it.

I COULDN'T REREAD IT—which leads to a more embarrassing reversal, though on a more intimate scale. After not very many pages and some honest consideration, I had to acknowledge that the reason I remembered so few specifics about *The Odyssey* was that I had never read it at all. Unfortunately, I had been brashly claiming to have done so my entire adult life.

I remember the little red version of the book I got in ninth-grade English, and I remember a color lithograph it contained of a bearded guy on a raft in a stormy sea. Seeing it on my reading list, my mother had assured me: "If you can get past the language, it really is just the greatest adventure story." The story of Odysseus, hero of the Trojan War, making his ten-year journey home from the Greek victory at Troy, *The Odyssey,* by the blind poet Homer, was one of the epic poems that constitute the foundation of Western civilization. Shipwrecks, storms, monsters, witches, pretty girls, gods and goddesses, archery, treasure, sword fights—all this awaited if I could "get past the language."

No chance. Homer's classical rhythms resisted me in adolescence as resolutely as Joyce's tortured syntax did in adulthood. All I remember now from that English class is a movie we saw of part of *The Odyssey*, in which a man wanders among stone walls, orating the story of Odysseus and the Cyclops. Odysseus and his men, trapped in a cave by the giant Cyclops, get the Cyclops drunk and blind him, then slip past him by hanging on to the bellies of his sheep as they exit the cave. Describing it, the actor brayed like John Gielgud: "My raaam," he moaned as the Cyclops, "my faaavorite raaam," and as he stood there swaying my momentary flicker of interest—a monster! A big stick in his eye! A daring escape!—vanished beneath the tide of well-meaning dramatization meant to impress ninth-graders.

We cheated on quizzes and dawdled through class, wrote themes and moved on to whatever was next, and that was my junior high school *Odyssey* experience. A color lithograph, a tiresome movie, a book I didn't read. And though one collegiate summer I filled a hole in my education and read *The Iliad,* Homer's other masterpiece, I never returned to *The Odyssey*. It was checked off that giant list of books you are supposed to have read, and I never went back.

Which is too bad, because from somewhere, elements of *The Odyssey* definitely did become part of my life. Its content creeps into our minds through back channels, like the symphonies we learn by snatches as background music in Bugs Bunny cartoons: half-understood college lectures; popular references to the danger of "siren songs" or being "between Scylla and Charybdis"; hints of *The Odyssey* in poetry and popular song. *The Odyssey* is a classic—it's one of those books whose stories we all sort of know, from somewhere, but in most cases don't really know from anywhere.

That vague understanding can be dangerous. I told people I had read *The Odyssey*. I deeply believed I had read *The Odyssey*. I have specific memories, in post-college years, of pontificating about the admiration I had developed for Odysseus; about Athena, the goddess of wisdom who is his special protector, and how one might please her; about traveling, about home, about challenge.

Some of what I said actually made sense. For example, I compared Odysseus to other protagonists in Greek myths and plays. At least one terrible thing happens to almost all of them: Agamemnon kills his own daughter and is killed by his faithless wife; Oedipus kills his father, sleeps with his mother, pokes his eyes out; Hercules goes mad and kills his own wife and children. Theseus causes his father's suicide when he forgets to signal his own safety; Perseus kills his grandfather with a discus; Atreus invites his brother Thyestes to dinner—and feeds Thyestes his own children. That's hardly the worst of it—consider Medea: to help her lover Jason, Medea kills and dismembers her own brother and boils Jason's uncle alive; when Jason then decides—can you blame him?—to marry someone else, Medea kills Jason's bride, Jason's father, and her and Jason's own two children.

Odysseus, on the other hand, manages to win the decade-long Trojan War (the famous Trojan Horse is his idea). Then, overcoming unimaginable difficulties on his way home, he eventually returns to find his only son healthy and grown, his wife faithful and safe, his father overjoyed. According to at least one version of events, Odysseus lives happily ever after.

That Cyclops episode, probably his most well-known adventure, represents my conception of him perfectly. He can't match the giant bad guy physically, so he outwits him—he calls himself "No-Man," so when the fighting starts and the Cyclops shouts that "No-Man is killing me," his neighbors figure he doesn't need their help. The Cyclops, like most of Odysseus's enemies, ends up claiming he was cheated. Odysseus wins, but not because he's biggest; he's just the sneakiest.

Baseball fans might compare Achilles, the vain, arrogant hero of *The Iliad,* with someone like Ted Williams: undeniably great, but not necessarily good for the team or pleasant to be around; Agamemnon might be Ty Cobb, vicious and dangerous but hard to beat; and Menelaus something like Mickey Mantle: great and useful but something of a blowhard. Odysseus would be Pete Rose: the sneaky little bastard who pulls off some kind of trick that you think is beneath contempt, but carries the day. The guy you call a liar and a cheat—unless he's on your team. Then he's just a guy who does what it takes to win. I began to think—and more than once said out loud—that a good way to live your life was to live it as much like Odysseus as possible. I said it often enough that I began to consider it one of my life's principles.

Thus, as we plowed through *Ulysses,* I was embarrassed to notice that I didn't have more than a vague notion of exactly how Odysseus had lived his life. And then, on my night table, that gift from my wife: *The Odyssey,* and the chance to really read it. Leave it to your wife to make you finally find out whether you really believe what you always say you believe.

IT'S ENOUGH TO MAKE YOU BELIEVE in the gods. Sure, *The Odyssey* is still a little long, still a little dense, and the epic poetic language does take some getting used to. Nonetheless I read it—on my own—and by the time I finished I felt the book had sought me out, that my need for *The Odyssey* had manifested itself and brought the book to me— "with the help of some god," as characters in Homer commonly say of remarkable occurrences. I had ignored it in the ninth grade and in my twenties blindly claimed to adopt its hero as my model. But when in my forties I finally actually read it, *The Odyssey* turned out to be every-thing I had ignorantly imagined it might be.

First, as my mother promised all those years ago, it's a great story. But there's a lot more, too: those famous stories we all half know turn out to constitute rather a small portion of the whole—about four chapter-length books out of twenty-four total. And the remainder, the parts of *The Odyssey* nobody talks much about—the wanderings of Odysseus's son, Telemachus; the struggles of Odysseus's clever wife, Penelope; the challenges that await Odysseus when he finally returns home—have a resonance I never imagined. A funny thing about the difference between fourteen years old and forty-four: This time *The Odyssey* spoke to me. This time I got the language. This time I couldn't let it go.

Episodes to which I had been referring for decades suddenly made sense—and stories whose fatuous morals I thought I knew (Rely on your wits, not brute strength! Choose carefully among difficult alter-natives! Don't seek to know more than is good for you!) turned out to have unexpected depth and complexity. Moreover, Odysseus spends a lot of time—a *lot* of time—in this book sleeping with goddesses.

This book got my interest. This was a book worth more than a simple reading. This was a book, at long last, worth the return. I read it again, then again. I came to see the passage of Odysseus from Troy to Ithaca as a metaphor, a series of adventures in which Odysseus demonstrates what he needs to learn—or unlearn—to live his life. *The Odyssey* became the book I carried around, dipping into in spare moments—while the car got an oil change; in the waiting room for the eye doctor; for a few minutes before sleep. I had a handbook: The oldest lessons in the world were still the lessons I needed to learn—and they were still waiting for me in *The Odyssey*. During those post-college years when I claimed Odysseus as my role model, I had been right. I hadn't known what I was talking about, but I had been right.

So Joyce's impossible *Ulysses* had done me a favor: Homer wrote down the Odyssey nearly three thousand years ago, and we've been constantly retelling it ever since, but I had still managed to miss it. Only by squaring off opposite *Ulysses* did I stumble my way back to the original, central story. It was *The Odyssey,* not *Ulysses,* that had something for me.

STILL, I DID PILFER one important idea from the *Ulysses* community: pilgrimage. Like opera buffs or *Star Wars* fans at a premiere, members of an entire subculture find in *Ulysses* a binding element for their lives. Its stories become central to them, known by heart and repeated, studied, appreciated. *Ulysses* serves as a lodestone text to which they return time and again for understanding.

And *Ulysses* fans return to more than just their book. Driven by obsession, they return, year after year, to Dublin itself, approaching Dublin as pilgrims, visiting its sites as shrines—going where Bloom went to see what Bloom saw, to learn what Bloom learned. Visiting the sites of the stories in *Ulysses* brings those stories home, gives them life and substance beyond the book. Through their travel these pilgrims thus go beyond merely reading *Ulysses*—in this small way they live it, and by connecting it physically to their world make it somehow even more their own.

Thousands of them do this every year.

Somewhere deep inside my brain, this started a train of thought. I wondered: Why don't I do the same? As I read and reread *The Odyssey*, as I returned to certain passages over and over, gleaning more each time, the book began to genuinely occupy the central metaphorical position in my life I had once claimed it did. So I thought: Why shouldn't I visit my sacred sites as the Joyceans do theirs? Whom would I meet? What would I find? Why don't I go to Troy, where Odysseus finished the Trojan War, and make my way to Ithaca, the western Greek island Odysseus called home?

I wanted to go where Odysseus went, to learn what Odysseus learned.

THE MORE I THOUGHT ABOUT IT the more sense it made. For one thing, the timing was right. Odysseus leaves for the Trojan War when he's a young father. He stays at Troy for a decade fighting, and after the war spends another decade making his way home, arriving presumably in his midforties. That's when *The Odyssey* is set—Odysseus tells the adventure stories largely in flashback. That is, at the time of the action of *The Odyssey*, Odysseus is my age.

Since we were the same age, I found comparison natural. Here's Odysseus at around forty-four: He has a grown son. He has won the greatest war of all time. Then, overcoming unimaginable perils, he has traveled not only the known world but the unknown, outfoxing monsters and bedding goddesses, making his way home to defeat a palace full of murderous rivals, reestablishing command of his island kingdom. Not bad. Okay, here's me: I had paid off my student loans. I had been employed significantly more than I had not. I had a failed marriage, though prospects for the second one looked pretty good. I knew that pouring gas in the carburetor will sometimes get a balky lawn mower to start. I had nursed fourteen years out of a pickup truck. I can hang a ceiling fan, build closet shelves, throw darts well enough to win a wall plaque. Interesting, but looking around me I saw no kingdom;

in the rearview mirror I saw no enraged monsters, vanquished by my hand, screaming for vengeance; in memory, depressingly few goddesses demanded my sexual favors.

Of course, I blame circumstances; my lack of heroic stature is not entirely my fault. After all, I lack heroic milieu. Despite war, global warming, terrorism, and a host of other troubles, for American suburbanites challenge is generally lacking. A big adventure means going camping and not bringing the cell phone; when we talk about challenge, we mean life without cable, a broken air conditioner, going out to get an ink cartridge and having to drive to two stores.

So you can't blame me for wondering: Is that all there is? I mean, worship youth all you want, remain youthful through diet, exercise, surgery, prayer. But whatever you do, by the time you hit your midforties, you're slowing down, and you've got to start approaching your life differently, shortening your batting stroke. Looking in the mirror at that guy hitting Odysseus's age and heading for decline, I had to figure: It's now or never. You want adventure? Time is getting short.

So perhaps my most powerful motive as I considered *The Odyssey* was simple: existential fear. I wasn't ready to be done adventuring, so the idea of retracing the route Odysseus took quickly began to feel inevitable: One last heroic, Joseph Campbell–style adventure to mark the passing of my adventuring years. In fact, Odysseus returns home so exhausted, so sick of war, so weary of travel and excitement that he hopes to never leave home again—a state of mind I couldn't imagine, but that I deeply envied. Wouldn't it be grand to feel so complete, so finished? I aspired to even a tiny piece of Odysseus's weariness, his gladness to be through with adventure, to be home at last. All I needed was a trip all over the known world and beyond.

OR A JOURNEY around the Mediterranean might work. For one thing, after several peripatetic years, my wife, June, and I had returned to our home and were just getting our lives organized; a big trip-sized lacuna could still probably find its way into my schedule. For another, I was no stranger to long journeys. A year abroad in college had taught me the rudiments of unscheduled backpack travel: creativity in sleeping arrangements, reliance on street-vendor food, and a willingness to try to make myself understood in a language unknown to me. Perhaps as a result, a lifetime of semiplanned travel—backpack, floppy hat, hiking boots, and all—has ensued. At forty-four and married, I had to figure that kind of travel, too, was unlikely to remain part of my world much longer.

So one more trip sounded like a grand last hurrah. I was owning my middle age. Instead of chasing secretaries or sports cars, I had found a better rite of passage. My old hero Odysseus and I would have a season together, and after that—well, after that I'd worry about what came next. Moreover, a trip is always a trip: You can choose where to begin, but you can't choose where, when, or how it will end and what you will find on the way. That's probably the moral of *The Odyssey*—as any competent ninth-grader could tell you—but as I pieced together my trip I failed to see it. Maybe I shouldn't have cheated on all those quizzes.

I sketched it out: For several months I'd haunt libraries, finding what I could about the route Odysseus took. In a considered, organized fashion I'd contact classicists, archaeologists, translators. I'd learn a few words of a few languages, make reservations. I'd load up on maps and euros and then, prepared, I'd set out in the wake of Odysseus. I had a plan.

ANOTHER PLAN—only this wasn't a mere claim about a book, this was an entire campaign, so you know what comes next. In this case it took less than a week.

One morning I mulled things over, lying in a pile of laundry on our bed. For how many months should I explore the libraries? People had been speculating on the route of Odysseus for millennia, with no consensus; from the arguments and suggestions, how ought I to choose my destinations? What experts might be able to help me find my way? What time of year ought I to travel the Mediterranean? How much time ought I to spend? What to bring?

Lost in thought, I cogitated until I became aware of a presence in the doorway. June stood there, a small smile on her lips. In her hand a pink plastic stick about the length of a thermometer, held in a towel. A pregnancy test.

"What do you think?" my wife asked me. "Do both of those stripes look pink to you?"

WE MADE A BUNCH OF DECISIONS QUICK. June had supported the trip from the start, and she had no interest in saddling our unborn child with the blame for a change in plans; we never even considered canceling the trip. In fact, impending fatherhood made the journey feel even more important. Still—you can't plan for surprise, and nobody wanted me out wandering the planet when June had our baby. The rank of calendar pages for my adventure, stretching gracefully into the limitless future, suddenly accordioned down. I could still retrace Odysseus's adventures of twenty years.

I just had six months to do it.

Chapter 1

No Greater Claim to Our Credence:

On the Isle of the Nymph Calypso

Now all the others who had managed to escape destruction were safe at home, untroubled by war or the sea. Odysseus alone, full of longing for wife and friends, was kept from returning by that beautiful nymph Calypso, the powerful goddess who hoped to make him her husband. . . . that luckless but clever man Odysseus, who far from his friends, on a lonely island at the great sea's very navel, has long been miserable.

—*The Odyssey*, Book I

I COULD START the tale of my trip at the beginning—telling you how I stuffed my backpack and was dropped at the airport by my wife, still early enough in her pregnancy that she radiated like fresh-baked bread. On a string around my neck I wore not just a charm bearing the image of an owl—Athena's symbol, for luck—but a ring of June's, one that during our courtship she used to "forget" at my house to remind me she wasn't far off. When I told her I planned to wear the Athena charm she suggested adding the ring. I had the support, she smiled, of not just mythological women. She wished me godspeed.

I could tell how I flew to Istanbul and stayed overnight with friends, how the evening before I took my first bus toward Troy, my host explained my upcoming trip to a friend over a late glass of tea on a plaza overlooking the Bosporus. How the friend, before leaving us, wished my host good night, then put his hand on my shoulder, fixing

[13]

me with a gaze: "And you," he said, shaking his head. "You have a long way to go."

I could. But that would be the wrong place to begin. In travel my model was Odysseus, and my goal was simple: to get from Troy to Ithaca, if decidedly by the scenic route. But I came on adventure looking for lessons, and this powerful lesson comes not from Odysseus but from Homer: The tale doesn't always start at the beginning. Homer starts nowhere near the beginning. So as teller of tales I follow Homer, and I start where he started.

The Odyssey begins with a ten-line proem, a prefatory passage invoking the muse and reminding us that the wily Odysseus will have many adventures, eventually arriving home safe but alone. The proem asks the muse to tell the story, "beginning wherever you wish."

The muse takes Homer at his word, beginning the story of Odysseus's return from Troy not by rushing to Troy, where such a journey presumably starts. Instead we go to Ithaca, exactly where Odysseus isn't, and we spend time with Telemachus, Odysseus's son, by now a young man of twenty. We learn about the many troubles Odysseus's long absence has caused Telemachus and his beleaguered mother, Penelope, and we even follow Telemachus as he takes a short trip looking for his missing father. Only after four entire books of such scene setting do we meet Odysseus. Even then, at the outset of Book V, we still don't go to Troy.

We finally join our hero on a tiny island: Ogygia, where he's spent the last seven years as sexual captive to the nymph Calypso. Nice work if you can get it, but Odysseus doesn't want it. That is itself a long story, and Homer makes good use of it—*in medias res,* the Roman poet Horace famously advised, "start in the middle of things," and a heroic adventurer weary of sex with goddesses and desperate for home sure sounds like the middle of something. So Homer starts with Odysseus on Ogygia with Calypso. And to get you to that island, Homer adds another to his list of literary firsts: He directs the world's first helicopter shot.

Book V begins with the gods on Olympus, among whom we learn that the hour of Odysseus's return has finally arrived. Zeus sends Hermes, messenger of the gods, to tell Calypso the news, and the scene reads like the alpine opening of *The Sound of Music*. Hermes dons his famous sandals on the mountaintop, "and from there he swooped to the sea, skimming over the waves. . . ." Then he arrives at the island, and the camera zooms in on Calypso's cave. It's a stunning beginning: breathtaking and cinematic, taking you from the mountaintop realm of the gods to, suddenly, an actual place on the actual planet.

I could ask for no better muse than Homer, so we start as he did. Carried by a smallish aluminum airplane instead of golden sandals, we go zinging above the ocean waves. And if no earthly island currently bears the name Ogygia, still we find somewhere to land.

MALTA IS A YELLOW PLACE. Yellow grit swirls on the roadways and drifts among outcroppings of dusty ancient limestone; the harsh Mediterranean sun glints off weathered yellow blocks of that same limestone in the walls of the buildings that line the steep, stairstep streets of the sixteenth-century capital city, Valletta. And yellow sand radiates beneath cloudless skies along the shore of Ramla Bay, one of Malta's only sandy beaches, though it wasn't the sand that drew me there. Ramla Bay lies directly below the cave identified as the home of Calypso, "the nymph with the beautiful braids," who's keeping Odysseus with her against his will.

Atop a rocky outcropping on the northeastern shore of Gozo, the westernmost of Malta's three inhabited islands, at the end of a dusty asphalt road, I found a concrete pad, the twisted remains of some pipe railing, and what seems to have once been an information kiosk. A sign points toward the cave. A gritty path, steps carved directly into the stone, leads downward to a natural ledge—to the right a lovely view down to the Ramla beach and the sapphire Mediterranean beyond; to the left the mouth of the cave, a triangular cleft about six feet tall in the limestone escarpment.

Homer calls this "the spacious cave where the nymph made her home," describing a forest of cypress and poplar, birds nesting, grapevines twining around the cave mouth—and inside, the beautiful Calypso sings as she paces before her loom. Four fountains sparkle nearby, water tumbling in four different directions; fields of violets and parsley complete the scene. "Even a god might gaze in wonder and delight," Homer says, at which point Hermes, now on the scene, does just that.

At the Gozo cave today, "wonder" may overstate the case. Less spacious (elsewhere Homer calls it "looming") than cozy, this cave is in reality barely wide enough to squeeze into at the mouth. It then widens, but if you wish to wiggle more than a few yards in, you'd better have a flashlight. And don't go looking for grapes, cypress, or violets, either—on this dry, rocky edge of the sea you'll find some low, dark-green shrubs, but little else grows among the pale rocks.

Still—I think "delight" is apt. For one thing, just getting to the cave from Valletta is delightful. A fleet of shiny yellow buses from the 1950s and 1960s constitutes Malta's public transportation system, their grilles like cartoon faces, with brightly painted trim in blue, red, and green; each has an elaborately scripted nameplate: "Paradise," "Meadow," "Life in Heaven," "Firefly." With their gleaming colors the buses seem like onshore versions of *luzzus,* the little gaudily painted fishing boats that crowd every Maltese harbor. The Maltese claim that *luzzus,* with apotropaic eyes on their prows (they ward off evil), are direct descendants of the trading boats used by the Phoenicians who colonized the islands around 800 BC. Maltese buses, then, continue a Mediterranean travel tradition little changed since Homeric times. Buses easily take you to Victoria, the tiny central town of Gozo, where you can rent a wonky bicycle and pedal the final few kilometers to the cave.

More prosaic than that, but possibly the best thing of all about Calypso's cave, is that it shows up on Malta's tourist maps. It's labeled, it's easy to find, and people have heard of it. After months of travel seeking the footsteps of Odysseus—and months of narrowed eyes, wrinkled brows, and shaken heads—an actual place on an actual map provided a genuine thrill. It's one thing to have someplace to go; it's another to know that when you get there, it will be there, too.

It was. I found that actual cave, just where it was supposed to be according to the map, which gave my visit to Ogygia—Homer's name for Calypso's isle—a sense of completion that some of my other Mediterranean stops lacked. I had a list, scrawled inside the cover of my copy of *The Odyssey*: I checked off "Calypso" with a flourish. Not only that, at the cave mouth I found more seekers after Calypso: three members of an international flight crew from Emirates Airline, out of Dubai. Beatrice was a flight attendant from Spain; Martina, also a flight attendant, came from Germany; and Thomas was a Norwegian pilot. They used English as their shared language, so we easily fell into conversation as they bemoaned the fact that without any light, they couldn't go into the cave. Well supplied from the months of travel that had led me to Malta, I provided two flashlights, which led us deep inside, stooping, then crouching, and finally duckwalking our way down the smooth, sandy floor until the cave petered out after ten or fifteen meters. No goddess, no fountains, no loom; just a smallish, dusty, empty limestone cave.

When we returned to the rocks in the sun at the cave mouth, Thomas explained that the crew was idling away a couple days on layover. What, he wanted to know, had brought me to Malta, and to Calypso's cave?

I said, "Funny you should ask."

And I produced from my backpack my little blue copy of *The Odyssey*. And there in front of Calypso's cave the four of us read aloud the episode in which Odysseus is released from his captivity by the nymph with the braided hair.

AS I'VE MENTIONED, Calypso's cave is the first time we meet Odysseus in the poem that bears his name. On Olympus, Athena, the goddess of wisdom, pleads the case for poor Odysseus, captive these seven years on Ogygia: "He stagnates still on an island, suffering much," she says, "the home of the nymph Calypso, who keeps him there by force." Zeus basically shrugs and tells her to go ahead and arrange things. Athena rushes off to western Greece to help Telemachus, Odysseus's son, whose story has occupied the first four books of the poem, while Hermes heads to Calypso's out-of-the-way realm with the new orders, finding her at her loom, amid the "sweet-smelling cypress" and grapevines "heavy with opulent clusters." Only then do we finally get a look at the main character: Odysseus, this hero, this "sacker of cities," as he's called, the greatest man of his age, the man who won the

Trojan War. And he's not eating grapes with the goddess, either; he's not building a boat; he's not praying to the gods for help; he's not even cursing his fate. No, Odysseus, when at last we meet him, is doing nothing more energetic than staring sadly out to sea in the direction of home.

And he's crying.

When Calypso tells him he can finally go, Odysseus, suspicious, makes her swear that she means him no harm. She takes the oath, acknowledging that he shows good sense by demanding it, and the two have dinner. Afterward, she tries to talk him out of leaving: "I cannot be less lovely than she, in face or figure," Calypso says of Odysseus's wife, Penelope, to say nothing of the fact that with Calypso Odysseus could live forever in luxury. Odysseus doesn't argue, using perhaps for the first time on record the "It's not you, it's me" excuse that men have been offering since then. He knows Calypso is prettier and has more to offer, he knows Penelope has surely aged—but "even so, all the time I yearn for my home and the day I'll return there." The goddess gives in, helping Odysseus build a boat, which she furnishes with water, food, and wine As a final gift she even gives thorough directions (he's to keep the Big Dipper on his left, thus sailing eastward) and a gentle homeward wind. And off he goes. Naturally Odysseus soon encounters trouble again—a terrible shipwreck this time—but by the middle of Book V Calypso is receding into the rearview mirror. Her entire role is to impede Odysseus and then, reluctantly, let him go home.

So leaving the cave should have been enough to stake my Calypso experience onto the Maltese shore. At each of Odysseus's stops I tried to find some place to stand or thing to do to symbolically complete my pilgrim's visit. Months before, on the island of the Cyclops, for example, I had found a cave to enter; at the strait between Scylla and Charybdis I paddled a rented kayak out between the two monsters and lived to tell the tale. On Malta, then, I planned to visit the nymph's cave and then make my way down to the beach, perhaps to stare longingly toward Ithaca. Staring toward Ithaca was easy—the Ramla beach and the cave both, in fact, face generally northeast, the direction Ithaca lies from Malta. More, after my long season of travel, my wife's pregnancy had reached its eighth month, so I had plenty of reason to genuinely long for home.

But the trail down to the beach was steep, and I had that bicycle, and if I went down I'd have to come back up again—a long hike just to sit symbolically on a rock. I was hot and the trail was dusty, and I thought maybe spending the remainder of the afternoon in the cool cathedral at Victoria might be more pleasant—it was supposed to have a remarkable trompe l'oeil dome painted on its flat ceiling, well worth a visit, according to *Lonely Planet: Mediterranean Europe*. My chance companions planned to head down for a swim, so I said good-bye and began walking up the road toward the rented bike. Then a hand on my arm—Beatrice—and a smile: "Come on, Ulysses," she said. "You don't use a bicycle." And then we were all walking down the steep yellow trail to the yellow beach, and my trip had suddenly changed direction, as it constantly did, almost always for the better.

MALTA WAS MY TWELFTH STOP in Odysseus's wake, and by the time I was there, I was definitely growing weary of travel on the cheap—of train station food and *Lonely Planet,* of not getting enough sleep and not knowing the language, of living out of a backpack and renting hotel rooms barely big enough to put a backpack in. My yearning for return had become something far more than a self-conscious part of my pilgrimage. I missed my wife. I was ready to go home, but it wasn't quite time. I was making my pilgrimage in order, following Odysseus directly: That is, I started in Troy in June, ending up (after a caesura back home) in Ithaca in October.

Which brings us back to Malta, twelve stops along and two to go.

About eighty-five miles south of Sicily, almost equidistant from the Lebanese coast to the east and the Strait of Gibraltar to the west, each about eleven hundred miles away, Malta lies at something like the geographical center of the Mediterranean Sea. Homer describes Calypso's island as "the great sea's very navel," so from the first attempts to place Odysseus's travel into the known world, people have taken Malta's Mediterranean centrality as evidence that Calypso lived there. As early as the early third century BC, Callimachus, the Greek scholar who cataloged the famous Alexandrian library, called Gozo (then known as Gaudos) "Calypso's little isle." Strabo, the Greek father of modern geography, lived two centuries later, and he defended Callimachus's identification. We might as well accept it, Strabo says, "since no other places are pointed out that have a greater claim to our credence."

Over subsequent years, many people have pointed out many places, of course, though with only varying claims to our credence. In 1969, Frenchman Gérard Pillot wrote a book claiming that *The Odyssey* was not just a good story—it was actually a complex encoded series of sailing directions around the Atlantic, and Pillot was certain that despite Homer's description of it as verdant and luxurious, Ogygia was Iceland. Equally adventurous theories place Ogygia everywhere from Romania (in one of many theories that have Odysseus's famous sea voyage occurring on land); the Seychelles, in the Indian Ocean; the Faeroes, north of Scotland; the Azores, off the coast of Portugal; and as far away as Kyushu, Japan.

It's like this for every spot Odysseus stops. From the moment *The Odyssey* first appeared in written form—around the eighth century BC—people have been debating whether those places existed in real life. *The True Voyage of Odysseus (Die wirklicke Reise des Odysseus)*, a German book written in 1983, surveys the history of attempts to find the true sites of the wanderings of Odysseus and describes almost eighty widely different theories of Odysseus's travels. To put it another way, regarding Odysseus's travels there have been nearly three thousand years of what a book entitled *Ancient Greek Mariners* calls "an ever mounting literature of 'higher' criticism, much of it full of absurdities and false logic, [which] only serves to confuse the issue."

Honestly, though, the absurdities and false logic are part of the fun. When I raced to the library to get information to outline my trip, it was like walking into a cocktail party where an argument had started hours before—there's no hope of getting to the bottom of the issue, so you just wade in and start yelling along with everyone else. "If we read the right meaning into each word in the text and exclude so-called 'poetic' renderings," says Victor Bérard, the French author of *Navigations of Ulysses*, "we can prove the truth of each single description, with finger on chart and *Sailing Instructions* and Travellers' Journals at our elbow to help us." As to the right meaning of each word, and which renderings are to be excluded as poetic? There, of course, you're on your own.

Theorists usually start soon after Odysseus leaves Troy, with a nine-day storm that blows him southwest as he tries to round Cape Malea of the Peloponnese Peninsula, the southernmost tip of the Greek mainland. They bring up the Aegean wind now known as the *melteme*, calculate Mediterranean sea currents, consider whether Odysseus's sail—the single square sail used by Bronze Age Mediterranean ships—would have been up, down, or shredded, and posit a landing in northeast Africa or, possibly, a sweeping passage right out through Gibraltar, and from there begin tracing his further journeys. No landfall is too unlikely, no theory too bizarre.

One participant in this millennia-long debate nicely sums up the genial, wild-eyed conclusion-leaping of the historians, geographers, and scholars involved. In his book about *The Odyssey*, English author Samuel Butler, working in the late nineteenth century, dismisses out of hand (apparently its topography is all wrong) the assertion by some villagers on the east coast of Sicily that a nearby island could have been the one mentioned in the famous Cyclops episode. "That it should be so confidently believed to be . . . the land of the Cyclopes serves as a warning to myself," Butler cautions, "inasmuch as it shows how easily people can bring themselves to accept any site for any scene if they make up their minds to do so." Butler's book on the topic, by the way, is called *The Authoress of the Odyssey*, and in it Butler claims that instead of a Greek poet living in Asia Minor, Homer was a nice young woman from an ancient Greek colony who never in her life ventured beyond her hometown of Trapani, on the western tip of Sicily. Butler is by no means the only author to believe the author of *The Odyssey* was a woman, but his point is doubly made: You certainly can fit any evidence to any theory if you make up your mind to do so.

Butler represents one type of *Odyssey* hunter, a genus that over the centuries has subdivided into three general species. You have true believers in one theory or another: Butler believed *The Odyssey* was written by a woman, and that most of its descriptions go no farther than the Sicilian shore. Iman Wilkens, in 1990, wrote a book called

Where Troy Once Stood, explaining that the Trojan War was actually fought in East Anglia in England, and that Odysseus's voyages took place across the Atlantic in places like the Bahamas—with Calypso's island turning out to be São Miguel in the Azores. For Wilkens, like for Gerard Pillot, *The Odyssey* is actually coded travel directions for traders. An example of the way the codes work: the description of the Laestrygonians spearing Odysseus's men like fishes refers to the zodiacal sign Pisces, indicating the proper time of year to trade with the Laestrygonians, who live, it turns out, in Cuba. True believers, these.

On the other end of the spectrum you have scoffers, who, like the author of *Ancient Greek Mariners,* focused on the "absurdities and false logic" of the true believers. Such geographical cynics have been around since the very beginning. The most famous is Eratosthenes of Cyrene, another librarian of Alexandria (he succeeded Callimachus), who actually coined the term *geography* and in the third century BC made what is probably the first reasonably accurate measurement of the circumference of the earth. (At noon on the summer solstice, Eratosthenes measured the angle of the sun at Alexandria, then measured the distance from Alexandria to Syene, where at the same moment the sun shone straight to the bottom of a deep well on the solstice; then he did the math.) With such a practical frame of mind, Eratosthenes was predictably skeptical of assigning actual places to the stops on Odysseus's fantastic journey among man-eating giants and hideous dragons, floating islands and prophesying ghosts. Referring to the episode in which Aeolus the wind king gathers all contrary winds into a bag, from which Odysseus can release them once he's safely home, Eratosthenes snorts, "You will find the scene of the wanderings of Odysseus when you find the cobbler who sewed up the bag of the winds."

To understand the cynics' view, imagine bringing the same zeal to a search for the sites Dorothy visited in *The Wizard of Oz.* People searching for the "real" Munchkinland would gather data on Kansas tornado frequency, speed, and direction (basing sensible presumptions about the time of year on Uncle Henry's clothing choices, the size of the pigs, and the early-twentieth-century travel patterns of vagabond showmen); they would estimate the weight and aerodynamics of Dorothy's house; and they would claim that Munchkinland had thus got to be . . . exactly, just . . . *here*. They would then estimate time and distance and begin digging at the exact place they determined Dorothy's travels would have led her to the Emerald City, which would perhaps turn out to be Chicago (green river?), until someone else theorized that the common wisdom had it all wrong, that the tornado was a predictive metaphor for intercontinental jet travel, and on and on and on.

The scoffers have a point, of course. On one hand, Wilkens, for instance, lays at least momentary claim to our credence that the stories we attribute to Homer came down to the Greeks with northern Europeans emigrating away from a catastrophic war over the rare resource of tin. But when Wilkens explains that the Delphi Homer refers to is actually Delft, in the Netherlands—overlooking that Greece has had a perfectly serviceable Delphi of its own for nearly three millennia— you can understand the cynics' desire to wipe away the cobwebs. "Have you gone mad?" you can almost hear them shout, grabbing fistfuls of hair. "This is fiction! It's a made-up story!"

The third group of Odyssean geographers lands, of course, in the middle and comprises most of those who have thought much about the topic. Strabo took this approach in the first century BC, and he still sums it up best. This ceaseless picking by one geographer at another is a waste of time, he says, noting that Homer is above all else a poet. "Poets, and Homer in particular," he says, "do not narrate pure myths simply but more often use mythical elements as additions to fact." The way to look at the travels of Odysseus, Strabo says, is as "stories which we should neither scrutinize rigorously, nor set aside as baseless and as without local setting." But try to make exact correlations at your peril. "It is ever the case," Strabo says, "that a person lies most successfully, when he intermingles a sprinkling of truth." He thus says of Homer what everyone else says of Odysseus: that he's great to listen to, but you'd be wise not to completely trust what he says.

ALL OF WHICH MEANT that when I was choosing my *Odyssey* destinations I had a wide variety of options. On one hand, I could have chosen one outlandish theory or another and traveled anyplace I liked; on the other, I could have cynically debunked the whole thing and never left home. Just the same, Peter Smith, a professor of classics I contacted when my interest in *The Odyssey* had passed all boundaries, told me that, at bottom, he agreed with Strabo. During the eighth century BC, when *The Odyssey* was committed to writing, the Greeks were colonizing Sicily, the Italian mainland, and other points west: "I think [*The Odyssey*] does reflect, in tone, the western Mediterranean," he told me. And that, in turn, finds a general consensus among the dozens of theories and maps of Odysseus's wanderings. Many vary only in particulars, showing a general swing to the west and then return eastward to Ithaca. If you distill them, you get a route that goes something like this: Odysseus started at Troy, in northwestern Turkey (there's been a general agreement on that since antiquity), and virtually all sources agree he then went north, to Thrace, and afterward was blown by a huge storm to the southwest, to the north shore of Africa. Thereafter, geographers plot his journey any number of ways among the islands to the south and west of the Italian mainland, from whence he eventually made his way back to Ithaca in western Greece.

And if Odysseus stayed in the western Mediterranean, then Malta functions perfectly as Ogygia, his almost-last stop, from which he finally made his way back to Greece. In any case, "since no other places are pointed out that have a greater claim to our credence," I stuck with Strabo and Callimachus and chose to visit Malta.

A good choice, too. Malta has been the crossroads of the Mediterranean for millennia. Whether goddesses have lived there or not, people have lived on Malta since just about the dawn of civilization: The Maltese islands hold ruins of temples built before 3500 BC; their still-standing portions are thus the oldest freestanding, stone-on-a-stone structures in the world (the Great Pyramid, for example, was built a good millennium later). But its location at the navel of the sea has always made Malta attractive to others, and it was colonized by the Phoenicians, the Carthaginians, and the Romans. It was supposedly converted to Christianity by Saint Paul, who shipwrecked there in the year 60—thus making Saint Paul, remarkably, only the second-most-famous person to wash up from the sea on the Maltese shore. Add in the omnipresent raids and the slave trade, and human flotsam has always been a big part of the Maltese experience.

Malta ended up in the eastern, Constantinople-ruled, half of the Roman Empire, but in 870 North African Arabs came and held on until they were expelled by the Normans in 1091. Feudal lords of a variety of flavors held Malta for the next several centuries.

The Spanish king and Holy Roman Emperor Charles V in 1530 gave the islands to the crusading Knights of Saint John of Jerusalem—the Knights Hospitallers—who supposedly paid rent by sending one live falcon per year (Dashiell Hammett, of course, famously expanded on that story in *The Maltese Falcon*). Napoléon took Malta from the Knights in 1798; the British got it from him in 1814, and in 1964 the Maltese finally took it for themselves, though they remain a Commonwealth nation. English gets you what you need all over the archipelago, though Maltese is a fabulous mélange of French, Italian, Spanish, and Arabic (there are few enough speakers of Maltese, in fact, that the EU is still looking for translators).

With a history like that, Malta turns out to be a great place to be stuck for a little while. Tiny details constantly remind you that you are in a crossroads, in some ways the northern rim of African Arab culture, in some ways the southern rim of Italian. In front of a market, for example, a child slips a coin into a slot and rocks gently back and forth on a mechanical camel, not a horsey. On the other hand, the complex language transliterated into little establishments like St. Paul's Bocci Klabb, in front of which six or eight old guys in sandals and short sleeves watched the harbor. Looking past, of course, a bright-red British-style phone box.

But Malta is above all Mediterranean. When there I looked at lace and glassware at the usual weekend market by the city walls; watched birds wheel in the wind during the ferry ride from Valletta to the strand at Sliema; visited the ancient temple ruins and the church dedicated to Saint Paul.

And, of course, visited Calypso's cave, where I met that flight crew and went to the beach.

WE FELL IN TOGETHER the way travelers do, tossing our day bags on such towels as anybody had, wading into the turquoise Mediterranean, conversation based on nothing, skipping along the surface. My local quest seemingly complete—I had seen Calypso's cave, I had even glanced longingly toward Ithaca—I had no further goals on Malta, and the day ticked along according to the rhythm of our idling. After an hour on the beach, we grew bored and conceived the next plan: I would ride my bicycle back to Victoria, then walk to the cathedral, where I'd meet them again and we'd continue exploring. As it happened, their circling hunt for parking brought them up in front of the garage where I was returning the bicycle, so I just bundled into their tiny rental car and off we drove. I never did see the trompe l'oeil at that cathedral.

I didn't mind. They had a plan to see the Azure Window at the far end of Gozo, a natural rock arch bending out into the Mediterranean. Near the Window is a little lagoon called the Inland Sea, which connects to the Mediterranean through a vast crack in its rocky surrounding wall. The crevice is probably less than twenty feet wide, but if you swim through it for about thirty yards you emerge in the sudden vastness of the Mediterranean itself, bobbing like a cork off Gozo's sheer cliffs and staring, your eyes at sea level, across the emptiness of open water. I had been traveling for a long time, I realized, but this was the first time I had found myself nothing more than a body afloat in the sea. There was no beach within yards to creep onto, no boat idling nearby with my well-being in mind, and the water is at least eighty feet deep where the crevice meets the sea, dropping off to much greater depth very quickly. With those three new friends, I floated in the sea, an object in motion, far far from home. I found the sensation helpful when considering the shipwreck Odysseus endures after leaving Calypso—he remains thus afloat for two days. I didn't last so long; the sun was beginning to set, and after barely fifteen minutes I was aching for dry land, so I was the first of our foursome to begin my careful breaststroke back through the crevice, to the Inland Sea and its stony beach.

ALL GREAT, AND ALL FUN. But none of this had got me any closer to the kernel of the story of Calypso and the seven grudging years Odysseus spent with her, crying during the day and sleeping with her at night. And this is where accidental travel companions can turn out to be actual emissaries sent by the gods.

We formed a nice little group, the Emirates crew and me—two young, attractive women, and two men, slightly older, married—off on adventure. It was hard not to think about what the evening might bring; after all, you're traveling, you're far from home, those special not-quite-normal-reality rules seem to apply, or you can tell yourself they might. It's largely imaginary, of course, but who doesn't like to imagine? Thomas, the pilot, though, seemed to be on a mission—like a border collie, if we strayed apart, he swung around and brought us all together, keeping us in a nice little pack. And after the swimming, driving, and shopping, during a nice long dinner beneath the stars in a plaza in front of a Gozo church, it was Thomas who ended any even imaginary flirtation.

At dinner, we compared the airplanes on which my companions worked with the trains, buses, and ships on which I'd spent most of my months of Odyssean travel. Airplanes are unique, I opined. When you're off one and waiting, you're desperate, and all you want to do is get on. But the second you're on one, nothing in this world is as important to you as getting off as soon as you can.

"Yes!" Thomas said, nodding. "Exactly! It's just like forbidden sex!"

Thomas and I laughed, but a chill descended on the table, and from that moment conversation with Beatrice and Martina lost its pleasant edge. The waiter, summoned, was dismissed without an order for more beer. Talk of moving on to a bar or discotheque in Sliema or Paceville, the entertainment districts across the Marsamxett Harbour from Valletta, quickly dried up. And so instead of some half-imagined encounter with a lovely flight attendant, I ended up having, when Thomas dropped me off, a long conversation about how nice it was being married, having children to go home to—or in my case a child soon to arrive. I could slip my pinkie into that ring of June's I wore around my neck and have that familial connection, that comfort, to ground me when I found myself far from home, wandering beaches and coves rife with temptation, whether from ageless nymphs or vacationing flight attendants.

WHICH, OF COURSE, finally brought me to the center of the Calypso episode, which I thought about as I returned to my cheap hotel room, no larger than the bathroom in an average American house. With Calypso, Odysseus finds himself, at the middle of his life, held in this strange sexual captivity, "his sweet life trickling away in his mournful yearning for home. The nymph he no longer found pleasing, though at night he still slept with her in the looming caves, an unwilling man by a nymph not at all that way." Which perfectly describes that immediately-after-forbidden-sex feeling: I no longer find this person pleasing, and suddenly, oh boy, am I yearning for home.

The Odyssey never tells the story of how Odysseus met Calypso—we learn later that Zeus destroyed Odysseus's last ship full of men after they left Thrinacia, the island of the sun god, and that Odysseus alone survived and washed up on Calypso's shore. His stay with Calypso is nearly his last stop on his series of adventures, but it's the first one we hear about. Thus reading about how weary he is of Calypso, we don't yet know that she's already the second goddess he's spent at least a year sleeping with, and that his tiring of her demonstrates that he's tired of just about everything and is finally truly ready to be home. And so, in some ways, we get to learn two lessons from this episode.

The first is the simple one—which Thomas and I discussed when he made his airplane joke. Odysseus has what looks to most of us home-bound nonheroes to be a pretty sweet deal: a hot goddess to share his bed, nothing to do all day but eat and hang around, and eternal youth. Everything but video games, televised sports, and calorie-free junk food. But he's learned the same lesson everyone who's ever fixated on the local hot goddess has learned: finally catching her is like getting on an airplane—it's like the Christmas present you dreamed of, like your favorite sports team winning a championship, like everything you desperately yearn for only to learn, once you get it, that the having solves nothing.

Calypso's name is based on the Greek root for "conceal," and a large part of her function in *The Odyssey* is to do just that: to keep Odysseus hidden in her tiny island outpost for long enough that the rest of the world has begun to get along without him. Odysseus has found that not only has the next in a series of pretty girls not really solved his problem; she's become his problem. Presumably she seemed nice enough when she fished him out of the water, and at first her bed was warm and her loveliness enthralling. But no matter how young she can keep him, Odysseus is a man in middle age. He has a wife and a child and a home, and he really wants to get back there—much like the guy who leaves his wife for the secretary only to find out that her youth isn't his youth. He yearns instead to return to reality, to his own wife, aged, less lovely, and mortal though she may be.

And that mortality, I think, is Calypso's second and most powerful message.

That is, Odysseus turns down more than a goddess, a comfortable cave, and all the grapes he can eat. By rejecting Calypso and yearning for Penelope, Odysseus is overtly choosing eventual death over endless life, the troubled reality of human experience over an endless leisure that is, finally, merely endless. Odysseus is choosing reality over fantasy, the weary predictability of daily life and eventual death over adventure and excitement and pleasure for all time. Of course, Odysseus has been facing nonstop adventure for twenty years, the last ten of which have been something like pure fantasy. Just the same, isn't that the ultimate choice of middle age? Don't we all have, finally, to learn the difference between fantasy and reality? And though choosing fantasy is tempting, even to the last moments (Homer says, after all, that Odysseus "no longer" finds Calypso pleasing, not that he never did), isn't the comfort of reality where we all hope to end up?

As a guy with a pregnant wife waiting half a world away while I finished a trip that may have been starting to go on just a bit too long, I deeply appreciated this choice of home above all. It's an overwhelming moment: You're nice and all, and living forever in this island paradise would have its charms, but frankly, I'd rather go home to my wife and eventually die. Odysseus, choosing a dangerous and uncertain journey to Ithaca over endless good times with the nymph, must really, really want to get home; he must want it about as badly as a person can want anything. There's lots more to learn about Odysseus, but that's a pretty good place to start.

THE CALYPSO EPISODE taught me one more thing, but that didn't show up until my final day or so in Malta. To be sure, with Calypso Odysseus learns that ultimate truth of middle age that the fulfillment of desire rarely yields satisfaction; for us mortals, home is always home, and one lifetime is enough. Odysseus also shows that he's clever, demanding that oath from Calypso. But beyond philosophical points about mortality and home, Calypso has something simple to say about life on her out-of-the-way island.

Before I left for my trip, a friend introduced me to someone from Malta, whose father would be glad to meet me and show me around. I thus met up in Malta with Narcy Calamatta, who with his charming wife took me to dinner at a restaurant overlooking Valletta's Grand Harbor, and the next day took me on a tour of the main island.

Narcy is one of Malta's most famous people. An actor, politician, producer, tour guide, and raconteur, he breezed us through turnstiles and everywhere greeted friends old and new. And though he entertained me with stories about the Maltese indigenes who built those ancient temples and fascinated me with visions of the blue water in caves, Narcy spent more time quizzing me than telling me about his homeland. I, however, knew I was on Malta for probably the only time in my life, and I wanted to learn what I could. We thus amiably wrestled the conversation—I would steer it to the ancient temple of Hagar Qim or the Knights Hospitallers; Narcy would riposte with questions about my Mediterranean travels or my wife and unborn child. We were, of course, participating in a travel tradition, an ancient competition between host and guest, and eventually Narcy had his way and the conversation went where he willed it.

When we stood on the parapet overlooking the harbor before we parted, I asked Narcy how, when I had come to his island to learn about it, we had ended up talking about my own travels instead of the history of his home, or even, if travel was our topic, the travels of Odysseus.

Narcy smiled. This, he said, was nothing more than the simplest lesson Calypso had to share, perhaps the main reason she kept Odysseus for so long against his will: He was somebody to talk to, somebody new, somebody fresh. Stuck on her island in the middle of the sea, Calypso was just lonely. "You have to understand," Narcy said, "we live on an island.

"We *wait* for people like you."

Chapter 2

Something to Say for Yourself—or, Among the Oar-Loving Phaeacians

My friend, be crafty no longer in answering these questions of mine. To be frank is much better. Tell me the name you go by at home—what your mother and father and countrymen call you. For no one in the world is nameless, however mean and noble, since parents give names to all the children they have. And tell me your country, people, and city, that our ships, having minds of their own, may take you there.

—*The Odyssey*, Book VIII

YOU DON'T NORMALLY HOP a cruise ship like an intercity bus. But when I learned that a luxury ship carrying some eighty passengers on an *Odyssey*-themed cruise around the Mediterranean would be sailing directly to Corfu at exactly the time I planned to leave Malta, I decided I'd try to press it into service. Corfu has long been associated with Scheria, where Odysseus washes up after Poseidon destroys the boat he built on Calypso's island. Scheria is home of the seagoing people Homer calls "the long-oared, ship-famous Phaeacians," magical seafarers who treat Odysseus fabulously, load him with treasure, and then deposit him, at long last, on the shore of Ithaca, his home. Corfu was thus my next—and next-to-last—stop.

I could board the ship docked in Sicily, less than a hundred miles from Malta, but I found it on the Internet before I left home. As I did my research about Odysseus's travels, I stumbled onto a website describing the ship's planned voyage, right around the time I was expecting to be nearing the end of my own trip. I thought talking with people on a journey somewhat similar to my own would be fun, so I contacted the line that runs the ship. A brief flurry of e-mails and phone messages resulted in an apologetic call from Travel Dynamics International explaining that using their ship as public transportation to Corfu might disrupt the enjoyment of their passengers, who would be expecting at the very least not to be importuned (the cheapest berth on the ship was $7,695), plus how would they prorate the cost? I completely understood and so began figuring out a basic passage from Malta to Corfu: ferry to Sicily. Train to Messina. Ferry to the mainland. A couple more trains, a couple more ferries, then, finally, Corfu. Inelegant, but functional.

Then I received another call, this time from the president of Travel Dynamics, who wanted to apologize personally for not being able to help me out, and incidentally to hear more about my little quest. The gods being the tricksters that they are, he had to turn out to be Greek; his son's middle name, he told me, was Odysseus. By the time we got off the phone an hour later, he had invited me to catch up with his ship on the dock in Messina and to enjoy the passage to Corfu. Payment was never discussed or requested. Odysseus, that famous fast-talker, would have been proud. When Odysseus left Ogygia he spent eighteen days on his little boat, followed by a storm and a shipwreck and two more days bobbing alone in the sea before he finally washed up, naked and exhausted, among the Phaeacians. I would make my final long Mediterranean passage in a stateroom whose bathroom alone was bigger than most of the hotel rooms I had been renting. After a forty-five-minute early-morning flight from Malta, I guessed right on the bus to the train station and thus a few hours later ended up under a cloudless cerulean sky in the center of the port city of Messina at the western tip of Sicily, an easy walk to the docks. A few minutes strolling the quay led me to the *Clelia II*, a clean, white five-story ship where the man guarding the gangway confidently put out a hand to stop me: Dirty T-shirt, hiking boots, and sagging backpack were hardly the hallmarks of his passengers. He reluctantly carried my name up to the deck, on which a smiling purser soon appeared.

My cabin had not only a hot-water shower but a nice fluffy terry-cloth robe.

I WAS A LITTLE ABASHED. Apart from the picture-window view of the ocean, my suite had rich wood paneling with brass fixtures; a separate sitting area; a bath with marble surfaces and a teak floor; and a color TV. The ship's five decks contained a swimming pool and a library, to say nothing of the restaurants, clubs, and lounges. As a nonpaying passenger I felt more than a little like an interloper.

In fact, my journal from my days aboard the *Clelia II* is full of self-recrimination; the luxury aboard ship felt somehow false, as though it negated the bare-bones approach I had taken through my months of travel. Hurried by June's pregnancy, my trip was only barely planned, though of that necessity I easily made a virtue. I was following Odysseus, after all, whose trip is the very definition of unplanned travel. What could be more fitting than to never quite know where I was going next, to show up unexpected in city after city? I traveled on the cheap simply because we don't have much money, which is fine, too.

Or more than fine: journey among the students, the footloose, the drifters of this world and you quickly learn that shoestring travelers wear their poverty with pride. Among backpackers, cheaper always trumps: If I found a comfortable room for $15 a night and you found an unheated pit without windows or a bathroom but it was only $12, then you win, and I am embarrassed. Above all, independent travelers eschew comfort and deride those who do not. If you didn't wake up with a scorpion in your mouth, you're a pansy and a Western-centric capitalist travel rapist. If you pay to get hot water, that's not traveling, that's pillaging. Of course, there's an element of truth to all that—who hasn't endured evenings with friends who went to Rome or to Hong Kong, and returned with tales about nothing but the hotel restaurant and the cute tour guide? Imagine if Odysseus spent ten years trying to get home from Troy and his stories all involved shoes lost by valets and unconscionable VAT added to café bills: avoiding the easy and the predigested does have value. I enjoyed having to think fast when I arrived in new places, spending nights in the cheap rooms I rented, the bed covered with maps, travel guides, train and ferry schedules, and, of course, *The Odyssey*. Just the same, one can take this too far— and when one is sneering at luxury travel because it's not grungy and difficult, one manifestly has done so.

In general, I traveled according to basic principles: I rarely made reservations, preferring to, like Odysseus, trust to the Fates when I arrived at any new destination. And I traveled as publicly as possible: I didn't want to be shut up in a car or, any more than necessary, in private cabins. I wanted to go where Odysseus might have gone but to be among the people there now.

I had started the trip as a farewell to adventure, an independent, almost fierce, last foray to the world's fringes, to the rocky shores of the Mediterranean, among the cheap travelers of the world, avoiding tours and guides, for one final time facing the world's far places head-on, showing up at dock or station unexpected, unprotected, alone— like my spirit guide, Odysseus. It should have at least crossed my mind that high summer season in the Mediterranean might not provide the kind of solo adventure I sought, but it never did. Still, I largely kept to my principles, so after months of crowded train passages and uncomfortable overnight ferries, of 20-euro rooms and street-vendor meals, the luxurious ship made me feel enough of a fake that only months later did I recognize that I had unwittingly won the shoestring travel championship: Not merely cheap, I was traveling free. Plus I had a bathroom and could drink the water. Not only that, the sumptuousness of the cruise was entirely appropriate to my destination.

When Odysseus, nearing the end of his journey, washes up on the island of the Phaeacians, luxury is what he finds. Great, even magical, seafarers—their boats can reach any destination overnight, effortlessly, and their legendary willingness to ferry passengers has begun to raise the ire of Poseidon—the Phaeacians treat Odysseus like the nobility he turns out to be, bathing him, feting him, and finally returning him to Ithaca. And though it's not his only good experience along the way, it's certainly the first time on his trip that he knows he's in no physical danger—and it's among the Phaeacians that he drops his disguises and tells the story of his wanderings. So, in luxury, did I. After enjoying the shower (and the terry-cloth robe) in my room, I wandered the ship, knowing it was scheduled to depart in the early afternoon, shortly after its passengers returned from a guided tour.

I was thus leaning over the rail when buses rolled down the quay, came to a stop, and disgorged two full loads of grandparents.

SANSABELT SLACKS, blindingly clean white cross trainers, or else those crepe-soled shoes that all people begin wearing at a certain grandparently age; men, wearing bucket hats, carefully led around by patient women in visors and sunglasses. Whatever age you are, these people were your grandparents. It makes sense—these luxury culture cruises are marketed powerfully through university alumni groups and the subscription lists of magazines like *Archaeology,* and the people in those groups with the time and money for luxury trips aren't midcareer professionals with jobs and kids to manage: They're mostly retired or semiretired.

Most of my fellow passengers took no notice of me as I watched them parade up the gangway, but I felt even further convinced that I did not belong on the *Clelia II.* As soon as they were aboard, the ship sailed and the crew served lunch, during which my pointless awkwardness intensified when one fellow diner, a scowling white-haired man, began for some reason angrily grilling me about my intentions aboard the ship (he did not approve), my work history (ditto), and my character, at which point his wife abruptly left the table. He was a one-time naval officer to whom grilling clearly came easily, and I was an abashed freeloader unwilling to justify the original concerns of my host by arguing with the paying customers, so the discussion ended in something of a rout. I was so embarrassed that I was very late emerging from my cabin for dinner, for which I borrowed a tie from the ship's cruise director. Just the same, aware that I was interested in speaking to other passengers about their cruise, the director had taken pains to seat me far from my antagonist. This time I joined a table of five women, ranging in age from their forties to their seventies, and while we consumed course after course of first-rate cruise ship food and glass after glass of absolutely free cruise ship wine they engaged me in talk.

I SAY ENGAGED ME because that's how it went. Though I had the goal of interviewing them about their travels, they quickly turned my inquiries aside. Certainly they enjoyed *The Odyssey* and its resonance, but like the rest of the passengers I eventually spoke with aboard the *Clelia II*, they had mostly joined the cruise because they wanted to see the Mediterranean or because it was the right time of year for a cruise and this one looked like fun. My lunchtime humiliation aside, the passengers were an extremely pleasant bunch who enjoyed the lectures and tours, but above all they were people who could afford to travel nicely, and traveling nicely in the Mediterranean happened to be what they were up to. ("I had a choice of two tours," one told me. "The other one was the Great Lakes.") On the other hand, cheerful or not, like Calypso on her out-of-the-way island, the *Clelia II* passengers were, like all cruise passengers nearing the end of their trip, rather past one another's company. Flung together by the fates for an eleven-day journey, these women had already shared such stories as they wished to share, made and evaded friendships and feuds (the tale of my ambush by the man the other passengers called the General provided a frisson as it spread), seen nearly as much of one another as they cared to. I was someone new; instead of asking questions, they hoped I would answer them. What adventure had brought me suddenly among them? Where was I headed? Whence had I come? What was I trying to do?

THE QUESTIONS couldn't have been more fitting. I found myself, among these magical seafarers, exactly like Odysseus, though with considerably less naked bobbing in stormy seas on my part. When Odysseus leaves Calypso, he steers eastward (with the Big Dipper on his left) for seventeen days, at which point he sees the mountains of the land of the Phaeacians.

Regrettably, at that point Poseidon, the god of the sea, happens to notice him. Poseidon has caused much of Odysseus's suffering, enraged because Odysseus tried to kill Poseidon's son, the Cyclops Polyphemus ("Ever since that day," Homer says in Book I, "Earth-shaking Poseidon, instead of killing Odysseus outright, makes him a wanderer and homeless"). Seeing Odysseus near land, Poseidon admits that Odysseus may be nearing the end of his journey, but "still I think I can give him his bellyful of misfortune!"

Cue sudden storm at sea.

Odysseus, storm-tossed and surely wondering, *What next?* envies those who died at Troy and at least received funerals and their share of fame for their exploits, whereas he seems fated to drown ignominious and unwitnessed. Fortunately, a sea goddess named Ino shows up and takes pity on him, urging him to take off the rich clothes Calypso had provided and swim to the coast. She gives him a magical veil to tie about his waist for protection, telling him to throw it back into the sea when he reaches dry land.

Mistrustful as ever, Odysseus does no such thing, planning to stay with his boat until he gets closer to shore. Poseidon has other ideas and smashes the boat. Clinging to a plank, Odysseus finally takes Ino's advice, flinging off his clothes and throwing himself into the roiling sea. Poseidon, satisfied that Odysseus "won't make many jokes about what [he's] been through," heads home, and Athena calms the seas, clearing the way for the wind to blow Odysseus toward shore. For two days he bobs in the ocean, near death from rocks and waves, until he finds a river mouth where he safely struggles ashore, remembering to return Ino's veil to the sea. Naked, exhausted, and alone, Odysseus covers himself in leaves and goes to sleep in the underbrush beneath olive trees.

The next morning, Athena orchestrates events. Nausicaa, the nubile princess of the Phaeacians, arrives at the seashore to do laundry with her maids. Odysseus hears them and, covering his nakedness with a branch, beseeches her for help. After Odysseus cleans himself up, Nausicaa sizes him up as potential husband material and contrives a way for him to make his way into the city without exciting idle talk or trouble. Once there, Odysseus throws himself at the mercy of

Nausicaa's mother, Arete, and father, Alcinous. They display tremendous hospitality, throwing celebratory feasts and competitions in honor of their guest, promising, as is their wont, to return him to his home in one of their magical ships, described as needing no steering or oars, simply reading their sailor's minds, traveling "swift as . . . thought itself." Though Odysseus dare not quite believe it, his travels are almost over.

"For your reassurance," King Alcinous says thoughtfully, "I shall set a time for your sending. Let tomorrow be the day." A small point in *The Odyssey,* this is a huge point to travelers. In the copy of *The Odyssey* June gave me—I carried it on my trip as a totem object—I have scrawled in the margin by this line, "He's got his ticket! He can relax!" Among its many other guises, *The Odyssey* is a travel book, and at this passage as near many others I put the words "Travel True!" which I used whenever my own experiences demonstrated how well Homer had painted the experience of being on the move. Traveling alone, you never completely relax; one hand on your passport and your money, one eye on your bag, your room key. Nobody really knows where you are. When you travel alone the back of your mind constantly hums: Where to next? How to get there? Where to stay? But, comfortable in one place, once you have chosen the next step and bought the ticket for the train, the bus, the ferry, settled up with the hotel, set the alarm for the next morning, you do feel a rare relief. Tomorrow is planned, the next leg organized: for now, then, with nothing more to do, you can relax. This Odysseus does, taking a peaceful night of sleep and comfortably enjoying the next day of contests and feasts held in his honor.

Or mostly enjoying. When the blind court poet entertains, he sings first about a quarrel (otherwise undescribed in ancient Greek literature; neither Homer nor anybody else ever mentions it again) between Odysseus and Achilles. As the poet sings, Odysseus hides his head and cries. Alcinous silences the poet, but later Odysseus himself asks for another song, specifically for the tale of the Trojan Horse. During this he weeps piteously, and Alcinous again stops the poet. Perhaps Odysseus is in some way connected to these events, he suggests. "Can it be that one of your kinsmen by marriage fell before Troy?" he asks Odysseus.

"Some splendid son- or father-in-law . . . ?" Above all, Alcinous finally begs one thing from Odysseus: Alcinous wants to know his name.

ASKING ODYSSEUS whether he lost some in-law at Troy is, of course, a great ironic joke—like asking Shakespeare whether he might have once written a greeting card or a limerick or something. Much more important, though, is the request for Odysseus to tell his name. Odysseus, in the middle of his second day among the Phaeacians, still hasn't mentioned it—this is the first ever example of the stock movie scene: "I'm sorry, what did you say your name was?" A beat of silence, then: "I didn't." Yet here this causes no discomfort. Instead, it expresses one of the central themes of *The Odyssey*: what the Greeks called *xenia,* which can be translated to "guest-friendship" or simply welcoming outsiders. According to this system, a stranger approaching a home could expect to be fed, offered a place to rest and wash up, and even offered a place to sleep. Only after that would he be asked to state his name and his business. The way you treated the stranger at your gates, that is, immediately demonstrated your level of civilization, both to the stranger and to yourself.

In the Bronze Age Mediterranean of the Homeric Greeks, with few amalgamated powers, nothing like laws about behavior in the space between them, and primary identification not with some state but with a family or tribe, a stranger approaching town was a matter of great complexity. Raider? Wanderer? Thief? Trader? Spy? Beggar? God in disguise? A stranger could be almost anything, and thus had to be treated with suspicion and care. To the stranger entering a new town, however, with no family or allies to protect him, the meeting was even more uncertain.

That's why the system by which strangers were welcomed, protected, and helped on their way was so remarkable: "It's amazing a system could be devised that someone would show up and it would be your duty," said Al Leonard, a pleasant classics professor who provided some of the expert commentary to the passengers aboard the *Clelia II.* "You would give them at least those three things"—food, shelter, and a bath. Leonard enjoyed the way the ship was providing for me exactly what the Phaeacians had provided for Odysseus, and he did his best to explain *xenia* to me.

"It's more than the guest and the host," he said. "It's almost like karma. Once you accept *xenia* it becomes your obligation to pass it on." Not necessarily to the same person who hosted you, but to any stranger or guest who came your way. "It's almost like a pyramid plan," he laughed. *The Odyssey* is filled, he pointed out, with good and bad examples of *xenia*. The poem starts out with a description of Penelope and Telemachus at home in Ithaca, desperate for Odysseus's return because their home is filled with suitors making a mockery of the custom, eating them out of house and home. Telemachus then travels in search of his father and encounters wonderful hospitality— counterexamples, showing what *xenia* should look like. Then the poem picks up with Odysseus, kept against his will by Calypso—who nonetheless rallies and not only sends him on his way but gives him food, clothes, the wherewithal to make a boat, and a fair wind. "Welcome the coming, speed the parting guest," a famous line from the translation of *The Odyssey* by Alexander Pope, may express the idea most simply. In the 1950s and 1960s, when Leonard hitchhiked around Greece, he said, "we could be in the smallest little town and someone would come out yelling *'Xeni! Xeni!'* [Stranger! Stranger!]," and then he and his friends would be offered a place to stay, something to eat, and a place to wash up. Even the state-owned Greek chain of American-style hotels at that time was called Xenia. Travelers and supplicants were considered to be under the special protection of Zeus, the god of hospitality, among his many other jobs, so no wonder the tradition dies hard.

But *xenia* offered more than ease of travel. Only partially a gesture of goodwill, it also presented an opportunity to feel out a situation. Thus the Phaeacians treat Odysseus like royalty—Odysseus is welcomed and bathed, offered comfortable bed and blankets, wined and dined and not pushed to state his business. His name remains secret—good for the Phaeacians, who thus need not yet react to his needs or background, and good for Odysseus, who need not yet divulge any personal information.

So when Alcinous asks, Odysseus finally, after two days of being his guest—and after a third of the poem that tells his story is already gone—speaks his name. "I am Odysseus," he says, "the son of Laertes, and I am known among men and gods for being able to use the mind I have." He describes his home in Ithaca and explains how Calypso has just spent seven years holding him hostage, as the witch Circe had done previously, but they couldn't keep him, "for no luxurious life in a foreign mansion can be so sweet as a man's own country and parents."

He settles down. "But enough," he says. "It's time for me to begin the story of the sad eventful return that Zeus decreed for me as homeward I traveled from the land of Troy." And then Odysseus tells the stories of his travels, the stories that will forever be associated with *The Odyssey*.

THE GENIUS OF ODYSSEUS telling the stories of his travels himself was explained to me by Peter Smith, my classics professor friend (classics professors are like potato chips: You never stop at one). Smith noted that Homer allows us to witness Odysseus divulging his character through his speech as well as through his actions; plus, we get to wonder whether he's telling the truth in his stories, since as Homer's listeners would have known, he rarely does that.

Perhaps more important, throughout most of its development *The Odyssey* was an oral tale, sung at parties full of nobles by a poet just like the poet singing to the Phaeacians. Homer's construction of the journey as a tale-within-a-tale allows the poet singing at dinner to narrate these adventures in the first person in Odysseus's voice: I met this person and fought with that one, I stopped here, ate there, the bard will tell his listeners; not speaking of some character, some third person, the poet will sing directly to his listeners of exploits. Nothing could be more immediate: a tale spoken, from mouth to ear. For a journey that has eventually come to feel like the vast human journey we all undertake, Homer's decision is pure magic. For the listener, Odysseus is there in the room, telling his tales—the poet becomes Odysseus, and the listeners themselves become the magical Phaeacians.

And then there was I, aboard the *Clelia II*, nearing the end of my journey, among Phaeacians of my own, in borrowed tie at a table full of nice women. No poet or singer entertained us—instead, I was the stranger passing by, the unknown quantity, the new guy. And as the Phaeacians did to Odysseus, my tablemates asked me: Who are you?

"Where shall I begin and how much shall I tell?" Odysseus asks Alcinous in response. It's a rhetorical question. Odysseus compliments the poet (Homer was a big fan of poets) and then he starts talking.

So did I. The whole point of my trip was to do what Odysseus had done. The ladies asked me, Where are you going? Where have you been? And why?

Like Odysseus, I started with Troy.

Chapter 3

Troy, Backstory Capital of the World

Famous Odysseus and his men were already sitting in the Trojans' place of assembly, concealed in the horse, for the Trojans themselves had dragged it within the high walls. . . . The sons of Achaeans poured out of that hollow horse, their ambush, and sacked the city, . . . this way and that they managed to level the lofty town, and . . . Odysseus went, like Ares himself . . .

—*The Odyssey*, Book VIII

BENEATH THE RUSTLING LEAVES of a fig tree, a bench. Beside the bench a folding card table, on which sits an urn of complimentary tea. Paper cups, napkins, and of course sugar cubes—you will not find tea in Turkey without sugar cubes. The bench is the only place in the ruins of Troy where you can catch a little shade; all else is bleached white stone, a stinging hot sun in a clear blue sky, and the ever-present blowing: "windy Ilium," Homer calls it, and he got that just right. Weeds, shrubs, and the occasional low trees grow among the ancient rocks, and you can wander among the scattered ruins as long as you care to, lingering over whatever stops you—a ramp, a wall; buried urns, shattered houses; a gate through which the Trojans may have dragged the famous horse. Troy stands on the very end of a long inland plateau, and so from the top of the ruins, where the plateau drops steeply off, you can see the coastal plain stretch a few miles to the sea, easily imagining the Trojan houses surrounding the citadel and, farther off, the Greek camp and ships that would have filled the plain for those ten years of war.

The site itself, only about ten acres in size, looms above the plain, giving it the kind of height advantage you'd want in a city built to withstand a siege. Nowadays paths and boardwalks curve in and around various parts of the site: here twenty-foot-high tapering walls built of stone blocks, there a deep trench to more-ancient foundations, now and then steep stairways—nominally off-limits—leading beside fortifications from the tops of the walls all the way down the slope to the plain. The guided tour stays on the paths, but even there you can lean against the very walls in front of which the Greek heroes supposedly fought and fell, wander among houses in which Trojans may have waited out the siege—or died in its catastrophic end.

After the tour, I sat on that bench with a young college student from Kazakhstan named Jafar, who had befriended me on the bus from Istanbul to Çanakkale. We had stayed behind to wander the ruins, finding ourselves after an hour or so trying to escape the heat by that tea urn. We talked about Homer, I started telling him other stories I had learned, and then Jafar asked a marvelously weird question: Why, he wondered, did I think the Trojans hadn't just left? If the Greeks wanted the town that much, why hadn't the Trojans just gone off and founded another? After all, according to our guide, Troy had been a bad-luck spot from the outset, rebuilt on the same spot nearly a dozen times. It's destroyed by earthquake; they build it again. Raiders burn it—they build it again. Why, Jafar wondered, didn't they just take a hint? I considered for a moment launching into one of those forty-four-talking-to-twenty-one lectures, but fortunately I did not. We talked briefly about current thoughts—that Troy was an important city for trade, controlling the mouth of the Dardanelles and thus well situated to exact tribute from ships waiting for favorable winds to sail north toward the Black Sea, and so attractive to raiders, like the Greeks, as well as traders, despite the tectonic fault on which it was built.

But in truth, the Trojans didn't leave because—well, because it was Troy. It was home and all, but moreover, it was Troy. There's just something about the place—the place makes heroes. That's why they stayed, and that's why we were there.

TROY, BACKSTORY CAPITAL OF THE WORLD

* * *

HERE'S THE *LONELY PLANET* GUIDE on Troy: "Don't get excited—there's little of Troy (Truva) to be seen and most people aren't thrilled by the tacky 'Trojan Horse.'"

The writers of travel guides must lead terribly exciting lives. Troy, with its bleached stone walls, ancient stairways and ramps, and grasses and fig leaves still rustling in the ceaseless wind, has a sense of place that fairly radiates into the brilliant blue sky above northwest Turkey. Here Achilles fell; here Agamemnon ranted; here Odysseus schemed. Into one of these portals Trojans may have dragged the famous horse, forever teaching the world to beware of Greeks bearing gifts. Helen left Menelaus to live here with Paris, making it the site of the oldest love story *and* the oldest war story in the world. Plus, that fakey-looking two-story Trojan Horse you could climb in? I had my picture taken leaning out a window in that horse; a key chain with a tiny wooden horse stands even now on my bookshelf. If ancient, ruined walls and the Trojan Horse aren't what you're looking for, why on earth did you come to Troy?

To visit Troy you stay in Çanakkale (rhymes with "the broccoli"), a Turkish city directly on the Dardanelles, dominated by the fort built in 1451 when Mehmed II, the conqueror of Istanbul, fortified the strait to better control shipping as the new Ottoman Empire stretched into Europe. The *Blue Guide* to Turkey tells you that Mehmed also visited Troy, where he "gloried in the fact that he had defeated the descendants of those [Europeans] who had destroyed the city. They had at last, he declared, paid the debt that they owed the people of Asia." The Dardanelles, the narrow strait dividing Asia from Europe (at Çanakkale barely twelve hundred meters wide) and connecting the Mediterranean with the Sea of Marmara and hence the Black Sea, have been important ever since: They were the site of a key battle in the Peloponnesian War in the fifth century BC as well as the catastrophic battle of Gallipoli in 1915—the northwest shore is covered with monuments. So I was far from the first on my pilgrimage to Troy. In fact, not just the site of the most famous battle in mythology, and not just situated at the mouth of a strip of water people have been fighting over since before history, Troy has another claim to immortality—as the birthplace of modern archaeology.

Following Odysseus, I wanted to start at the obvious square one. Homer's two poems, *The Iliad* and *The Odyssey*, deal with the war at Troy and its aftermath; Odysseus left for Ithaca from Troy. Thus I felt confident that since it all started at Troy, so could I. But then I started reading, discovering not only that Homer's stories don't really tell much of the story of the Trojan War but also that they fit into a vast interconnected series of myths called the Epic Cycle, which forms a unified narrative, starting with the beginning of the world and ending with the returns of the heroes from Troy—Odysseus, of course, being the last one home. That is, *The Odyssey* was only the last chapter in a saga that started, literally, with the dawn of time. Far from the Beginning of Beginnings I expected, modern Troy turns out to be the back-story capital of the world.

THAT'S A LOT OF BACKSTORY. Imagine my relief, then, when I learned that outside of Homer, a mere 120 lines or so of the poems in the Epic Cycle still exist. They are summarized by various ancient authors, though, and by sifting through the summaries and later compilations, you can put together an easily digested narrative. Not only does that put the Homer stories in an enlightening context, the other myths yield wonderful information about Odysseus himself.

Okay, backstory. The tale of the Trojan War really begins with the marriage of Peleus, a mortal, and Thetis, a sea nymph. Zeus, king of the gods, has eyes for Thetis, but she is fated to give birth to a son who will outdo his father—which vastly diminishes the interest of Zeus, who thus gives Thetis to Peleus. They have a child, by the way, who turns out to be Achilles, whom Thetis tries to render immortal, either by holding him in fire or by dipping him in the river Styx, depending on which myth you read. Either way his heel doesn't get the treatment, setting the stage for future events.

But the trouble starts long before that. The wedding of Peleus and Thetis is attended by all the gods—all, that is, but Eris, goddess of discord, who naturally isn't invited. True to character, she returns the favor by writing "for the fairest" on a golden apple and rolling it into the festivities. Of course, three goddesses demand the apple: Athena, goddess of wisdom and craft, patron of warriors; Hera, wife of Zeus and goddess of marriage and women; and Aphrodite, goddess of desire. Discord, indeed; Zeus wisely refuses to get involved, again dumping the problem on a mortal, choosing a young Trojan shepherd named Paris. Paris has his own backstory: Born to the queen of Troy, who had a dream that she had given birth to a flaming torch, Paris was considered the seed of Troy's eventual destruction and sent off into the mountains to be killed. He lived—a mythological commonplace—and the gods seek his judgment for the award of the apple.

For the world's first beauty contest, the goddesses never consider a fair fight—they each offer the best bribe they can think of. Hera offers dominion over all Asia; Athena offers wisdom and victory in war; and Aphrodite offers the most beautiful woman in the world: Helen, who lives in Sparta. In what is known as the Judgment of Paris, Aphrodite gets the apple—Paris is a man, after all. Back among the fold in Troy, Paris is sent as an envoy to Sparta, where he stays as a guest with Helen—and her husband, the Spartan king Menelaus. If there's a better way to disrespect the guest-friendship traditions of *xenia* than by running off with your host's wife, nobody's thought of it yet, but that's what Paris does. The angry Menelaus applies for help to his brother, Agamemnon of Mycenae, chief king among the Greeks (called Achaeans or Argives by Homer, since this all took place long before Greece formally existed).

Okay, more backstory: Helen and Menelaus. Helen is the most beautiful woman in the world and destined to be queen of Sparta, so everybody wants to marry her. Her father, the current Spartan king, doesn't know how to avoid the trouble certain to ensue when he awards her to only one of her many suitors, so he takes a good piece of advice from a young prince from the faraway island province of Ithaca—a tricky fellow named Odysseus. Odysseus suggests that all the suitors take an oath to support the eventual winner of Helen, thus not only protecting their own possible interests before the choice, but also preventing trouble afterward. Helen's father agrees; Menelaus gets Helen, and all the princes are thus bound to defend the new couple. Odysseus, called by Homer "peer of Zeus in counsel," thus demonstrates his cleverness the first time he shows up in mythology. For his good advice he's also awarded Helen's cousin, Penelope, though other sources say he won her in a footrace. Either way, Odysseus was unlikely to win Helen (he's supposedly the only suitor who brought no gifts) and well suited to her crafty cousin.

Odysseus and Penelope happily return to Ithaca, where they have a baby boy, Telemachus. Thus, after Paris runs off with Helen, when Agamemnon and Menelaus show up demanding that Odysseus honor his pledge and join their party to reclaim Helen from Troy, Odysseus has a lot to leave behind (he's also heard a prophecy that if he goes, he'll be gone twenty years). Looking for a way out, Odysseus feigns insanity, donning a peasant cap, yoking together an ass and an ox, and plowing the sand, throwing over his shoulder salt instead of seeds. One Palamedes, a member of Agamemnon and Menelaus's party, isn't convinced. He snatches the infant Telemachus from the arms of Penelope and places the infant in front of the team, which Odysseus, of course, instantly stops, demonstrating sanity. Three thousand years before *Catch-22,* Odysseus fails to get his mental health deferral and goes off to war.

Subsequent stories about Odysseus also focus on trickery. Thetis knows that her son Achilles is fated to live either a long, dull life away from the war at Troy or a brief but glorious one if he goes. She sends him to hide at the court of a friend, where he dresses as a woman in a harem (if Odysseus prefigures *Catch-22,* Achilles foreshadows Corporal Klinger from *M*A*S*H*). Odysseus, sent to fetch Achilles, places among gifts to the women a sword and armor, then has accomplices feign attack; unable to resist a good fight, Achilles seizes the sword, revealing himself. Later, when Agamemnon needs to placate the gods to get fair winds to sail to Troy—by sacrificing his own daughter—it's Odysseus who lures Iphigenia to the port by claiming she's wanted as a bride to Achilles. On a more personal note, Odysseus, not quick to forgive, eventually frames Palamedes for treason and has him stoned to death by the Greek army.

Again, this all comes to us from sources other than Homer, and almost entirely from sources describing other, vanished sources. Then, finally, comes Homer's *Iliad,* set in the tenth year of the war.

*   *   *

THE ILIAD describes the terrible results of the titanic sulk thrown by Achilles, who refuses to continue fighting after Agamemnon appropriates a captive woman to whom Achilles has taken a liking. The arrogance of the two as they engage in their bitter feud while Greeks and Trojans fall in droves around them forms the center of the poem, though Homer describes plenty of Greeks killing Trojans and vice versa, and the gods stay deeply involved on both sides. Finally enraged by the death of his friend fighting in his place, Achilles does reenter the fighting, killing the Trojan champion Hector and outraging his body by dragging it around the city walls. He calms down and returns the body to Hector's father, the Trojan king Priam, and with Hector's funeral celebrations *The Iliad* ends. There's plenty of war left to fight, during which Achilles will die—a wound to that heel, of course—and the Greeks eventually win.

Odysseus plays a vital role in *The Iliad,* as much respected for his abilities with words as with weapons. Agamemnon sends Odysseus to try to convince Achilles to rejoin the battle; Odysseus sneaks into Trojan territory and interrogates, and then murders, a soldier. A short-legged, barrel-chested guy with reddish hair and beard, Odysseus pacing in front of his soldiers looks like "a great wooly ram ordering his ewes"; and though he's much shorter than Menelaus, when they're seated it's Odysseus, not Helen's husband, who radiates royalty. More, when he's trying to convince you of something, "words came driving from his deep chest like winter snow before the wind," says the Trojan elder Antenor, who unsuccessfully negotiated with him to avoid the war. Odysseus "excels in all manner of stratagems and subtle cunning," Antenor says; in such matters, "there was none to touch him."

And what Odysseus is most remembered for in the Trojan War is just such a matter of sneakery: coming up with the scheme to finally win the war by hiding soldiers in the Trojan Horse. *The Iliad* ends long before the Greeks come up with that strategy. *The Odyssey* does mention the Trojan Horse, but it tells only fragments of the story—once Menelaus describes for young Telemachus the feeling among the soldiers inside the horse as Helen, then still among the Trojans, imitates the voices of the soldiers' wives in order to trick anyone hidden inside the horse to cry out and give away their position; Odysseus, Menelaus says, clapped his hand over the mouth of one who almost couldn't resist. The other time the story comes up is among the Phaeacians, and it causes a weeping Odysseus to finally reveal his identity.

The story is told in detail by the Roman poet Virgil in *The Aeneid* and summarized by other ancients like Apollodorus and Quintus of Smyrna. At the suggestion of Odysseus, the Greeks seemingly abandon their camp one night, burning their tents and sailing their ships beyond a nearby island. The only thing remaining besides their still-smoking fires is a gigantic wooden horse, in which the greatest of the Greek heroes silently hide. As the Trojans pour out from their city and try to make sense of the thing, Trojan soldiers capture one Sinon of the Greeks, who claims to have been abandoned. Sinon explains that the horse, an offering to Athena for safe passage home, has been made so large to prevent the Trojans from dragging it inside their gates and thus using its protection for themselves. The Trojans naturally want to do just that, ignoring the warnings of sensible oracles among their own people who suggest throwing it off a cliff or cutting it open. According to Virgil, it's Laocoön, a Trojan prophet, who says, "I am nothing but apprehensive of the motives of Greeks, even as bearers of gifts." However, immediately thereafter, he and his children are attacked by giant snakes, perhaps reducing the effect of his warning.

In goes the horse, and the party starts. That night, when after their drunken revelries the Trojans collapse into sleep, Sinon releases the men inside the horse, raises a signal fire to the returning Greek ships, and opens the gates—and let the rout begin, as after ten years the Greeks finally win the war.

THAT HORSE is key to it all, really. People have heard of Achilles, of Agamemnon; people know of Helen of Troy and Odysseus. But the Trojan Horse—that's a metaphor we all use, even if we don't know the story well. It's the sneaky surprise we still worry about in computer software, the trick ending of all trick endings, neatly summing up both the complex story behind it and the character of Odysseus, who thought it up. I read a short story once about a boy hiding inside a couch to gain access to an apartment—its title, "The Trojan Couch." *Trojan* is universally understood code for "watch it—surprise inside." So naturally the first stop on the tour of Troy is the big fake wooden horse built near the grounds of the archaeological site.

It looks much like a knight off a chessboard—about three stories tall, with that characteristic vertical head and castellated mane, and facing of narrow brown planks. Entirely wooden, its open stairwells and shuddery planking gave it less the feeling of an engine of war than of the stairs and decking of a beach rental. But it was a giant horse, and I was at Troy, and I had my picture made. And though I emerged back into the light to tour the ruin instead of sacking the city, still— something felt completed.

After that, with my travel guide, a sheaf of photocopied descriptions from archaeological texts, and *The Odyssey,* I joined a small guided tour and stalked the grounds. Our guide—an archaeology student named Baris—walked us through the many levels of Troy. There turn out to be nine, all built one upon the other—occasional placards of large Roman numerals now hang on the strata of rubble to identify the levels. Level I, built on the surface of the plateau around 3000 BC, starts sixteen meters above sea level. By the time the Romans, tracing their imaginary lineage back to the Trojan hero Aeneas, gussied up Troy IX, the foundations stood twenty meters higher. That's more than sixty vertical feet of constant rebuilding, as earthquakes and fires destroyed a town and the people rebuilt on—and with—the rubble of their predecessors. Troy I was founded long before the events Homer describes; and Troy IX was the product of commemorative Roman rebuilding around the time of Jesus. Levels VI and VIIa, generally associated with Homeric Troy, certainly do fit the bill. Troy VI was a prosperous kingdom with wide, sloping walls and tall watchtowers, with a rock cistern that could have supported the population during a siege. It appears to have been destroyed by earthquake in the mid– thirteenth century BC. Troy VIIa was rebuilt directly atop the ruins, and its ruins in turn show signs of a sudden climb in population within the city walls—as though people used to living outside the walls had moved inside, as if during a siege. There are also sling bullets hoarded as for self-defense—and, of course, it was destroyed by fire around 1200 BC, remarkably close to 1184 BC, the date for the fall of Troy widely held in antiquity, calculated by Eratosthenes himself. Human bones found there suggest violence.

Our guide pointed out a gate through which the horse might have rolled, showed us ruins of buildings added centuries later by the Romans, showing how the site was rendered even more complex when each generation of builders gathered building materials from previous ruins (though the sun-dried bricks of the first few layers can be used only once and thus remain relatively intact). Then he gathered us in the ruins of a Roman amphitheater to remind us of only one thing: Archaeology or no, what we know of Homeric Troy is speculation. "Homer tells the story the way he wanted," Baris said. "He most probably changed the whole story." When challenged about this, he made an excellent point: "I would not have accepted the horse into the city—would you?" He shook his head. "Trust me," he said of Homer. "He is the best liar ever in the world."

Which makes this a good place to introduce yet another heroic liar into the mix. His name was Heinrich Schliemann, and here at Troy in 1870 he invented modern archaeology—by taking mythology's most important archaeological site, getting a bunch of locals with shovels, and having them wreck it.

THE BEST WAY to imagine Heinrich Schliemann is to think of Indiana Jones in *Raiders of the Lost Ark,* only if in that famous first scene with the idol and the bag of sand, instead of the whole business with the shoulder shimmy and the weighing and the quick exchange, he had just said, "The hell with it, let's get this party started," and revved up a backhoe. Not surprisingly for Troy, a little backstory clarifies things.

Schliemann was born in 1822 to a poor family in a small German town. He claims in his book *Troy and Its Remains* that his father entertained him as a child with stories of the Trojan War. When at age eight Schliemann mooned over a picture in a history text of the Trojan hero Aeneas leaving the burning city, his father told him it was just a work of the imagination. "If such walls existed," Schliemann remembers replying, undeterred, "they cannot possibly have been completely destroyed: vast ruins of them must still remain, but they are hidden away beneath the dust of ages." This being the way few eight-year-olds talk, skepticism among readers can be forgiven. "At last we both agreed that I should one day excavate Troy." Elsewhere, Schliemann describes working as a retail clerk when a drunken miller came in and, lacking money, paid for his goods by reciting "about one hundred lines of [Homer], observing the rhythmic cadence." Schliemann spent "the few pence that made up my whole fortune" to keep the miller liquored up so that he would repeat the lines. Nothing says "fourteen-year-old" like paying the local drunk to recite verse in a language you don't understand, right?

In any case, Schliemann wrote all this well after he had become world famous for his discoveries at Troy. Nonetheless, whether or not he went back and reorganized his memories to support the inevitability of his discoveries at Troy, Schliemann led a remarkable life, the facts almost embarrassingly unlikely. Leaving his poor village seeking his fortune, he was shipwrecked near Holland; finding employment there, he used a natural flair for languages to become valuable to a trading company, eventually settling in St. Petersburg but traveling the world. In California during the gold rush, he made a fortune as a banker, leaving in 1852 under a cloud of suspicion. Though unhappily married to a Russian fortune hunter, he continued to find success in trade, multiplying his profits through possibly crooked military contracts during the Crimean War. He visited the Homeric sites in Greece in 1868, eventually writing a book about his experiences. He moved to the United States in 1869 to take advantage of American divorce laws, then instructed friends in Greece to choose for him a nice Greek wife who would match his current obsession with things Homeric. Scholars still debate whether this interest arose during his unhappy marriage or during his childhood, as Schliemann eventually claimed; in any case, he would hardly be the only person to have ever conceived a sudden interest in Homer in middle age. Forty-six at the time, he chose from photographs a sixteen-year-old named Sophie; and just as Steve Guttenberg in *Diner* required his fiancée to win his love by demonstrating knowledge about the Baltimore Colts, Schliemann demanded that

Sophie recite some Homer. She apparently did well enough, for they were married within three weeks of their meeting.

To the ancients, the historicity of the Trojan War had been unquestioned. Only in the century or so before Schliemann's birth had people begun believing that Homer had created Troy and its events out of whole cloth. ("[The city] was looked for to little purpose as long back as the time of Strabo," wrote one Robert Wood in 1769.) So when in the 1860s people began trying to locate the historic Troy, many considered the effort entirely wasted. Just the same, Herodotus said the Persian general Xerxes stopped at Troy in 480 BC and sacrificed a thousand oxen on his way to fight the Greeks; Alexander the Great, who slept with a copy of *The Iliad* under his pillow, visited in 334 BC, going the other direction. So practitioners of the nascent field of archaeology had begun rooting around northwestern Turkey looking for the site of the historic Troy, if there was one.

Several sites received attention, but accepting the advice of Frank Calvert, an expatriate Englishman who worked in the U.S. consulate and in his spare time practiced archaeology, Schliemann focused on a mound called Hisarlik, half of which Calvert owned. Calvert had dug unsuccessfully in several other locations, and though light digging at Hisarlik had yielded promising artifacts, he could not convince the British Museum to fund his work. Schliemann, with almost unlimited personal wealth, was glad to take over and began digging in 1871.

The digging quickly showed that the mound had been someplace important, plainly rebuilt time after time. Convinced that the Homeric Troy would be at the bottom, Schliemann set about getting to the bottom as quickly as possible—by having his workers dig a massive trench bisecting the mound. Photographs of the site at the time show huge piles of material from the trench unceremoniously dumped onto the nearby plain; writer Michael Wood has since called Troy "the ruin of a ruin." While Schliemann's methods make moderns tear at their hair in grief over what has been lost, remember—Schliemann was himself inventing the science of archaeology on the fly. The state of the art was to find a mound, dig until you found treasure worth telling the newspapers about (and selling), and then write a book to capitalize on your popular success.

Schliemann had quite some success. According to his own accounts, as he wandered through the site one day, a glint of gold caught his eye and he began digging with his bare hands, shouting for Sophie to send home the workers. Alone, they uncovered a cache of rings, diadems, cups, and other gold jewelry that he instantly dubbed "the Treasure of Priam," presuming that it was hastily buried as the Greeks fired the city. He and Sophie hid the gold in their clothing and made off with it. Pictures of Sophie wearing "the Jewels of Helen" appeared in newspapers throughout the world, making Schliemann famous.

The good news was the world had its historic Troy back; the bad news was just about everything else. Schliemann's trench had destroyed irreplaceable artifacts, helping make a hugely complex site even more so. And though Schliemann's site did appear to be Troy, experts quickly doubted whether the stratum at which Schliemann found the gold was really Homeric Troy. Many doubted the gold itself, wondering whether he had moved it there or even had it manufactured. (Later researchers have proved, for example, that Sophie was in Greece on the day Schliemann claims they found the hoard.)

Questions remain. Schliemann eventually spirited virtually all of the treasure away from Turkey; shown in German museums, the gold vanished at the end of World War II. If the gold was found where Schliemann claims to have found it, the pieces date probably from Troy II or III, which puts them nearly a thousand years before the Homeric Troy. As for the gold, it resurfaced in the 1990s in Russian museums and is now the subject of what some have called the second Trojan War—a tug-of-war between Turkey, Germany, Russia, and the Calvert family, all of whom claim legitimate title to at least some of it.

His success at Troy encouraged Schliemann to dig at Tiryns and at Mycenae, home of Agamemnon, where he had even more remarkable success, finding more treasures and artifacts, including a golden death mask he called "the mask of Agamemnon," now on display in Athens. His finds there suffered from the same degree of his own overstatement and a resulting backlash (the "mask of Agamemnon" is itself sometimes called a fake). Though "he gave history its missing childhood," according to a placard at the museum in his house in Athens, "fate is hard and hubris great": In 1890, "at the zenith of his worldwide recognition . . . sick and almost deaf, death struck ignominiously" as Schliemann traveled in Naples, and he died there, "alone and unknown." He left behind a columned mausoleum for his remains, which still stands in an Athens cemetery, bearing the legend "For the Hero, Schliemann." Most of the names associated with the Trojan War ended badly— Schliemann, then, may have gotten as close to Troy as you can.

SO ANYWAY—this Troy stuff: big mojo. As our little tour group walked the ruins, our guide, Baris, told us stories of Schliemann and Homer, of current experts finding mentions among Hittite ruins of an important city called Wilusa (Homer calls Troy Ilios, Latinized to Ilium), where the locals had trouble with a group called the Ahhiyawa (the Greeks, remember, were called Achaeans)—all supportive of a historic war at Troy, between European proto-Greeks and Asians from around Troy. Troy, with its prime location at the end of the Dardanelles, could easily have been the powerful city many conceive it to have been, a site where ships had to wait for the rare favorable winds from the south to go north through the channel, against a strong southward current. Taxing—or raiding—those ships would have made Troy rich, and attractive indeed to the Greeks growing in power. The Trojan War was, according to some current thinking, simply a war of acquisition, with Helen the equivalent of phantasmic "weapons of mass destruction" or the battleship *Maine* used to justify the attack.

In any case, theories of Troy, the Trojan War, and the Trojan Horse, Baris effectively demonstrated, are exactly like those surrounding the places Odysseus supposedly stopped: rife with uncertainty, with plenty of debate keeping things lively. On the other hand, there is a general agreement that this pile of rubble is indeed the place the ancients called Troy; that, from the evidence, there was a war and probably a siege here around the thirteenth century BC; and that the city was then destroyed by fire. Was it the war Homer described? None can say. As Baris pointed out, whether Homer was the biggest liar who ever lived, he surely told the story the way he wanted to, as has every author before and after him.

And honestly, I never felt like I had to make a choice. Walking those stone pathways, placing my palm against those heavy gray rocks, feeling the heat they absorbed from that unblinking Mediterranean sun, I was perfectly confident I was where Achilles fought and the Trojans foolishly trusted Greeks bearing gifts. Whether it was all a true history, a complete invention, or the likely human reimagining built up in layers on the armature of a few bare events like the rising city of Troy itself made no difference. For three thousand years people have looked to Troy as the battle at the beginning of Western culture, as the moment Europe and Asia turned from one another and parted, following separate destinies. That cultural significance was good enough for me. Here a city had stood—as a place for a settlement it was so worthy that it was rebuilt time after time. For millennia people called it Troy; then, for a few centuries, we thought differently, but now we're back to calling it Troy, and Troy it was as far as I was concerned. I sat in the grass for twenty minutes and sketched a wall identified as one from the Homeric Troy. I can't say I heard the hoofbeats of Achilles' horse as he dragged the corpse of Hector around and around the walls; I can't say I saw the flames rise as Odysseus and the others poured from the horse and fired the city. Even if I did, I'd only be saying what Schliemann said, and he turns out to be—like Odysseus, like Homer—a big liar.

But I thought about those things, and as I walked among the ruins I didn't think "there," I thought, "here," and I was glad. Queen Anne's lace grew in the weedy places, and the blossoms bob and twirl in the wind. For ten years that wind would have been the constant companion of Odysseus as he racked his brain to solve the impenetrable riddle of the conflict. Whether those ten years were fictional or real seemed utterly beside the point: The wind was real—eternal and real.

AFTER A COUPLE HOURS among the ruins, Jafar and I ignored a fence or two, climbed down steep ancient stairs to the base of the mound, and ran down the slope to the plain, setting off along farm roads, hoping to reach the Dardanelles. Among the farms and fields in the midday sun we wandered long enough that our water bottles ran out and we got a little turned around, so we gave up on walking to the sea. Returning to the ruins, we found fences that had been easy to hop on the way out not so congenial on the way in—Troy looked down on us, unconquerable as ever. So we had to make our way around the mound and into the little sunbaked town of Truva itself, a few streets of tiny block houses with clothes hung to dry, dogs and tractors patrolling in the dust, and a tiny store where we got cans of orange Fanta and directions back to the main road. We pawed through souvenirs and drank coffee while we waited for the minibus back to town; I bought a bracelet of protective evil eyes, like those carved into the Trojan walls, for my wife. Back in Çanakkale, Jafar, already headed out of town, caught another bus and I was on my own.

I spent the early evening on the rocky jetty along the harbor, dangling my feet in the Dardanelles and watching fishermen sell fish that slapped and flopped in the lids of five-gallon buckets along the quay. Ferries, caïques, tiny fishing boats, and huge freighters plied the waters, shockingly clear there at the gateway to the Mediterranean. I bought a kebab from one of the street vendors setting up for the evening and ate watching the orange sun sink into the Mediterranean at the mouth of the channel.

I found the Dardanelles themselves almost as inspirational as Troy. They're one of the world's pressure points, after all—the fracture between two continents, two cultures (when you land at the Istanbul airport and drive across the Ataturk Bridge, you see a sign, "Welcome to Asia," which is like the world champion Rotary Club–style "Welcome to Town" sign). People have been fighting there basically forever, and coming here to pay homage—whether Xerxes and Alexander looking for Troy, or Byron, in 1810, swimming across in homage of the legendary Leander, who swam across every night to Hero. They're a place people go looking for something—because they're a place where a lot of things have been. Baris, our guide, reminded us that Troy was a treasure hunt, whether we sought the historical treasure of the site itself or the treasure of the golden artifacts long before pillaged from the site by its first excavators.

But there was one more treasure, of course—the story. Told and retold in countless ways, both before Homer and after, the stories of Troy constituted the treasure I was after. The most thrilling thing of all about Troy was, finally, that it *is* backstory. Odysseus does remarkable things at Troy—but those things function only as background to his final story. With all that background finally under my belt, I was ready to go where I had set out to go—where Odysseus had gone. Among the ruins of Troy I found, at least, a place to start. From there, it was time to make my own way.

Chapter 4

Losing to the Twelfth Seed:

Surprised by the Cicones

From Ilium the wind carried our ships to Ismarus, home of the Cicones. There, as I commanded, we sacked the city and killed its defenders, dividing their wives and possessions as equally as possible among us. Then I ordered my men to return to the ships with what they had, but the fools did not obey me.

—*The Odyssey*, Book IX

THE FIRST THING ODYSSEUS DOES after leaving Troy is absorb an ass whipping. That is, he and his men commit a pirate raid on a people called the Cicones that ends in disaster.

Don't get the wrong idea about the raid. For Odysseus this pirate raid is, basically, like stopping for gas. In *The Iliad* Homer mentions the Cicones fighting on the Trojan side, rendering them perfectly fair game for raids by returning Greeks. Think of the journey from Troy to Ithaca as a long road trip; Odysseus and his men are just setting out, so they make an early pit stop to pick up some things for the road. But where we would stop at the Quickie Mart for twenty-ounce beverages and packets of junk food, seagoing war parties in the Bronze Age Mediterranean would stop at a coastal town and make off with food, treasure, and captives.

That is, making a pirate raid wasn't considered a bad thing—in *The Odyssey,* men arriving in new places are often blithely asked whether they are travelers or pirates, the way we ask someone we meet at a hotel whether he's traveling for pleasure or business. Thucydides noted that Bronze Age Mediterraneans located many of their towns a few miles inland just so they wouldn't be easy prey for such sea raiders. Though no picnic for the victims, pirate raids were just part of the game—and perfectly reasonable work.

As for the the Cicones, Herodotus, writing in the fifth century BC, places them in the northeastern Aegean district of Thrace, and four centuries later Strabo does the same. Thrace, just up the coast from Troy and the Dardanelles, would be right on the way home for Odysseus. In fact, there's virtually no disagreement among geographers ancient or modern that that's where the Cicones belong. Odysseus tells of raiding their coastal town called Ismarus, and today, at the base of a peak called Mount Ismarus in coastal Thrace, lies the little town of Maronia, near which is a broad archaeological site right on the sea, believed to be a Bronze Age town. Later in the poem we learn that a priest named Maron gave Odysseus gifts of wine and other treasure for sparing him during the raid, so those ruins near Maronia at the foot of Mount Ismarus thoroughly satisfied me as Odysseus's first stop. The nearest large town was Komotiní, where *Greece: The Rough Guide* promised I could find lodging, though I wasn't expected to like it. From there I could get a local bus to Maronia and then walk to visit my first purely Odyssean site. A glance at the Greece and western Turkey page of my atlas showed the red line of a highway wiggling north from the Dardanelles up toward Bulgaria, and a similar red line running from Istanbul west into Greece. Those lines crossed in far western Turkey at a place called Keşan. Though not described in any of my guidebooks, Keşan looked like someplace I could probably catch a bus for Greece.

The early ferry from Çanakkale was peopled almost entirely by old women in floral dresses, babushkas, socks, and sandals. They chattered among themselves in what sounded like a half-dozen languages—certainly at least Turkish, Greek, and Armenian—and alternated between two expressions: resignation and disgust. I felt like I was on a ferry with two hundred of my grandmother. We landed at Eceabat and I got on a bus.

* * *

RULE ONE OF WORLDWIDE BUS TRAVEL states that if you must take a long bus ride, take it in Turkey. A ride on a Turkish intercity bus is like a ride on an international plane used to be. For the moment leave out the clean, air-conditioned buses, the soft upholstery, the oriental rugs down the aisle instead of runners, and the omnipresent Turkish pop music (a hypnotically listenable mix of something like Europop and hip-hop, with a strong Arabic undertone). And look past the regular circulation of the attendant—there is one—with little complimentary cakes and cups of chai, *kahve,* water, or soda. Instead, consider this: On a Turkish bus, every hour or so, the attendant comes around with a bottle of cologne and a towel—you put out your hands, he holds the towel beneath them to catch stray drops, and he pours a dollop of cologne on your hands, which you apply to forearms, face, and neck, often running the last drops through your hair.

It's comforting in an almost apologetic way: "Nobody likes being cooped up on a bus for hours," it admits, "and we'd all probably like—and could use—a bath. In the meantime, here's something to refresh us all, and to keep us from offending one another." It's kind, decent, and fundamentally human, something that can be said about relatively little contemporary travel. The cologne smells almost exactly, by the way, like the ancient bottles of bergamot found at Schwab's general store in Memphis—*bergamot* has, it turns out, a Turkish root. As I marinated in that aroma north of Eceabat, fields of brilliant yellow sunflowers rolled by the windows.

Thus it was something of a shock to descend from the bus into the overexposed midday sunlight of the vast, rolling emptiness surrounding the Keşan bus station. Lithe dark men shouting, *"Grek! Grek! Grek!"* raced up, surrounding me and competing to wrestle away my backpack. After a moment of confusion, I decided that people screaming destinations in my face—"Athina! Personal! Okay!"—probably weren't official greeters, and I seized my pack and entered the bus station, a dim, one-story octagonal building that had almost certainly been mopped at least once since Turkey became a republic in 1923.

The walls of the bus station were pierced with tiny walk-through offices, each for a different bus company going different places. Only a few of those seemed to be open, staffed by men in white shirts that stuck to their backs. The office windows were covered with unrecognizable, wild-looking words—*yolcu, derya, gideceği yer, maliye bakanliği*—all surrounded by the accents that render Turkish terrifying to the uninitiated. Place-names were even worse—for example, Yunanistan. Not seeing the name of the country you hope to visit is disconcerting; seeing listings for countries you've never even heard of makes a bus station a forbidding place, especially a gloomy, echoing half-empty concrete bus station on the edge of a small Turkish town. I wandered the halls, occasionally sitting on the slatted wooden benches, consulting my guidebooks, and wondering what to do.

On about my fourth cycle around the octagon a man approached, plainly seeking to know where I wished to go. "Komotiní?" I said. A pause. I added, "Greece?" He looked momentarily perplexed: "Komo- . . . Ko- . . . ," and then he brightened. "Greek," he said, and walked me into an office. I heard a few guttural words, saw nods. The man behind the counter smiled and showed me a photocopied schedule, and I quickly understood: Yunanistan is what the Turks call Greece, and Komotiní was also known by another name: Gümüljina. I could catch a bus—the next day. I nodded thoughtfully, but I didn't have long to wonder: The man scrawled the name "Ahyon" onto a piece of paper and smiled at me. "Hotel!" he said, and I smiled back and bought my bus ticket. He led me outside, past several taxis to one he considered trustworthy, handed the slip of paper to the driver, and off I went.

The mostly empty Ahyon Hotel clearly served the few foreign visitors Keşan saw. My small room had a tiny orange flame bulb in the wall sconce, as though to remind me I was in Turkey, the mysterious Orient. They didn't need to: I felt as far from home as I'd ever been. On the TV were reruns of *Scooby-Doo* dubbed in Turkish. I took out *The Odyssey* and read about the Cicones.

WINNING THE WAR is the second-worst thing that could have happened to the Greeks. Sure, they want to win, and what with Odysseus and the horse and all they surely do, but they've been there ten years, and more than a little frustration has built up. The sack of Troy becomes a bloodbath, in which the victorious Greeks disgrace themselves.

Think of the Greeks as a football team. What they've done, finally, is win their championship. What happens, you might say, is they demonstrate excessive celebration, dancing like fools in the end zone, while their hordes turn over cars and loot downtown furniture stores—only in this case celebration involves burning the town and murdering children. Above all, the lesser Ajax (there were two Ajaxes among the Greeks) drags Cassandra, daughter of Priam, from the temple of Athena and rapes her.

Call Athena the referee, then, because she is outraged by what Ajax has done—especially since she has been supporting the Greek cause the whole way—and calls a penalty on the Greeks, sending a huge storm to bedevil them as they try to make their way home. Odysseus has a special relationship with Athena, but he suffers just the same. Her displeasure is apparent before that very first stop among the Cicones. Before even sailing away, the Greeks begin bickering among themselves. Agamemnon favors remaining at Troy long enough to make a mollifying sacrifice to Athena; Menelaus figures it's too late for that and the thing to do is head home, and fast. Half of the vessels go with Menelaus, but they, too, quickly factionalize, and some go back to Agamemnon. Odysseus and his twelve ships rejoin Agamemnon.

With sacrifices performed, Odysseus and his ships again get going from Troy, and almost immediately they pull over at the land of the Cicones, where, Odysseus later tells the Phaeacians, "we sacked the city and killed its defenders." Simple stuff. He orders his crew to load up and move out, but they're not having any of it, partying down with wine, mutton, and some nice fresh-captured Ciconian women. Odysseus doesn't mention it yet, but Ciconian wine is strong stuff, which might explain some of the men's actions. In any case, the party goes on until dawn—at which point Ciconian reinforcements arrive, descending on Odysseus and his bleary-eyed crew "as thick as the leaves and flowers of spring." The Greeks escape, but not before losing about seventy men. They row off, grieving. And with the exception of that powerful Ciconian wine that Maron gave Odysseus, which reappears down the line, that's the Cicones episode.

On the one hand, this is thin stuff. A real place, a skirmish, on to the next. It's like a speeding ticket near Indianapolis, a bar fight in Kansas

City. No exotic locale, no remarkable bad guy, not the highlight of your story when you tell friends about your trip. It's hard to understand until you remember a point Strabo makes about Homer: "A man will lie more plausibly," the geographer says, "if he will mix in some actual truth." That is, if you want your story to work, you don't start with the most preposterous element—you start with something normal and work your way in. *The Wizard of Oz* starts with an unhappy girl in Kansas, not with talking trees and flying monkeys. Just so, Odysseus's tale starts somewhere very much on the map, among a people widely known—the sex-hungry goddesses and man-eating giants can come later. With the Cicones, Homer has Odysseus lay the groundwork, presenting his bona fides as a reliable narrator. Especially since the episode doesn't make Odysseus look like much—this is Odysseus as bad boss, a guy who either can't manage his employees or doesn't bother to, and the result is grim, at least for seventy or so of them. Nobody would make up a story like this to tell on himself, so it must be true.

In modern terms, the Cicones episode smacks of post-victory letdown. Returning to the metaphor of the Greeks as league champs, the voyage home is their next season, with their first game against some second-division nobody. The Greeks run up a big score at halftime—and then forget about the second half. They just beat the Trojans in the big one, so you can't be surprised they let their guard down and manage to lose the next time they take the field. It's a stretch, of course, but the point remains: Odysseus, "peer of Zeus in counsel," the brains behind the Trojan Horse, was the MVP of the Trojan War. He and his twelve ships of loot, slaves, and conquering heroes make a quick stop at the Cicones for a little more loot—and through lack of focus and discipline they blow it.

THERE'S ANOTHER WAY TO LOOK at the debacle against the Cicones, though—and that's to see it as evidence that Odysseus and his men are traveling without protection from the gods.

The gods play active roles in Homer and in all the tales of the Epic Cycle—in fact, in all the stories of ancient Greece. They take sides, getting personally involved in one-on-one fighting. *The Iliad* can be frustrating to a modern reader because every time some conflict seems about to be finally resolved, some god intervenes and changes everything. For example, Menelaus and Paris agree to meet in single combat to settle the dispute over Helen once and for all. Menelaus quickly knocks Paris over and is dragging him back to the Greek camp—until Aphrodite swoops in and spirits Paris back to Troy. It's not enough that the men have to fight each other—they have to deal with the gods, who are capricious, petty, childish, self-interested, and cruel.

Which, miraculously, is perfect, once you get used to it. Doesn't that unpredictability exactly represent how life really is—that you're getting the upper hand in some personal conflict, you're about to achieve your goal, and then from nowhere comes something completely unexpected? The polytheistic Greek way of looking at things comes closer to offering a sensible explanation for the vagaries of our daily lives than any organized religion since. It doesn't merely offer some vague notion of a rewards-based afterlife; instead, it explains why things are so difficult right here on earth. Every monotheistic religion has as a central tenet the unknowableness of God. The book of Job, the prodigal son, the admonition to turn the other cheek: All are variations on a theme, which is "Don't try to figure it out—just trust us on this." With a single deity this stinginess with explanation begins to seem like churlishness. But many gods, with different ideas and personalities, pursuing conflicting goals? Now you're getting somewhere—no promise of heavenly rewards, but as a model of explanation it works great. Take, for example, the Anopheles mosquito, which spreads malaria. Which current religion gives you a good explanation for that biological treat? But let's say Athena is helping foreigners dig a canal; the locals appeal to Apollo for help; and here comes the Apollo-blessed mosquito to spread disease among the interlopers. Now you've got an explanation.

So when we try to understand the collapse of Odysseus's troops at Ismarus, we should remember: For ten years, this crew has been fighting with Athena at their backs. Not only that, Athena more than favors Odysseus; she's practically his girlfriend. The relationship between Odysseus and Athena is like no other between man and god: "Never have I seen the gods so openly loving as Pallas Athena was [at Troy]," the Greek hero Nestor tells Telemachus, Odysseus's son, "standing out in full view by your father's side." So Odysseus's men are used to solid protection, and leaving Troy after a halfhearted attempt to placate Athena, the crew may not yet have had it sink in that they're traveling without their usual guardian. Then things don't go well at Ismarus. And it turns out that's just the beginning.

INDEPENDENT TRAVELERS develop a list of frustrations to which their pursuits render them vulnerable. Among these are being constantly hit on by unattractive members of the gender you find least appealing; laundries in which people whose language you do not speak do things to your clothing you would never have thought it would cross the mind of a person to do; or confidently ordering unusual-looking food from a street vendor and discovering with the first bite that this is one of those countries where it's normal to eat guts. (I did this in a Keşan park; I suspect the vendors there still chuckle. Word to the wise: a vertically spinning rotisserie is *döner* kebab, delicious and similar to the Greek gyros; a horizontally spinning rotisserie is probably *kokoreç*, which is sheep intestines, and tastes like sheep intestines.)

But atop this list lies arriving, late in the day and unprepared, in a city entirely unknown to you. There you stand, utterly alone, knowing that not a single person you know has the first idea of where you might be, and for a moment, without resources, you freeze: You haven't got a map, you don't know where the tourist agency is, and the sun is going down. It's a tough way to roll into town, and it usually happens when a plane is delayed, a train breaks down, a boat is missed.

Or when the bus from Keşan makes a not-sharp-enough left turn, smashes a Greek "Don't Walk" sign off a light pole, and comes to a sudden stop at the curb of one of the main streets in Komotiní. Maybe the bus always disgorges its intercity passengers by the side of the road, or maybe it usually goes to the bus station, but the driver, anxious to flee before anybody thought to write down his bus number, just took the opportunity to throw my bag—and me—off the bus and go. In any case, before I had a moment to collect my thoughts, I was standing on a sidewalk, nearby people were pointing at twisted metal and broken glass in the street, and the bus was grinding away in a cloud of exhaust. Every sign I could see around me was in Greek; if Turkish is scary, at least they use the Roman alphabet. And the sun was going down.

I started walking.

But one of the benefits of independent travel is that you learn to solve problems quickly, because what are your alternatives? Plus, I was on the street of a medium-sized European city, where downtown is still downtown; and whether you know the language or not, when you walk into a hotel carrying luggage, they have a pretty good idea of what you want. I found a nice cheap room on the main street, next to a souvlaki place that supplied a dinner I could bring up to my room. Instead of *Scooby-Doo* dubbed in Greek, I found on the TV the European football championship, with the Greeks, tremendous underdogs, playing in the final. When they won, I could hear the cheering outside. Walking to the city's central plaza, I found celebration, but not excessive: no cars turned over or fires set, but a good deal of fireworks, smoke bombs, and blue-and-white Greek flags, to say nothing of beer and ouzo in abundance. Early the next morning, on the half-hour bus trip to Maronia, the radio blasted pop music—cheerful, sunny stuff, with bouzoukis marking it as unmistakably Greek—but periodically paused for a replay of the call of the game's lone goal, and everyone on the bus would smile and smile.

The bus drove through little whitewashed towns where you have to slow down for the tractors. Maronia was the last stop, a tiny town center arranged around a little loop in the road at the wooded top of a hill. A cafe offered retsina and beer; I made a mental note for later, but I headed south out of town, following the main asphalt road toward a sign I had seen on the drive in: "ΑΡΧΑΙΑ ΜΑΡΩΝΕΙΑ ΚΛΑΣΙΚΟ ΤΕΙΧΟΣ"—"Ancient Maronia Classical Fortification Wall." It pointed down a brown dirt road that quickly degraded into a bumpy path as it meandered into the foothills covered by low sage shrubs, the conical peak of Mount Ismarus looming to the left. It looked lonely, hot, and dry, with no source of shade under a sun that though it wasn't yet 10 a.m. already looked angry. Walking out of Maronia I had passed a little corner grocery, and I considered climbing back up the hill to supplement my couple bottles of water. But going a half mile back uphill sounded awful, plus the sketchy reference in my guidebook assured me the archaeological site was a mere four kilometers (a little more than two miles) away.

While I dithered, a dark-haired woman in a black housedress and flip-flops shuffled from a lonely white house at the crossroads and slowly crossed the main road to a cemetery, where she gathered some rosemary from among the white crosses and bright-red roses, then slowly climbed back through her doorway, vanishing like a ghost. I probably should have made note of her sepulchral pace. Instead, impatient enough to forgo extra water, I charged down the rocky dirt path that wound among the fields and rolling hills, generally descending toward the sea. Within a few minutes I was hot enough to remove the zippered trouser legs from my pants—and to recognize that my two half-liter bottles of water would require careful management during my hike.

The road wound long enough that I had time to begin wondering whether I had missed a turn—the occasional dusty turnoffs never seemed likely to be the right way, but after about an hour I had to figure I had gone, all downhill, at least four kilometers. Even if I had spoken Greek, there was nobody to ask—I hadn't seen another person since the woman gathering rosemary had disappeared back into the dimness of her house. Even the road—sometimes dirt, sometimes concrete—seemed confused itself as to whether it was worth all the trouble to get to this place. Just when I was considering wandering back to one of the turnoffs, I finally came upon a sign, and then the ruins of an ancient theater. Built probably in the third or second century BC, with three rows of marble seats I could still sit in, the theater reflected Maronia's status as an important city in classical Thrace. Wandering the site a little farther—it stretches about two kilometers—I found Roman gates, the ruins of a temple, and a signposted stretch of "ancient Maroneia city wall"—a bunch of rocks among what looked like purple loosestrife. The thing that thrilled me most, for some reason, was the vast number of shotgun shells scattered among the ruins. Greeks, it seems, enjoy themselves the same way Americans do: by going to quiet, beautiful places and shooting off guns. Utterly alone, I rested beneath the boughs of an old olive tree at the front of the theater as the cool sea breeze evaporated my sweat.

The marble seats and carved walls were lovely, though far later than Odysseus's period. I found the older, rough-hewn stones of the ancient walls, which may well have been from the second millennium BC, strangely unaffecting: old rocks, covered by earth, then uncovered by archaeologists; no trace of the sense of place I felt at Troy. I couldn't for a second say I felt the geographical memory of twelve ships pulling up to the shore or even of what life might have been like for those living on the slope of this mountain before those ships came. Neither the village nor the battle came to life for me—not surprising, since Homer describes neither: "We sacked the city and killed its defenders," Odysseus says, then points out that further defenders show up and return the favor. Not much to relive at Ismarus, really, and it seemed a dubious first stop on a long journey—that, at least, Odysseus and I had in common.

I took a few sips of my precious water, closing my eyes and concentrating on the cool breeze. I heard dogs barking, the wind in the trees, and goat bells—a wooden, hollow, almost magical sound never far from the ear in rural Greece. The shaded air beneath the olive was a degree or so cooler than that surrounding, so each new breath of breeze brought first the hot air from the sunny, sandy clearing around the tree, then the cool air that pushed it. I could smell the sea.

And I got an idea. I walked back up to the uncertain road and scouted the territory. Olive trees poked out here and there, coalescing into groves farther up the slope, but near the bottom the land was scrubby and sere, a cross between pebbly dirt and sand. Due south, though, the Aegean glittered. The Thracian coast is mostly rocky, with steep faces of ten feet or more descending directly into the water. Just the same, I was hot, I was tired, and I had approached my Odyssean site entirely by land—it seemed like a good time to go to the sea. I walked along the road until a scrubby, unmarked way presented itself—then I fairly ran, following descending plateaus of barer and barer rock until, on a little promontory, I found a place to scrabble down a steep, crumbling slope to a small crescent of pebbly beach. Backpack and boots were off in seconds, and I waded into the relief of the deep-blue Aegean.

The clear sea lay still, so calm that as I floated I kept on hat and sunglasses to protect me from the harsh sun in the absolutely cloudless sky. Tiny fish darted through the swaying sea grass in the clear water, and a million perfect skipping stones competed for attention. Give me a bottle of retsina and a crushing victory to celebrate and I could suddenly understand why a place like this would be hard to row away from. Swallows zipped by, but otherwise the only sound was the peaceful murmur of the pebbles turning under those gentle ripples at the shore. I swam, sunbathed, napped. Only when a boat putted by and slowed down to check out the lone figure on the beach was the spell broken. So I dried off and headed back. I got somewhat lost among the tracks back to the road, and my water was long gone in a half hour. Near the main road I stumbled across a sign I had missed the first time: "Οδῦσσειο Ρειθρο, 7, Αρχαια Ισμαρα, 6"—Odyssean Channel, 7 kilometers; Ancient Ismarus, 6 kilometers. Though it clarified why it took me so long to find the ruins, it made me curious enough about what the Odyssean Channel could be that I considered turning around and walking back. Without water, fortunately, I clung to sanity.

When I reached the little store, I drained two liters of water sitting on its steps. The little café in the town center was out of retsina, so I sat with a beer, and a local who spoke a little English helped me piece together the meaning of the signs I had seen. He was familiar with the archaeological site, though he'd never been there and didn't know it had any connection to Odysseus; about the Odyssean Channel, he had no clue. He called a few other Maronians on his cell phone and got no better information; he smiled, shrugged, wished me well, and left me in the shade to wait for my bus back to Komotiní. I took out my *Odyssey* and read again about Odysseus and the Cicones.

I TRIED TO FIND A MESSAGE in the episode, I really did. But the best I could muster, taking into account Odysseus's dithering back and forth between Agamemnon and Menelaus when leaving Troy, and his inability to get his troops off the beach after the initial success at Ismarus, was not to stay too long at the fair. If Odysseus and his troops had moved out immediately after drubbing the Cicones, they'd have escaped a beating; and if they'd left Troy once instead of twice—well, who knows what might have been different for them? For Nestor, who told that story, the journey home passed like an afternoon sail on a sunny day; Menelaus, with him, eventually made it home safely, too. Agamemnon, whom Odysseus turned around to rejoin, ended up killed by his faithless wife and her lover. To be fair, that seemed like overanalysis: Odysseus never looked back at those decisions, though he clearly learned from them. Odysseus just kept moving.

Which, if you're looking for a message, actually works pretty well, as advice in travel—or in career or family, for that matter. Just put one foot in front of the other—keep going and you'll probably get there. Odysseus gives a great example of what *not* to do, and honestly, when I hesitated, waterless, at the sign on the dirt road, I consciously thought back to his mistakes. I had seen ancient Ismarus, I was out of water, and it was time to head back. Maybe I had missed out on something and maybe not, but Odysseus's missteps made the point clear: Make your stop, do your best, then get going. Don't go back to start again; don't wait around for the reinforcements to come and kick your butt. Just keep going.

So I kept going. Back in Komotiní I did what was already becoming a routine: spread out on the bed my travel guides, maps, and *The Odyssey* and began planning my next destination. After that, with the remaining light I saw what I could of Komotiní—a low clock tower from Ottoman days looms regally over an old bazaar, with narrow streets, tiny stores selling clothes, notions, souvenirs, and, of course, coffee. Plenty of mosques mix with the churches, though the large Turkish population frustrates some of the Greeks. I got into a conversation about this with the woman who sold souvlakis next to my hotel—your souvlaki, by the way, comes wrapped in pita with French fries, and if there's a better meal on this planet I have not yet encountered it.

Her name was Marina and she spoke excellent English; since I took most of my Komotiní meals from her little takeout, we became familiars. She spoke rapidly and had quick dark eyes, and I spoke to her whenever I could; she pointed me in the direction of train and bus stations, gave me negotiating tips for taxis, suggested routes for walks, and, of course, fed me. We had discussed my journey, and I suggested that the seemingly peaceful mixture of Turks and Greeks in Komotiní indicated that though from the Trojan War through modern times Turks and Greeks have been at odds, old wounds were finally healing. A dark cloud passed over her face.

"You know," she said, lowering her voice, "they do not even call Komotiní." She shook her head. "They say: *Gümüljina*." She almost spat out the word. Then she leaned closer, pointing generally east. "And you know Constantinopoli?" I did. "They do not call Constantinopoli. They call *Istanbul*." She opened her eyes wide, spread her hands, palm upward: Can you believe it? "Is *not* Istanbul," she fiercely said. "Is Constantinopoli! They have different word for *everything!*"

A stranger in a strange land, I could but agree. Of course, I had agreed days before when, in that dim bus station in Keşan, two young Turkish men heading north for a hiking vacation had expressed concern when I told them I was going into that wild land of Yunanistan. I wouldn't consider going hiking with them instead? Nothing could dissuade me from my foolish decision? Okay, they ceded, but among those Greeks I was to be very careful. One actually shook a finger: "They will burglar you."

I spent many weeks in Greece, and nobody burglared me; the Greeks were if anything the only equals to the Turks in hospitality I met on my journey. Turks pushed extra cakes and sodas on me during bus rides, forced me to sample several dishes before ordering in restaurants, tried to refuse payment; Greeks took me by the hand and led me to bus stations, translated menus and maps, stood me drinks (when a man behind a Komotiní coffee bar learned I was in search of the Cicones and their famous wine, he poured me a free glass of *tsipouro,* a less-flavored cousin of ouzo). Among descendants of both Menelaus and Paris, the tradition of *xenia* lives on. Just not, it seems, for each other.

I was sorry to leave the Turks behind, and sorry to leave the borderlands where differences as old as the Trojan War remained. But if the Cicones episode taught anything, it was to do your business and move on. So I moved on.

Chapter 5

Acropolis Now:

Athens and Other Places Actually on the Map

But come, let me have a swift ship and twenty oarsmen, for I shall journey to Sparta and sandy Pylos to learn what I may of my long-lost father's return, hoping to hear some word from mortal men, or, what is more likely, from Zeus himself.

—*The Odyssey*, Book II

YOU HAVE TO CLIMB a lot of steps to get to the Acropolis. This sounds like an opaque piece of advice some uncle might give you, but it just means when you get there, you'll be hot. Of course, it's Greece, in July, and you're standing atop a vast outcropping of pale limestone with nothing around you for shade but ruined marble buildings— you should expect hot. Anyhow, hot scarcely matters: you're on the Athenian Acropolis, gazing at the Parthenon, the fundamental image of our cultural dawn. Those dun rows of fluted Doric columns supporting ruined pediments barely suggesting a triangle represent everything classical to Westerners. The shrine to Athena, goddess of wisdom, in the city that shares her name: the center of ancient Greece, the birthplace of the West. You can see across the coastal plain to the Aegean from up there—and you can see the Acropolis, hundreds of feet above the surrounding plain, from nearly everywhere in Athens.

In fact, that's why you came: What you do in Athens is look at up at the Acropolis, the "high city" of ceremonial buildings, dominated by the Parthenon. You take the funicular car up Lycavitos Hill, one of eight huge hills that dot the plain of Athens, and in front of the tiny church at its height you look across at the Parthenon. You stand upon the rock Areopagus—the site of the ancient civic court, not far from the world's first democratic meeting, which gathered a few steps away on the Pnyx hillside—and you look up at the Parthenon. You wander the tiny streets of the old Plaka district or pay $5.50 for an orange juice at a shaded table on the Monastiraki Plaza, and you look up. Stark in the sun or magically illuminated at night, wrecked by age and war (damage to the Parthenon occurred mostly when it was used as a gun-powder magazine in a seventeenth-century war between the Turks and the Venetians), the Parthenon on the Acropolis represents the West giving birth to itself, seemingly squeezing that miraculously proportional, columned temple out of the fertile Greek rock.

Not to say there's not plenty more to do in Athens, with a great archaeological museum, wonderful markets and parks, and no short-age of other ruins. The easternmost outpost of the West, Athens crawls with Byzantine churches to constantly remind you that you're closer to Istanbul than to Rome, though you hear church bells instead of muezzins throughout the day. Actually, though, you don't hear much of either—you hear mostly traffic. Traffic chokes Athens's streets, the constant hooting of car horns and the beeps and whines of scooters and motorcycles overwhelming any church bells except when, like those of the church next to my hotel, they ring madden-ingly for hours. Athens is hot and gritty, a dirty, decaying city of end-less white apartment blocks, bumpy sidewalks, and a downtown mixture of every century from the sixth BC to the twenty-first AD, all beneath the gaze of that looming Acropolis. Few tourists stay much longer than it takes to see the Acropolis and the National Archae-ological Museum, then grab a souvlaki and board a bus to one of the ports for the islands. Just the same, hot and dirty or not, Athens makes being a tourist easy—it's been hosting tourists for as long as anyplace on earth, with the probable exception of the Great Pyramid. Odysseus never saw the Great Pyramid. Then again, he never saw Athens, either.

*　*　*

ODYSSEUS DEPARTS FROM THRACE after the debacle with the Cicones; leaving their companions dead on the beach, he and his crews sail on, "glad to be alive," he says, "but grieving for our good friends no longer with us." He leaves behind a lot more than Thrace and his dead companions, however—he leaves behind the real world. Soon comes another indication, following their drubbing by the Cicones, that they have no friends among the gods: a monstrous storm, stirred up by Zeus on behalf of the affronted Athena. As the flotilla tries to round Cape Malea—the southernmost tip of mainland Greece, only another couple days' sail from Ithaca—a raging north wind propels them southward for nine full days: far from home, far from Ithaca, far from the mainland. In fact, that storm blows Odysseus right off the map. After the adventure with the very real Cicones in the very real location of Thrace, while trying to round the very real Cape Malea, the men are blown to the highly imaginary land of the Lotus-eaters. And until he finally lands—gently—among the semireal Phaeacians, Odysseus stays off the map for the next ten years.

I did not yet leave the map. For the only time, in fact, I diverged from my straightforward progress along his path. Odysseus stopped next among the Lotus-eaters, which since before Strabo geographers have associated with the North African coast. But unless I planned to charter a yacht directly from Thrace, the way from Komotiní to North Africa went through Athens. And though Athens barely rates a mention in *The Odyssey,* I didn't race through Athens in a hurry to get someplace else.

Equally important, Athens made a great base from which to visit two sites directly related to *The Odyssey.* The beach town of Pylos (Homer always calls it "sandy Pylos"), home to the old warrior Nestor, was only a few hours away by bus; and Sparta, home of Menelaus and Helen—the sick little family whose marital troubles lay at the very heart of the Trojan War—was even closer. Add in that Mycenae, the home of Agamemnon, was the easiest bus trip of all, and Athens became inevitable. I rode the train from Komotiní, rocking past Mount Olympus, veiled in cloud. I drew sketches as we went by.

* * *

THE ADVENTURES OF TELEMACHUS—sometimes called the Telemachiad—take up the first four books of *The Odyssey* and make a light early counterweight to the adventures of Odysseus that constitute the poem's center. Odysseus goes to a dozen places, most of them magical and unknown, and meets challenges of all kinds; his son goes only to two places, both utterly quotidian, and meets with nothing but wonderful hospitality—a perfect, tame first outing for a young man of twenty.

Book I focuses on Ithaca, and on just how badly things are going in the absence of Odysseus. On Olympus, Athena convinces Zeus to let her free Odysseus. After suggesting that Hermes go to Calypso's isle to take care of the details, Athena herself heads to Ithaca to help prod Telemachus along into manhood.

In the guise of Odysseus's old friend Mentes, Athena stops at the door to the palace. It's full of suitors, some 108 of them, flouting the laws of hospitality, partying in Odysseus's home, trying to force Penelope to give up on Odysseus and marry one of them. They've been at this for years. Telemachus, grown near to manhood wishing for his father's return, treats the disguised Athena with respect—fulfilling his duties as a host. She encourages Telemachus to grow up and tell off the suitors, which he does, in Book II calling a town assembly (the first since Odysseus left), where he tells the suitors to lay off.

The suitors defend their conduct with the famous story of Penelope and the shroud. They're only hanging around, they claim, because Penelope has promised to marry one of them as soon as she finishes weaving a funeral shroud for Laertes, Odysseus's father, who has in disgust moved into a shack out in the fields. He's old, he may die soon, and Penelope claimed she refused to consider him dying without a shroud to honor him. The suitors acquiesced, and for three years Penelope publicly wove by day—and then, by night, secretly unraveled what she had done, thus visibly busy at her task but never nearing the goal she didn't wish to reach. It's a brilliant plan, showing sneaky Penelope to be an obvious match for the equally sneaky, if absent, Odysseus. Regrettably, one of her servants eventually leaked, and the suitors have been even more aggressive since the story came out.

Telemachus still demands that the suitors leave. He also announces that he plans to set out by ship seeking news of his long-absent father.

Now in the guise of Mentor, to whom Odysseus had trusted management of his household twenty years previously, Athena helps Telemachus organize his departure. The faithful maid Eurycleia helps, too, provisioning Telemachus for his journey and keeping the news from Penelope. The suitors, naturally, determine to murder him on his return, and at the end of Book II Telemachus sails away in secret. He makes for Pylos, a city on the southwestern shore of the Peloponnese Peninsula, home of Nestor, the oldest of the heroes who fought at Troy.

SURROUNDED BY CAFÉS and almost completely shaded by a vast spreading plane tree, Platía Trión Navárhon, the main square of Pylos, sits directly on Navarino Bay, protected from the Mediterranean by the long island of Sphacteria. Little blue fishing boats bob in the gentle wavelets that make it as far as the quay along the squared-off harbor, and you can watch them from one of the round marble tables beneath the tree and sip lemonade—or beer or ouzo—for hours without running up much of a tab. When you get hot or bored, you can walk a few steps to the public beach and cool off in the bay. At dinnertime the cafés that not only surround the square but run up the quay compete to serve you fresh fish, salads, and aromatic grilled meat at tables under tents, overlooking the water. You easily find a cheap and friendly hotel by walking up one of the streets that rise steeply from the square, and from your window you see palm trees, bleached-white walls, tile roofs, and the deep blue Ionian. Near the far southwestern tip of the Peloponnese Peninsula, Pylos would have been an easy sail from Ithaca. For his introduction to adventure travel, Telemachus had it pretty good.

About sixteen kilometers north of the square lies an archaeological site, discovered in 1939, left untouched during World War II, and then excavated according to modern principles to reveal the finest and best-preserved ruins of a Bronze Age palace in the Peloponnese. Given that it's so close to the Pylos Homer described, it's been referred to as Nestor's palace since its excavators revealed it in 1952. I checked with a local bar and reserved a scooter for the next morning, then spent the afternoon and evening floating in the Ionian and sipping drinks beneath the plane tree. Tiny lights in the tree illuminated the main square as kids played soccer, teens cruised in cars and scooters, and families still talked and laughed at well past ten, when I finally returned to my room to read about Telemachus and Nestor.

His friends probably called Nestor garrulous; his enemies would have just rolled their eyes. Nestor, in *The Iliad* and here in *The Odyssey,* was a talker—the old man of the bunch, always speechifying and regaling the soldiers with tales of his own exploits, back when men was men. Most of his advice, however, proves good—in *The Iliad* he counsels the Greeks to build a protective wall near their ships, and he tries hard to get Agamemnon and Achilles talking. And when Athena calls up those storms against the victorious Greeks on their return trip, Nestor is the lone Greek captain who encounters no trouble, simply leaving Troy and sailing home.

Telemachus, traveling with Athena (still disguised as Mentor), finds Nestor sacrificing cattle to the gods on the sandy beach. Nestor and his sons welcome Telemachus and Athena, pleasing the goddess with their hospitality. When after dinner Telemachus identifies himself, Nestor describes his own uneventful return from Troy, mentioning that he last saw Odysseus returning to Agamemnon. He also relates the tragic tale of Agamemnon, killed upon his return from Troy by his faithless wife, Clytemnestra, and her lover, who were themselves thereafter killed in revenge by Agamemnon's son, Orestes. If Telemachus needed examples of what a household should look like after Troy—and how a son should respond when it doesn't—Nestor provides them all. Nestor also, of course, gives Telemachus the meal, bath, and night's lodging expected; he even has Polycaste, his own comely daughter, provide the bath.

A POINT ABOUT BATHS, of which *The Odyssey* is full. I usually scanned those blithely: "Yes, yes, another bath—on to the good part." After all, what host wouldn't offer a guest a bath? So do we all today: "Here's a towel, and you'll find in the medicine cabinet a selection of soaps and tiny bottles of shampoo filched from our nation's finer midlevel motels. Knock yourself out." But I got a sense of why Homer finds these baths worth mentioning when in Istanbul, at the outset of my trip, my friend Andrew paid our way into the Çinili Hamam, a magnificent stone and tile building built in 1640 that looked like a mosque.

We each got a private room in which to disrobe, and a long, wide cotton towel called a *peshtemel,* to be wrapped around the waist for modesty throughout the bath. We stopped first on the central slab, above the boiler, where we lay briefly to begin sweating, below a dome punctured by circular glass skylights, through which rays of sunlight illuminated the moist air in the echoing room. We went next to semi-private areas called *halvets,* where at personal taps, using water scoops and soap, we lightly bathed, taking care of personal areas. Finally, though, came the *tellaks*—the men who would actually bathe us. Led into the hotter, outer rim of the circular *hamam,* each of us was seated on an individual pad and ministered to by a heavyset guy with a Saddam Hussein mustache, his own *peshtemel,* and hands stronger than stone. With no more than words of greeting and thanks in Turkish I could say nothing to my *tellak,* and with no English he could do no more, yet his hands communicated every move I needed to make, every shift of my weight to enable his wool loofah to remove layers of skin I didn't even know I had. He moved with such practice and confidence that any hesitation or resistance I harbored melted in seconds; I think in such a bath an adult approaches the feeling a baby must have when its parents wash it. A brief massage followed, after which my *tellak* stood before me and with a firm final nod shook hands, ending our relationship.

Fluffy towels and a little glass of Istanbul's famous tea awaited in our private dressing rooms, where Andrew had to knock on the door to rouse me from ecstatic repose upon my couch. I doubted I had ever before been so clean. "After one of these," Andrew said, "I feel like I even *see* better."

COINCIDENTALLY, NESTOR'S PALACE contains a perfectly preserved ceramic bathtub. By the time I stood in front of it, I wanted to climb in. My scooter rental fell through—the definitions of "morning" and "scooter" apparently change across cultures—so I grabbed the only

Sunday morning bus from Pylos to the palace site, figuring I'd worry about getting back when that became important. The walk from the bus stop to the palace wasn't a quarter mile, but away from the sea breeze, the day was extremely hot.

Just the same, atop Englianos hill and mercifully shaded by a metal shed roof, the palace site rewards your sweat, commanding a great view of the harbor to the south. Roses, geraniums, and sunflowers pepper its areas of open lawn, and vines with peach-colored trumpet flowers snake up the surrounding olives and palms. A uniform terra-cotta brown, the ruined palace walls remain several feet high—thus rather than among the foundations, I felt as though I actually stood in the two-story palace. The megaron, or throne room, with its vast plastered floor and central hearth, has a waiting area with benches that I could easily imagine crowded with supplicants; storerooms with huge buried pithoi (urns) of olive oil demonstrate the importance of oil in the Bronze Age for both cooking and lighting; guard posts at the main entries show how secure the palace would have been; and stairwells to the second floor reminded me that I saw only half at best of what was once there. Though Nestor is an old guy whose stories tend to go on, he's got a hell of a place, and I could see why Telemachus enjoyed his visit. I got an even better sense of the palace at the tiny museum in the nearby town of Hora, which has not just the usual selection of cracked pithoi and amphorae and some silver jewelry in cases; it also displays an artist's re-creation of the palace throne room as it would have been in its glory.

Color is what stops you. Fragments of frescoes from the palace remain, but only in the drawing do you realize: Bright blues, reds, yellows would have adorned everything, from the capitals atop the megaron columns to the coffers in the ceilings. Similar displays in the museum atop the Acropolis in Athens make the same point, but I had to constantly remind myself: Our whitewashed vision of the ancients just means we've looked at too many statues and temples after the paint has worn off. The world of Pylos—and the entire Greek-dominated Mediterranean—would have looked a lot more like our colorful conception of ancient Egypt than the atonal grays and whites we see in museums and public buildings that have affected classical columns but not their coloration. The world of Odysseus would have sparkled with the bright reds and golds of those Maltese *luzzus* and buses rather than the faded browns and ecrus of the ruins we visit.

Glad I visited that little museum, I was especially glad I didn't have to walk there. I had shouldered my little day pack, sipped some water, and started toward Hora along the hot asphalt street, sweating and immediately resenting my unfulfilled scooter reservation, hoping that I made it to town before the museum closed and that I hadn't missed the afternoon bus back to Pylos. Before I had gone much more than a couple hundred yards, though, a tiny blue rental car beeped and pulled over, and I was invited inside by a Dutch family whom I recognized—they had wandered the palace at the same time I had. The father and fifteen-year-old daughter spoke perfect English and the mother smiled pleasantly, and since they were headed to the same museum I was we put our heads together to decode street signs and reeled around the tiny town of Hora. More, they were staying in Pylos not far from my hotel; I thanked Athena. After we wandered the museum together and drove back, we had tea on the waterfront at one of those tiny circular tables beneath the plane tree. I spent another couple hours in the Ionian, then planned my next passage, because the palace visit is all Telemachus does in Pylos. As Mentor, Athena tells Nestor to give Telemachus a chariot in which he and Nestor's son Peisistratus can leave for Sparta; the goddess then turns into a hawk and flies off. Impressed, Nestor does as he's told, and off goes Telemachus.

A WORD, BY THE WAY, ABOUT MENTOR. We use *mentor* to mean a trusted guide or counselor—someone older who takes us under a wing, tutors us, teaches us. The word comes, we are told, from Mentor himself, the old man Odysseus left in charge of his household when he left for Troy. But here in *The Odyssey*, twenty years later, Odysseus's house is beset by suitors, eating Odysseus's stock and insulting and plaguing his wife; his son, with no other guidance, is leaving to wander the planet; his father has moved out of the palace and lives in the bushes. And from this we use *mentor* to mean someone dependable and experienced?

Not exactly. Meet François de Salignac de La Mothe-Fénelon, a seventeenth-century French archbishop and man of letters. In *Dialogues on Excellence,* Fénelon wrote that *The Odyssey* contained "on all sides, a thousand moral instructions for all the situations of life." Naturally, though, a thousand moral instructions weren't enough, so Fénelon in 1699 published a book called *The Adventures of Telemachus,* in which Athena, disguised as Mentor, takes Telemachus much farther than merely to the Peloponnese; together they go on a series of adventures that parallel those of Odysseus, though Mentor uses the incidents to teach about the duties moral and civic of an enlightened monarch. As a book of political philosophy critical of the excesses of Louis XIV, it influenced Montesquieu and Rousseau and is considered the most widely read work of Grand Siècle France, even though by criticizing the king it helped ruin Fénelon's career. In any case, in Fénelon's book, Mentor—Athena in disguise—provides wonderful guidance, nothing like the old man who impotently watches things go wrong in Homer. That's probably where we get our usage of the term.

HOMER DESCRIBES TELEMACHUS AND PEISISTRATUS taking a chariot from Pylos to Sparta, and the bus hadn't traveled five minutes along that route before I thought of the description as Homer's great in-joke to the geographers he somehow knew, down the millennia, would leap to preposterous conclusions about the locations in *The Odyssey.* Unless Nestor lent Telemachus a four-wheel-drive chariot, that trip strains credulity. It took half a day of climbing and descending two mountain ranges on three separate buses to get the sixty kilometers or so from Pylos to Sparta; people may have made the trip on horseback or on foot, but it's safe to say nobody has ever made it by chariot. Homer is giving a stage wink here, I decided: This is a story, and people go where I say they do, how I say they go. It may not correspond to your physical reality.

Not that I objected. The mountains of the southern Peloponnese, peaking at about twenty-four hundred meters, are fierce and steep, limestone outcroppings alternating with lines of pine and gray-green olive as the twisting road hugs sheer cliffs. Little shrines dot the curves in the tortuous road, and the bus leaving Pylos putted along, passing tractors pulling hay carts on which sat old women wearing babushkas—local public transportation, it appeared. At one point a car sped past us and then pulled over, waving down the bus, which stopped—and our driver laughingly took on a young woman from the car. Later, the bus paused in a tiny hamlet; the driver opened the doors, threw out a couple bundles of newspapers, waved, and then on we went. At Kalamata I changed buses and had time for breakfast in a greasy spoon by the bus station—tea, bread, cheese, and, of course, Kalamata olives. The next bus stopped atop the Taygetus Mountains at a little store, where the passengers all got out for water, ice cream, or cigarettes, as we looked across a steep valley at another wave of mountains. After a few minutes we heard a bus from Sparta grinding up the other side of the mountain. It arrived, the two buses exchanged passengers, and down we went to Sparta. This transit, coordinated and doubling as delivery service, stopping for a bite along the way, seemed sensible and civilized.

IN SPARTA, Telemachus gets another lesson in hospitality, visiting Menelaus and Helen. He finds them celebrating two marriages: of their daughter to the son of Achilles and of their son to a local girl; the family welcomes him as hospitably as Nestor's had. Helen instantly makes Telemachus for Odysseus's son, and Menelaus and Helen share Trojan War stories concerning Odysseus. Menelaus describes Odysseus's fierce concentration inside the Trojan Horse, and Helen describes a spying mission he undertook, dressed as a beggar, into Troy; Telemachus for his part tells of his troubles at home without his father. It's all very nice, but there's a tinge of pain there. Menelaus expresses, perhaps a shade too strongly, outrage about the conduct of the suitors and disgust with the story of Agamemnon, which he again relates for Telemachus's benefit. Helen adds occasional demure self-chastisement (she calls herself "shameless" and regrets her "stupid infatuation," which caused so much trouble), and also puts into everyone's wine a drug that banishes sorrow. That after the tremendous bloodletting and all that's happened Helen and Menelaus have some-how re-created a family seems both remarkable and somewhat icky; the visit feels like an evening with a couple who drink just a bit much and begin exchanging smiling but intimate insults in front of the guests.

Eventually, Menelaus tells of their return from Troy—seven years of wandering, all to real places: Egypt, Phoenicia, Cyprus, Ethiopia, and Libya all appear in his rather pedestrian journey. The one fantastic adventure he did have concerns Proteus, the shape-changing Old Man of the Sea, whom he and his men wrestled to the ground and forced to explain what was keeping Menelaus from reaching home. Proteus did, relating the fates of the other Greek captains as well; Menelaus repeats the stories, updating Telemachus—and us readers—about what's hap-pened to the principals since the end of the war. Among his tales Pro-teus tells Menelaus that Odysseus, the lone hero from Troy not yet either killed or home, is held captive by Calypso, on whose beach he sits and weeps. Menelaus then offers Telemachus a gift of horses and suggests a long visit, but Telemachus says he'd prefer a gift more suit-able to his small, rocky homeland. Perhaps sick of adults telling him long-winded stories, Telemachus also proposes to leave the next morn-ing instead. And there Homer leaves him.

SPARTA IS HOT. When I got off the bus and stepped from the shade of the station into a vicious sun it couldn't have been noon, but it was so hot that I thought about turning around for the first bus to Athens, or bet-ter yet back to Pylos, by the sea. While the Ionian breezes had gently lifted my arm hairs in sandy Pylos, things inland had gone from swel-tering to miserable, temperatures climbing deep into the nineties every day.

So I was unprepared when I emerged from the bus station, which at least cast a shadow over the disembarking passengers, into the searing midday sun above the Spartan plain. Homer refers to the Spartan countryside with phrases like "the rolling country of Lacadaemon" or, better yet, "the land of many ravines," referring to the bowl in which Sparta sits, a fertile plain utterly surrounded by stark, forbidding mountains. But it's easy to remember, when you squint into the sun at those harsh peaks, that the Spartans were the Klingons of Greece, the fierce warriors who valued discipline above all. The remains of one of the temples where Spartan boys entered manhood through flogging rituals still stand east of town.

Thucydides said of Sparta that if the city faded and future viewers based their impressions on the foundations of its public buildings and temples, "there would be a strong disposition . . . to refuse to accept her fame as a true exponent of her power." That is, Sparta's strength was in people, not buildings. When asked why Sparta had no surrounding wall, Lycurgus, one of Sparta's earliest kings, said, "The city is well fortified which hath a wall of men instead of brick." Walls of men leave scanty ruins, making my visit to the Spartan acropolis at first seem rather sad. After Athens, almost any other city will offer just another acropolis, but with the requisite Roman theater, a few ancient foundations, a stone path among some scraggly olive trees, and almost nothing else, the Spartan kept me there for barely half an hour. Ancient Sparta's disappointing habit of having decayed into dust meant that the two main things connecting Odysseus to Sparta that I'd have most liked to see no longer exist.

I learned about those things from Pausanias, who had been there before me—two thousand years before. Commonly called "the Greek Baedeker," after the nineteenth-century German who perfected the modern guidebook, Pausanias was a second-century-AD native-Greek geographer and traveler who wrote a guide to Greece for an audience of the Romans who were running things by that time. With most of ancient Greece still standing, Pausanias wrote ten books of plainspoken description covering mainland Greece just before the long centuries of neglect that left it in ruins. He spends a lot more time giving details of mythological and historical background than in describing what he sees: "I am not going through everything in order, but selecting and discussing the really memorable things," he says, sifting out "the mass of worthless stories which every people will tell you about themselves." Two thousand years later his work remains a huge help to archaeologists. He's probably done as much for geographers of ancient southern and central Greece as Strabo has for the rest of the Mediterranean.

Thus, though Pausanias has little to offer concerning Odysseus's destinations, he has plenty to say about Pylos (he describes Nestor's palace perfectly) and Sparta. And though virtually everything he describes in Sparta is long gone, it's fun to know that near the Spartan marketplace Odysseus supposedly dedicated a temple to Athena in honor of having won the footrace for Penelope there (in the alternative to the story line that he earned Penelope through his cleverness in figuring out what to do with Helen). The temple stood at what was then named Leaving Street—"obviously Odysseus won," Pausanias says, "but the others were left behind in Leaving Street." I'd also have loved to see a statue called *Modesty,* also based on the courtship of Odysseus and Penelope. When attempts to convince the couple to remain in Sparta failed, Penelope's father supposedly followed their cart out of town, begging Penelope to stay behind. Unwilling to use force, Odysseus stopped the cart for Penelope to make up her own mind; she spoke not a word, merely modestly veiling her face, as befitted a married woman, whereupon her father admitted defeat. According to Pausanias, "They say Penelope had come this far along the road when she hid her face." That statue, too, is long gone.

The shrine to Penelope's more famous cousin, Helen, had more luck.

SOME TOUR BOOKS REFER obliquely to something they call "the Menelaion," which they describe as an ancient residence or sanctuary of Menelaus and Helen. Pausanias cuts to the chase: "the story is that Menelaus and Helen are buried there." To me, that sounded worth finding, even if it was several kilometers out of town, on no bus route—a long walk along a barren asphalt two-lane. I bought an extra two liters of water and headed out.

No more than forty minutes out of town, a sign pointed me up a dirt road into the hills. A long climb ended at a little white stucco chapel (locked, but candles burned inside) at the end of even the dirt road. A footpath continued up the hill for perhaps another mile, where it abruptly leveled, heading through olive orchards onto a little knob with a breathtaking view across the Spartan plain to the Taygetus Mountains I had crossed by bus on the way into town. After walking an hour in heat that later proved to be over a hundred degrees Fahrenheit, I must have been exhausted and sweating, but I never noticed, because the moment I reached the top I received an omen from the gods. On my right I saw at once, surrounded by pine trees, a ruined but still easily identifiable pyramid, four-sided, of hewn stone. The Menelaion—like all Neolithic sites, perfectly located, with a view of the Spartan plain, the Evrótas River, the stark, forbidding mountains in the background. And on it sat doves, which flushed when I stepped toward them, rising at once into the sky—four white, four black. Startled, I followed them upward with my eyes and saw, directly above the monument, slowly circling, a single hawk. And then suddenly, blown in by the steady, brisk wind, the site swarmed with monarch butterflies.

The ancient myths are full of this type of thing: A snake consumes eight baby birds, then the mother, convincing a seer that the Trojan War will consume nine years and conclude in the tenth; Athena leaves Nestor and Telemachus by turning into a hawk; dueling eagles above the Ithaca council of Telemachus presage the return of Odysseus. But above all, time and again: birds on your right? That's a good sign. And then I flush four light and four dark doves on my right, and look up to see a lone hawk. Then, suddenly, butterflies. I actually got chills. This was an omen.

Of course, without an oracle handy, try to interpret. Four good hotels and four bad hotels, lots of little pleasures on my trip, but above all Athena would look out for me? The missing and catching of eight buses, trains, boats, and uncountable people I might meet? The eight—uh-oh, by this point less than six—months remaining until the birth of my child? Lacking the skills to understand it, I did little more than glory in the unlikelihood of this mysterious event—that and found a shady spot to have lunch.

Or tried to. In the heat, lunch pretty much failed. The cheese had melted and dry bread made me queasy. I settled for cookies and plenty of fluids, though the water from my backpack was already warm enough to scarcely refresh. Panting in air redolent with the smell of the pines and the omnipresent sage covering the hills, I listened to chirruping insects and caught my breath. As homage to Menelaus and

Helen, I cleaned up a little trash from previous visitors. I considered staying up there among the butterflies and the sound of the wind, perhaps even napping, but it was terribly hot, and I had a long way to walk back. I headed down.

Every few minutes I stepped into whatever small shade I could find—an olive tree, usually—and sipped water, but soon the water from my backpack was too hot to drink. I plodded slowly on, worrying less about caution among the few but speeding drivers than about illness from the heat. I walked for nearly an hour before, close to my turn back to Sparta, I found a farm on which icy water flowed in an irrigation ditch between olive trees. I drank none, but using my hat and the bandanna from around my neck I drenched my head, neck, wrists. On my way into town, I stopped at every store I passed and bought—and drained—a water or an orange Fanta. Overheating transformers had failed, so the bus station power was out. The clerk handwrote my ticket for Athens, and waiting for the bus felt like a Beckett play, passengers in dim silence, swatting flies. When I went to the restroom faucet to refill my water bottle, the water I emptied from the bottle was hot enough that I jerked my hand away.

The dirt-cheap hotel I found in Athens at midnight gave me a fan. It didn't work.

TWO DAYS LATER I walked up the aisle of a moving bus and crouched by the driver. *"Signomie,"* I said. *"O leoforio . . . stasi . . . ya Mykines, ne?"* I was going for "Excuse me, this bus—it stops for Mycenae, yes?" The driver scowled. *"Ne, ne,"* he said, jerking his head and waving me back to my seat.

I was thrilled. He hadn't tried to help me, hadn't spoken to me in baby talk, hadn't sighed and pulled the bus over to puzzle out with me what I wanted, hadn't spoken to me in English. "Yes, yes," he said, basically. "Siddown." Three minutes later, when the bus stopped at the crossroads for Mycenae, I descended the steps feeling expansive, sweeping my gaze around the dusty white countryside—intrepid traveler, considering his options. My gaze swept past two men sitting on a bench, then jerked back to them. Both stared impassively, right arms up, extended to the right, pointing straight out along a single track: "That way, stupid." And off I went, just another goob with a floppy hat, a backpack, and a guidebook.

No matter. I had done what I hoped: I had learned enough Greek to get by.

The Odyssey never depicts Odysseus—or anybody—speaking a different language. Odysseus blithely lands in place after place, speaks his own presumably western island dialect of Bronze Age proto-Greek, and so does everybody else in the world. I didn't have it so easy, and before the trip was done I'd tried to get by in pidgin Turkish, Greek, Arabic, French, Italian, and Maltese. My high school French proved surprisingly helpful in Tunisia, with its French colonial history, and helped with Italian, too. Still, I commonly found myself knowing just enough to sound foolish. Especially in Italy, where for a period, whenever reduced to speaking English slowly and hopefully, I inexplicably contrived to do so in an Italian accent. I can't recall why I thought this would help, but I do know that I sounded like Rosemary Clooney singing "Mambo Italiano."

Tour books provide in the back universally useless short phrase lists: *"Xejn ma jiskantani"*—Maltese for "Nothing surprises me." In my worst moments I agree, but I'd have preferred the absent "Please, can you tell me, where is the bus station?" Relying on such a digest during the early days of my trip had left me mere greetings in Turkish, and frustrated in less-touristed Thrace among the Cicones, merely parroting phrases taught me by my friend the souvlaketeer. So when in Athens continued linguistic incapacity caused what I began calling "the thirty-euro laundry incident," I made a Greek phrase book a housekeeping priority. Athens had an English bookstore, and with a thorough phrase book I bought there I began learning the language. Before I left Greece for good, I could count to twelve, confidently order food and arrange transportation and lodging, resist confusion at *ne* for yes and *oki* for no, and, as I mentioned, stammer out the occasional germane question.

That linguistic accomplishment was actually the high point of my visit to Mycenae, home of Agamemnon. Not that Mycenae, the city that gives its name to the period in Greek history in which the Homeric events took place, isn't worth visiting—it has marvelous tholos tombs (the ones shaped like beehives) and a ruined palace complex nearly as well preserved as the one at Pylos, only many times bigger: the same low walls, decorated floors, and even a dark cistern you could descend into by a curving set of stairs. Just the same, neither Telemachus nor Odysseus visited this palace—Agamemnon is long dead by the time of *The Odyssey*. His saga was important as background, and so a brief time walking the site satisfied me. I enjoyed a cheap and delicious omelet at one of the many empty restaurants that lined the streets (the heat and the euro, my host told me, were killing business). I walked back with Sylvester and Béata, a Polish couple. When a brief downpour caught us enjoying a beer beneath an awning as we waited at a café back at the crossroads, Sylvester thought to pick up my knapsack. A minute later the sidewalk where it had sat was under three inches of water. When we boarded the bus for Athens ten minutes later, the sidewalk was bone dry again.

MY LAST DAYS IN ATHENS were given to housekeeping. Laundry, e-mailing home, purchasing tickets for my next segment, a visit to the English-language bookstore for a new novel (I had finished Jeffrey Eugenides's *Middlesex*; I traded it in for Thackeray's *Vanity Fair*). I visited the house of Heinrich Schliemann, the archaeologist of Troy. Now a coin museum, it has a display on his history, and the walls still sport his bizarre original decorations: naked cherubs carefully digging through an archaeological site. At the National Archaeological Museum I gazed at statues of Athena and Odysseus, but the thrill was gone; finally, I ended up just walking the city, stopping constantly for water or soda at the little street kiosks that sell candy, drinks, bus tickets. Waiting a day and a half for a plane, I was just killing time. Homer was done with the Telemachiad, and I was ready to be done, too.

The last segment of Book IV nicely summarizes the story so far. Penelope learns of Telemachus's journey and fears for his safety—and ultimately for her own. With Telemachus far from home, the suitors planning ambush and murder on his return, and Penelope alone and terrified, Homer finishes the first four books of *The Odyssey* by setting them aside completely. We won't hear of Telemachus or Penelope until Odysseus's journeys are through, nine books later.

It's the first cliff-hanger in literature.

BOOK IV, ABOUT SPARTA, is the longest book in *The Odyssey*, by a quarter. It's long because it finishes giving the complete lay of the land for not only Telemachus but the entire Greek force returning from Troy. Not only that, those early books also coyly refer to almost every other episode coming up in the poem. Telemachus's bath prefigures those later baths; the hospitality he receives contrasts with the suitors at home and the many inhospitable places about which Odysseus will later tell. Menelaus tells return stories—called *nostoi* by the Greeks—that perfectly set up the big tale Odysseus tells. I think of this chapter like the early black-and-white scenes of *The Wizard of Oz*, slyly hinting at everything to come.

In retracing the Telemachiad, I enjoyed the ease of Peloponnesian travel. After less than a week in Istanbul, Troy, and Komotiní, I had barely firmed my travel muscles. A couple weeks in Greece, seeing four cities, all well on the beaten path, let me gain a little comfort in my capacities, get used to managing a backpack, a passport, my personal comfort, all in highly accommodating circumstances.

I loved seeing the Acropolis—after having seen Rome once before, ancient Athens had remained the only classical site I felt absolutely obligated to see before I died, and it didn't disappoint. From the beginning of my association with Odysseus, back in my twenties, I had conceived a loyalty to Athena, his patroness. In Nashville, where I lived when my *Ulysses* claims started this whole chain of events, they have a full-scale replica of the Parthenon, replete with a forty-foot statue of Athena—the largest indoor sculpture in the West. I used to go sit on the steps of that fake Parthenon and gaze in at the statue, communing. Thus, finally seeing her home temple made me feel like I had demonstrated my fealty, made a true effort to earn her patronage.

Much more, though, I had seen real places actually mentioned in *The Odyssey*, places about which there was never debate, ancient or modern. Sand from sandy Pylos lies even now in the center crease of my journal; at the tomb to Helen and Menelaus in Sparta, I witnessed a genuine omen. I participated. I did what Telemachus did—I wandered in an easy way through the Peloponnese, learning what I could and getting ready for something. Every man is a son before he's a father, and *The Odyssey* puts the pieces in appropriate order: four books about being a son before the rest of the story about manhood. In my life back home, I had been a son all my life and was about to face the unimaginable journey of becoming a father. Just so on my trip: I had enjoyed the reality of the son. Now I was ready to seek the mythology of the father.

I headed for the Athens airport.

Chapter 6

A Drink with an Umbrella in It:

The Honeyed Fruit of the Lotus

For nine long days we were pounded by the howling gale through the teeming sea-water, but on the tenth we reached the land of the Lotus-eaters, who feast on fruit. . . . I chose two men and another to act as their herald, and sent them to find what kind of men took their nourishment there. They went, but we got no word from them, for the Lotus-eaters had received them kindly and served them the honeyed fruit of the lotus to eat, a meal which deprived them of any desire to return or send word. They were content to stay with the Lotus-eaters, consuming the luscious fruit and forgetful of home, but I brought them back to the ships by force, three weeping men, tied them up and dragged them beneath the benches low in the hull. Quickly I ordered the rest of my trusty friends to board the swift ships. . . . Soon aboard, they took their seats, and all together they struck the gray sea with their oars.

—*The Odyssey,* Book IX

TUNISIA GETS much of its popular music from Egypt, so everywhere you go you hear a mesmerizing mixture of ululating vocals, brass percussion, and sinuous violin or sitar, reminding: You are in the Arab world. The music gets under your skin and feels central, even necessary. So when the café in the Tunis airport turned it off at 2 a.m., I noticed. Suddenly almost the only sound echoing through the boxy two-story passenger area was the gentle humming of a Zamboni-style waxer going up and back, up and back, waxing the stone tile floors. Ceiling designs looked like the snaking mosaics found in mosques, though internally lit screened windows along the departure lounge made the place feel more like the interior of a vast jukebox.

More important than the silence was its implication: If the music was off, the café was closed. With regret I gave up on my tepid tea and moved to a row of seats along the balcony. Seats, of course, and not a bench, which made lying flat for a few hours' sleep impossible. On paper, a brief night in the airport always sounds easier than finding a hotel after a late flight and returning to the airport for an early flight. Why not just cadge a few hours' sleep on an airport bench?

Because airports aren't hotels. So airports have uncomfortable plastic seats, not benches. So I had time to regret my decision. A long time—the music didn't come back on until 4:15.

AIRPLANE TRAVEL makes bus travel look civilized. Deposited in some featureless, gray, carpeted airport in some city, you are funneled down tracks and tubes like a UPS package—sorted, stamped, scanned, and impersonally handled. You eventually find yourself folded like a lawn chair and strapped into a hissing, smelly aluminum tube with wings, where they got a big canister of air in 1987 and they've been recycling it ever since. Air travel may once have had romance, but never again: "in reality it is uglier than any other way of traveling in the history of man." That's writer John Fowles—and he made that journal entry in 1966. I don't think things have improved much; especially after spending that night among those plastic seats—and the following morning arguing in high school French that I had a seat on a flight to Jerba, which a collapsed computer system could not verify.

In fact, travel itself, in my own lifetime, has changed depressingly— or not so much changed, perhaps, as nearly vanished. When I traveled by airplane in 1977 to visit a college, I was only the second member of my family to fly. When in 1979 I spent a year in England as an exchange student, going to Europe was still something you hoped to do someday, but it was expensive and if you couldn't, there was always Yellowstone. No blank spaces remained on the map, to be sure, but travel beyond the beaten path remained rare and set the blood racing. George Bailey in *It's a Wonderful Life* says the three most exciting sounds in the world are anchor chains, plane motors, and train whistles, and presumably part of the reason he thought so was that when he heard that plane motor he wouldn't be squashed into a 727 with 150 middle schoolers from Dayton on their class trip to Singapore, Hong Kong, and Japan. Back then I looked forward to going places that people I knew had never gone and would never have thought of going. In those days everybody's grandparents didn't send Christmas photos of themselves atop the Great Wall of China. Fuel policies? Deregulation? The vast disposable income of a bored and indulgent society? Explain it how you will, there's now no hamlet in Africa, no Asian backwater, no South American mountaintop that doesn't have its own Lonely Planet guide, districts of cheap hotels filled with loud American college students and nicotine-stained Eurotrash.

It's hard to travel when there's no place left to go.

Odysseus had every place left to go, and following him I tried to reinvest travel with that romantic sense of the undiscovered. Thus I strove to avoid air travel at all costs; apart from crossing the Atlantic, the passage from Greece to the isle of Jerba in southern Tunisia was virtually my single air trip. From Athens to Tunis by surface would have taken at least two train rides and two ferry rides and an intervening stop in Italy; probably at least two days of travel, at no savings of cost.

At first I regretted the plane trip: You stand in line in Athens, you sit on a plane for a couple hours, then you're disgorged late at night in another airport that could be anyplace on the planet. Travel, the essence of space and motion, on an airplane becomes its opposite, an exercise in remaining still in a confined place. Yet a plane trip, in fact, came as close as a storm-induced boat journey to approximating Odysseus's abrupt arrival in Lotusland.

LIKE DOROTHY'S TORNADO, the gale that blew Odysseus off course from Cape Malea transported him to a fantasy world: a place of bright color and unusual vegetation, where he meets people of unusual size and species, sometimes remarkably wicked or afflicted. Like Dorothy, Odysseus wants to go home but doesn't know how, so he stops where he can and asks whomever he meets. The Lotus-eaters are the first of them. And though the Lotus-eaters populate the shortest of all the sto-ries Odysseus tells the Phaeacians (it runs a mere twenty lines; even the Cicones got more than that), they have inspired disproportionate interest.

With an actual starting place and straightforward travel directions, people have quibbled little about where the Lotus-eaters lived. Look at any map and consider a boat blown southward from the southernmost point of mainland Greece for days. Where's it going to land? Some-where in North Africa, to be sure. Strabo tells us that the historian Polybius in the second century BC placed the Lotus-eaters on what was then called the isle of Meninx, now called Jerba, in southern Tunisia; Herodotus had them in pretty much the same place. Strabo concurs, and they've remained there ever since.

What happened to Odysseus in Lotusland would take longer to summarize than it took to read in this chapter's epigraph. A few guys get into a mix-up, Odysseus fetches them bodily, and off they go; in this episode Odysseus hasn't done anything more heroic than grab a couple guys by the nose. Moe of the Three Stooges does this ten times per movie: "Come on, you knuckleheads!" And nobody bases their life's journey on Moe.

A highly unscientific personal survey lasting several years suggests that the *Odyssey* adventures divide into four tiers of recognition. In the first tier you find the three sibilants: the Cyclopes, the Sirens, and Scylla and Charybdis. Everyone has heard of these monsters; they were the three episodes I remembered from junior high. When the newspaper cartoon *Baby Blues* ran a strip in which the father compares a shopping trip with his children to *The Odyssey,* the artist shows him tied to the mast of his ship as it sails among a big one-eyed mon-ster, singing women, a sea monster, and a whirlpool. Everyone gets that joke.

In the second tier I place the nymph Calypso and the witch Circe, commonly conflated; people who remember a little more of their *Odyssey* remember at least something about a sexually aggressive god-dess. The wind god Aeolus makes this category, too—maybe it's Aeo-lian harps in people's backyards, but people at least remember the name. The third tier comprises solely the visit to the land of the dead—only a few people remember that Odysseus made this visit, but those who do usually know a lot about it. The four remaining episodes, which nobody ever remembers, populate the lowest tier: the cattle of the sun, the Laestrygonians, the Phaeacians, and the Cicones. Even people who remember *The Odyssey* well can't summon these episodes, and it makes sense: the two quasi-real episodes that bookend the journey, and the two episodes that serve mainly to kill off Odysseus's crew—eleven ships' worth butchered by the Laestrygonians, and the rest drowned after eating the cattle of the sun. In some ways these visits amount to narrative housekeeping.

The Lotus-eaters fall into the second tier—not as widely known as, say, the Cyclopes, but pretty familiar to most people. "The Lotos-Eaters," for example, one of Tennyson's most famous poems, goes on far longer than Homer (Tennyson's poem is 173 lines), suffused in images of music that falls softer "than petals from blown roses," as the sailors lie in "dreamful ease" among the "mild-eyed melancholy Lotos-eaters." Speculation about the lotus itself has also kept the episode fresh. Herodotus, naturally, weighs in first, discussing a fruit "about the size of a mastic berry, and is as sweet as a date." Later writers like the Greek Theophrastus and the Roman Pliny suggest other fruits found in North Africa—which show, sadly, no trace of magical properties when tested. Mindful of the hypnotic, addictive qualities of the literary lotus, moderns invariably suggest hashish—implying perhaps that Odysseus's men consumed some wicked brownies.

I came to a different conclusion entirely.

JOURNAL ENTRY, Tunisia, Day 3: *Dreaming in broken French almost exclusively now. Weird. At the Melia Djerba Menzel, where the plates might or might not be almost clean, where the tea service is missing either cups or saucers, where they'll rent you a beach towel for 10 Tunisian dinars [$8.00]; where you're on half-board, but it's the half that doesn't include water, which they'll sell you for 2.5 TD. Where the stiff onshore breeze drives half-clad Germans and French and Danes and Italians from the sandy shore of the Med. to the rims of the 4—or 5? 6?—pools, where they strategize against one another for the seizure of patches of umbrella shade* *or the few chaises that have adjustable backs—these 6-foot Alsaces, this hinged lebensraum on wheels—and roll their eyes at the behavior of one another's children.*

The Lotus-eaters, it came to me, didn't offer drugs or alcohol or anything so complex as that. The Lotus-eaters simply ran the world's first Club Med, where you could drop your troubles at the door, roll your bags into your suite, and commence lolling. My hotel actually sat in the *zone touristique* on the island's eastern shore, between *two* authentic Club Meds.

I ended up at a resort because I had a spasm of fear about entering a Muslim nation as a lone American during a time when Muslim nations in general did not appear cheerfully disposed toward my country. I'm not proud, but I admit: I quailed, and I decided against showing up in a new country on a new continent in a possibly hostile culture without a place to stay. Now, Tunisia is nobody's idea of the Middle East; its recorded history starts with the Phoenicians in the first millennium BC, who were conquered by the Romans in 146. After that came the Vandals, the Byzantines, the Arabs, the Ottomans, and in 1881 the French, who left in 1955. One of the most moderate Arab countries by Western standards, Tunisia may just have the patience born of age: according to archaeologists, people have lived there for nearly ten thousand years. The word *barbaroi,* by which the ancient Greeks referred to people who spoke an unfamiliar language, probably lies at the root of the name *Berbers,* Tunisia's oldest inhabitant group.

Still, Tunisia was new to me. A flurry of e-mail resulted in a reservation made by a friendly British travel agent, and a three-day stay in the Melia Djerba Menzel, a down-at-the-heels package resort. I hadn't spent half a day among the resort's uncountable pools, cavernous and depressing dining hall, and sandy beach with uncomfortable beach chairs beneath faux-palm-frond umbrellas before I wanted out. I never would have thought that watching topless European gamines apply suntan oil to their breasts would fail to fascinate, but the stone expressions I saw chilled my blood. Everywhere else I went I had conversations with fellow travelers, locals, workers, but inside the walls of this Tunisian resort I lived in silence. And whereas people usually at the very least smile for cameras, the northern Europeans populating the

Melia Djerba Menzel appeared to take their holidaymaking seriously: My few attempts at smiling and nodding met with such frozen stares that I spent my time either beachside, where the other guests never went, or poolside, under my hat, reading *Vanity Fair*.

I shared Odysseus's feelings entirely: Numb is no way to be; let's get out of here. In fact, I think the entire point of the Lotus-eaters episode comes in that simple act of renouncement. In Tennyson's poem, the Lotus-eaters wonder of men, "why should we only toil" when "all things else have rest from weariness?" That's what Odysseus wants, right? Rest, and an end to his wanderings. So why not just stop? Odysseus answers simply: This isn't where he's going. The point isn't stopping—the point is getting where you set out for, *then* stopping. Or maybe Odysseus just didn't want what they had.

I sure didn't. Lying on my butt in a second-rate resort among sullen Europeans felt like a kind of death—which I suppose the Lotus-eaters really represent anyhow: What else would you call giving up, forgetting your goals, and never leaving where you are? This may have been the first moment in which I found a way for Odysseus's travels to address my life directly, and I felt good. Call the lotus television, then, or money, or blind faith, or any of the comforts that discourage engagement and challenge. Like Odysseus, I had no interest in anything that bleeds away desire to grow and move forward.

So I wanted to get moving. Just the same, the next ferry from Tunis to Sicily—my subsequent stop—was days away, and I had paid in advance for my stay, leaving two more days to kill on Jerba. There's only so much reading by a pool a body can stand, and I began to think about something I'd very much wanted—but failed—to do back in Pylos when I tried to get to Nestor's palace. I went to the front desk of my resort hotel and made plans for the next morning.

YOU DON'T WANT TO USE the front hand brake on a motorbike; squeeze too hard and you'll flip, and since in Tunisia it doesn't occur to them to give you a helmet, flipping would be real bad. So you stick with the back brake, and on a yellow motorbike rented for the day you speed off toward the center of Jerba, which apart from the *zone touristique* and its main town of Houmt Souk is basically a desert island with a few tiny towns of smooth whitewashed walls and fortified mosques, separated by long expanses of sandy soil studded with palms and occasional olive and date orchards.

The motorbike came to me on "E," so I stopped at the first opportunity—a tiny single house alone along the empty road, where a pleasant woman wrapped in a black tunic emerged to dispense gasoline, which they call benzene, from an old-fashioned gravity pump. I saw people wrapped in similar tunics all over the island, learning only later that the tunic color and decoration identifies its wearer by village and marital status. Some claim the robes are little changed from those worn when Jerba belonged to the Roman Empire, others that they go further back, to the Berbers themselves. I headed for Houmt Souk (*souk* means market in Arabic), but long before I reached the main road I began to notice something unsettling. Periodically I came up behind people walking beside the road, and as I passed, their glances always seemed vaguely annoyed. Only after seeing a few other scooters— never occupied by only a single rider—did I understand: On a scooter, I had obligations. The next time I saw a pedestrian, I passed slowly, pulled over, and waited. The young man, carrying a briefcase and wearing Western dress, shouted, *"Merci!"* above the rattle of the engine and climbed on behind me. As we putted along we had a shouted conversation in which with my broken French I managed to understand that he was headed to El May, that I gave him pleasure by leaving the *zone touristique,* and that I ought to visit Guellala, on the island's south coast, where I could buy pottery. At El May he waved as I turned toward Houmt Souk on the island's north coast.

An Arab market town out of a picture postcard, the tiny Houmt Souk is a maze of whitewashed walls and pale blue doors and shutters, with the requisite spaghetti tangle of alleyways and passages in the central market, a couple streets of which form a traditional *qaysarriya,* or roofed bazaar. The usual assortments of tiny little boxes, fabrics, jewelry, pottery, rugs, and woven mats and baskets greet you in every stall; along the passages men work at sewing machines. Outside, in the central plaza, I sipped water beneath spreading trees, surrounded by Jerbans drinking coffee and talking. Only when I wondered at the lack of clicking did I notice that nobody seemed to be playing backgammon, unlike any public place in Turkey and Greece, whose GDPs would surely double if connected to turbines powered by the rotations of backgammon dice. I regretted not choosing to stay in one of the converted fonduks—colonnaded courtyards that once sheltered visiting camel trains—but I remembered my lesson from the Cicones and kept my eyes forward.

That meant that after a few hours in Houmt Souk I was back on the scooter, where I continued playing my supportive role in the Jerban public transportation infrastructure, got a piece of sand in my eye that caused discomfort for the rest of my journey, and crisscrossed Jerba, stopping to look at sand-colored mosques (tourists from the outside only, please) and tiny crossroads markets where I continually resisted the opportunity to buy a clever clay vessel in the shape of a camel that when tipped over resisted spillage. Guellala truly turned out to be filled with beautiful, simple pottery, but most of the pots were the size of my motorbike, and I found nothing small enough to fit in my backpack and survive the rest of my journey.

On the advice of my *Rough Guide* I rode all the way out to Ajim, the island's main port on its southwest tip; Jerba commonly shows up as a movie location, and in Ajim I could expect to find "the entrance to the bar at the space port of Mos Eisley where Luke and Obi-Wan meet Han Solo in the original *Star Wars*." A few kilometers north on the unpaved road along the island's west coast sat Obi-Wan's house. I had no luck at all finding the space bar, and that was the easy part. As I ground more and more slowly up the sand road north of Ajim, the parties of beachgoers I passed on the rocky coast gave fewer and fewer smiles, and I turned around after coming to several conclusions at once: first, that if the sandy road injured the scooter, I was in big trouble; second, that I was way off the beaten path and long past any form of welcome; and third, that if there's anything more ridiculous than making a pilgrimage to sites related to *The Odyssey*, it's sidetracking from that to visit sites from *Star Wars*.

The next day I flew back up to Tunis.

*   *   *

SOLO MALE TRAVELERS MUST APPROACH WOMEN the way you approach giving your credit card number over the phone: If you didn't start the interaction, proceed with extreme caution. Thus, when I found myself wandering the mazes of the eighth-century medina, or walled city, of Tunis in the company of an attractive young woman, and we unexpectedly picked up a friendly guide who had lots of time on his hands and lots of places to show us, I continued enjoying the trackless warrens of the ancient city, but I began looking for my exit and kept a hand on my wallet.

It started pleasantly enough in yet another Internet café, this one a block away from my hotel in central Tunis. The Maison Doree didn't have Sydney Greenstreet and Peter Lorre skulking in the stairwell, but that was all it lacked for atmosphere: deep-brown wooden doors whose locks still used skeleton keys, a dim lobby with pale yellow walls, polite men in middle age to serve you a beer or water at the bar, and at all times, with the curtains drawn against the midday sun, at least one employee, wearing a vest and bow tie, gently slumped on the lobby's leather sofa, snoring. All that and an Internet café within a block and my 20 dinars per night felt well spent.

In the café I wrote, as ever, to June, to friends—complaining about Jerba and checking news from home. The Tunisian keyboard, with its accommodation for Arabic letters and French accents, was something of a cipher, and as I puzzled it out the nice young woman next to me offered to help. She said her name was Rym, and after we conversed briefly she cited Tunisian hospitality and offered to show me the medina, Tunisia's ancient market and main attraction, though she had only an hour or so before her next college class. Men traveling alone are subject to constant scams, usually involving an attractive young woman as bait and ending in bars full of equally friendly locals, culminating at departure time in shockingly high drink tabs and considerably less friendliness. But Rym seemed genuine and pleasant, plus how could I turn down her offer of guest-friendship? I cautioned myself and accepted.

The streets closest to the entrance of the medina bustle with energy—shops selling everything from toothpaste and shampoo to spices and souvenirs compete for attention, and you jostle along in the narrow, cobbled streets, trying to keep your cool in the crowd. But even a few streets in (the medina stretches nearly a mile in length) the crowds dwindle, and Rym and I wandered long narrow alleys snaking between tall white-washed walls. Everywhere we passed beneath stucco arches, looked up at wrought-iron balconies and light brackets, put our hands on the peeling paint of ancient wooden doors—many the same dreamy blue as those in Jerba. Sometimes a door swung open and I got a glimpse inside—a dirt floor, an old carpet—and the sinuous, omnipresent music rose briefly in volume. Three turns or less from the main section I was utterly lost, dependent on my guide—and her guide, an unshaven old man with a walleye who in response to Rym's query for directions attached himself to us and led us up and down tiny streets, past shops selling cloth, souvenirs, tiles, tobacco, and everything imaginable to both tourist and local. Rym translated into a mélange of French and English that I mostly understood as he pointed out doors with two knockers (which supposedly meant a married couple lives within), eighteenth-century schools, lovely second-floor gallerias, a building that in the fourteenth century housed the historian Abd ar-Rahmān ibn Khaldūn, and eventually—inevitably—a carpet shop, where I was warmly welcomed.

Still, he led us to the roof, which had a remarkable view—fabulous tile-covered walls and arches, and a mixture of broken tile fragments and concrete made the entire floor a masterpiece. The fearsome four-square minaret of the Jamaa ez Zitouna (the Great Mosque) towered above us nearby, with the Kasbah Mosque, its thirteenth-century inspiration, some blocks farther north. The sell inside the carpet shop was soft indeed and there were no hard feelings when I left, nor was I particularly put out when the 5 dinars I preemptively offered our self-appointed guide were firmly refused—"Ten," he said, in English, for the first time meeting my eyes. It was worth it—I wouldn't have found the carpet-shop roof in a week of solo wandering. Just the same, the smoothness of the transaction raised questions. A long silence accompanied me and Rym as we made our way out of the medina, and when Rym suggested that perhaps she could skip her afternoon class just that once, a look passed between us that did not convey trust. I was alone, and I chose caution. Rym and I exchanged fractured smiles and went our separate ways on the Avenue de France.

*   *   *

SO, THE LOTUS. Eating what you shouldn't eat has got many a one in trouble—ask Goldilocks; ask Snow White. For that matter, ask Eve. Here Odysseus is more like Adam, almost getting into trouble for something somebody else decided to eat. Odysseus makes a better choice, though, and keeps his mouth shut—perhaps the first lesson of travel: Keep your mouth shut until you're sure about what you're eating or saying. The ancient Greeks told the myth of Persephone, snatched away to be queen of the dead by Hades. Her mother, the fertility goddess Demeter, was about to free her when Persephone ate a few pomegranate seeds—and was thus condemned to remain in the underworld one month every year for each seed she ate (her arrival is associated with spring, her departure with fall). Similar myths are found among people as far afield as the Maoris and the Zulus, the Finns and the Japanese. The point: What you eat binds you to where you are. Be careful.

But you can take this too far. You may be wise to resist the uncertain temptations of unsettlingly friendly locals, but just the same you do have to eat. Thus, that night in Tunis I set out looking for food, prepared to find something to take away and then walk the French-style Avenue Habib Bourguiba late into the evening along with almost everyone else in town: If there's one thing Mediterraneans like to do, it's walk around town in the evening, the chief entertainment in every Mediterranean city. Not far from my hotel I ran a gauntlet of cheap eateries, each with someone out front encouraging you to come in. Many such restaurants are scams, providing expensive and poor food to the uninitiated, so I kept my head down, until I brusquely passed someone who murmured, in English, "Looking for something to eat, sir?" I had gone nearly a block before I thought, "You dope, you exactly are looking for something to eat!" And I went back, glanced at the menu in the window, smiled, and went inside—and had the cheapest and best meal of my trip. The Tunisian specialty is couscous, served with any combination of potato, sauce, fish, chicken, and vegetables. I sat at a long table covered with a plastic tablecloth, with a smattering of locals, and ate a dish of chicken couscous with a red sauce and potatoes that was tender, spicy, cheap, and unimaginably filling. I dipped my bread into the little pot of *harissa,* a very hot pepper sauce, and earned pleased smiles from the staff. Above me a television showed the news, and I caught a glimpse of Colin Powell doing the YMCA dance. I was glad to be far from home.

THE FERRY FROM TUNIS TO SICILY runs only once a week, so I filled my remaining days among Tunis's most famous tourist attractions: the ruins at Carthage (across the bay from Tunis, easily reached by train) and the Bardo Museum, not far from the town center on the trolley, which left only a block or so from my hotel.

The Phoenician outpost of Carthage rose to prominence in the western Mediterranean in the sixth century BC and remained so until the Punic Wars with Rome began in 264. Decades of war seemed to swing in the Carthaginians' favor with Hannibal's famous campaign over the Alps, but the Romans fought back and thoroughly defeated the Carthaginians in 202 BC. A shaky peace followed. But when Carthage fought a Roman ally in 150, the Romans decided they'd had enough, and in 146 didn't merely defeat Carthage but vaporized it, demolishing the buildings and selling its inhabitants into slavery. Carthage thus left little behind; in fact, what you find today is mostly ruins of the city rebuilt by Julius Caesar. Just the same, you can visit ruins of a Carthaginian harbor, and best of all on Byrsa Hill a few narrow cobbled streets of ancient Carthage have been excavated from beneath the ruins of something the Romans built on top of them. Atop the hill itself is the Acropolium, once the Cathedral of Saint Louis (who died hereabouts during a Crusade) and now simply a rentable performance space, a fitting monument to a place always being recaptured that has time and again resprouted as itself. The Berbers, Phoenicians, Romans, Vandals, Byzantines, Arabs, Ottomans, and French have all claimed Tunisia. Like Troy, it doesn't know it's doomed and so continues to grow.

Carthage doesn't share the sense of connection with Virgil that Troy has with Homer. The Roman poet Virgil, of course, in the first century BC wrote *The Aeneid,* the Roman answer to Homer's poems, tracing the

Trojan hero Aeneas as he flees from Troy, has various adventures, visits Carthage, where he falls in love with—and betrays—Dido, and then goes on to conquer pretty much everything in sight, eventually leading the way to the founding of Rome, taking care to leave as descendant Augustus, coincidentally the Roman emperor at the time Virgil wrote the poem. It's a kind of Roman *Odyssey* and *Iliad* all in one, and though it has its champions I've always found it flat, derivative propagandizing. The actual history of Carthage was much more engaging than its mythological association with Aeneas. As I sat on a white-washed wall in the leafy, lovely tourist mecca of Sidi Bou Said, one metro stop north of Carthage, staring out over the Gulf of Tunis, I didn't think about Aeneas. Instead, I focused on the young woman who sat nearby and was convinced I would look just great if I paid her to put a henna tattoo on my arm. I listened to the sea breeze rattle the eucalyptus leaves and thought about leaving town. I didn't get the tattoo.

The difference between Virgil and Homer came clearest to me in the Bardo Museum the next day. A palace turned into a museum, the Bardo has formal rooms and staircases, with Moorish arches and elegant tiles, but it also has the largest collection of Roman mosaics in the world. Two mosaics spoke directly to the issue. One shows the episode of Odysseus and the Sirens—Odysseus lashed to the mast, looking at the singers, as his men row diligently on; a lovely representation of one of the most famous episodes in all of literature. The other shows Virgil, thoughtfully seated in a writing pose, flanked by two muses: Melpomene, the sad-eyed muse of tragedy, and the severe Clio, the muse of history.

A scene of action and great tension from the greatest story in the world, or a static representation of the author with his serious-minded inspiration. Which poem do you want to read? There were tile representations of lotuses, too, of course. I took a picture.

FINALLY, THE LOTUS-EATERS proved most satisfying in where they lived and how I left there. Tunisia is in Africa, which means that in his point of departure and his first two stops (Troy, Thrace, and Tunisia), Odysseus has visited three different continents. I've checked the globe, and the eastern corner of the Mediterranean is the only place on this planet where you can easily do this. When you travel there, you realize: Geography has meaning. Continents are more than just lines on a map. To get from one to another you have to cross mountains or water—they truly divide the world. Those continents contained all the different peoples pursuing all the different destinies known to the Old World, and by the time he's made his second stop Odysseus has been to all three. It's something of a feat for a traveler, and around this time I began thinking of myself as traveler rather than tourist. Nothing, then, satisfied me more than leaving Tunis not on some anonymous, depressing airplane but by the weekly ferry to Trapani, on the west coast of Sicily—conveniently, my next destination. I would go through passport control and spend an entire night crossing the sea, which felt like an appropriate length of time to cross a frontier between continents, even ones so close to one another. I got to the ferry station a few hours early, spent my remaining dinars on portable food and drink, and sized up my fellow passengers. They seemed divided about equally between seasonal workers and sunburned teenage Italians, carrying stuffed camels, too much luggage, and clever clay vessels that when tipped over resisted spillage.

Not a large crowd, fortunately, because it appeared we had all purchased only deck passage instead of more-expensive cabins, and boarding the ship would be a process of racing to the main deck seeking benches in public space for ourselves and our luggage. Tensions rose comically when the ticket agent abandoned his velvet ropes and simply led us down the stairs to the quay, where we naturally bunched around him like savages, each eager to beat the others on board. He would grab one of us, bark fiercely at the others, then back away to examine passport and ticket. As soon as he looked down we'd creep forward, freezing like cartoon monsters when he glanced up. By the time the last of us boarded he had been backed up all the way to the bottom of the gangway. No matter; the ship was nearly empty and we all had plenty of space in the saloon bar.

I fell in with Masanori, a young Japanese fellow who turned out to be following the path of Hannibal. We chortled about strange pilgrimages, drew maps of our itineraries, drank a beer, showed each other our totem objects—for him a copy of *Hannibal Crosses the Alps*, for me, of course, the copy of *The Odyssey* from my wife. Stewards checked on the crowd once, demanding that people remain upright while the saloon served sandwiches to the few passengers who had booked cabins. An hour later Masanori took off his shoes, put in his toe separators, and lay back. We stretched out feet-to-feet on the surprisingly comfortable upholstered bench seat, our bags between us and an armrest each for pillow; every one of us in steerage had similar comfort. Before long we heard only the throbbing engines and light snoring, the room smelling comfortably of relief, drying sweat, and feet. The air-conditioning cycled on, and we slept.

Chapter 7

Where No-Man Has Gone Before:

In the Cyclops's Cave

Soon that stake, though green, began to glow a terrible red, as if it would blaze any moment. I took it from the fire, and as my men gathered around me a god inspired our hearts with tremendous courage. Then they took that pointed pole of glowing green olive and plunged it into his eye, while I bore down on the shaft from above and spun it around. . . . As the eyeball sizzled and its roots crackled, his lids fell completely away, and his brow began to blister . . . Horrible were the screams that rang from wall to rocky wall, and we shrank back in terror. He tore the stake from his eye, all dripping with blood, and frantically hurled it away. Then, throwing himself wildly about, he shouted as loud as he could to the neighboring Cyclopes, who lived out there in caves among the windy mountains.

—*The Odyssey*, Book IX

THE PROPRIETOR OF THE PENSIONE MESSINA, a fourth-floor walk-up in the center of the old quarter of Trapani, at the very western tip of Sicily, explained the doorbell code. His close-cropped head and days of stubble made him look like one of those faces on which children use magnets to arrange iron filings as beard and hair. He stared at me: "*Uno, due,*" he said, counting intently. "*Uno, due—sì?*" Whether because of the mirrors and garden sculpture on the landings along the stone stairs up from the courtyard or the stuffed bookcases and the desk piled high in the tiny office in which the proprietor lurks, the Messina felt a bit like Grandpa's house—or, considering the volume of stuff, a house occupied by, say, five grandpas. My cheap room was charming enough, with a basin, louvered shutters over the casement window, and four walls all painted different colors—and, of course, a number. But instead of giving me a key to the front door, the proprietor preferred that when I wished to enter the hotel, I buzz the doorbell a number of times corresponding to my room number. I had room two: thus, *"Uno . . . due! Uno . . . due! Sì?"*

Sì. Groggy after my night of public sleep aboard the ferry, this was all I needed. I had offered my passport as identification when checking in, and the proprietor put it in a drawer, plainly planning to keep it until I checked out. When you travel abroad, your passport is your identity, so giving it up feels profoundly wrong. Yet I lacked the wherewithal—and the Italian—to protest. Then he told me the only way back in was by secret code, and I wandered from the Messina in a fog, luggage and passport in his care, with neither identification nor key. Rattled by the weird meeting, instead of spending the morning getting my bearings, I stumbled wearily into a peaceful stone piazza, near the harbor, and sat on a bench. Fishermen sat on the ground mending nets, green nylon stretched between benches as they lashed in the little glass flotation balls Mediterranean fishermen have used for centuries. Shouts echoed from the morning produce markets, and old women leaned out of windows and watched the street. People hung laundry. A Mediterranean morning, a moment to relax and savor— perhaps find a cappuccino, a *cornetto,* and inhale the rich scent of the coffee, the yeasty bread, the sea air. Instead, for reasons I can explain only by saying that proprietor just freaked me out, I suddenly determined to leap, unplanned, onto a hydrofoil for the island of Favignana, twenty minutes away. When you've been traveling awhile and don't know quite what to do next, sometimes you just find the closest moving thing and jump on it.

YOU CAN ACTUALLY FIND A FRAGMENT OF MOTIVATION for my precipitous ferry trip in the Cyclops episode of *The Odyssey.* Odysseus and his fleet initially land not on the land of the Cyclopes (that's the plural) but on a small fertile island just off the coast, where they catch and cook a hundred or so of the innumerable goats wandering there. Among the geographers who favor western Sicily for the Cyclops,

Favignana tends to stand in as this island (in Roman times it was actually known as Aegusa, "Goat Island"). It's not much—a small island associated with goats near another place where you can find a cave—but it's about all the geography you get. Thucydides places the Cyclopes among the earliest inhabitants of Sicily, though he refers readers vaguely to "the poets" for more information, leaving you right where you started—and that's about it from the ancients. Moderns like to place the Cyclops near Vesuvius or Aetna, the description of him "standing out like a lone peak" and his ability to throw entire mountaintops at ships suggesting that he's perhaps a kind of personification of a volcano.

Otherwise, Odysseus offers precious few geographical clues. Leaving the Lotus-eaters, he says, "from there we sailed on with hearts full of sorrow till we came to the land of the Cyclopes." Try to get Google Maps to give directions from "on" to "till" and it asks whether you mean Stoke-on-Trent.

Thucydides did say the Cyclopes lived on Sicily, but I especially took as my source in this matter Samuel Butler, the British essayist, novelist, and journalist of the late nineteenth century. Butler's wry take on the action of *The Odyssey* makes *The Authoress of the Odyssey* one of the most fun books about Odyssean geography. For example, Butler believed Penelope's weaving and unraveling of Laertes' shroud might have overcomplicated her efforts to get rid of unwanted suitors. "Did she ever try snubbing?" he wonders. "Then there was boring—did she ever try that? Did she ever read them any of her grandfather's letters? Did she sing them her own songs, or play them music of her own composition? I have always found these courses successful when I wanted to get rid of people." Butler made great company despite his somewhat outlandish conclusion that every stop past the Lotus-eaters (including Ithaca) has its original somewhere on the island of Sicily. His point is less that Odysseus stopped in these places than that the places inspired the descriptions by the author of *The Odyssey*—who was, according to Butler, a young woman who lived in Trapani.

Geographers look for plenty of other Cyclops clues. The Cyclops is traditionally represented as having only one eye, but academics like to argue about whether he didn't really have two, since Homer never describes his single eye (though Hesiod, Homer's contemporary, does in another poem), and they go back and forth about the relation of these Cyclopes to the mythological Cyclopes who supposedly help Zeus by forging his thunderbolts and are kept otherwise busy in construction (many preclassical walls in Greece are called Cyclopean, since later Greeks believed that only the giant Cyclopes could have built them). Theorists have brought up tribes hither or yon who supposedly had a third eye tattooed on their foreheads, and others wonder whether skulls of dwarf elephants, with massive central sinus cavities, didn't perhaps set people wondering about one-eyed giants.

For my purposes, Butler thought *The Odyssey* originated in Trapani. The ancients called Favignana, just off Trapani, "Goat Island." And most of all, Butler's book includes a fabulous photograph of a cave near Trapani that in the 1890s locals identified for him as the cave of Polyphemus. So I went to Trapani.

And then I impulsively jumped on the ferry to Favignana.

Where not much happened. The island feels like a kind of sickle curved around the port, a castle glowering above it atop a large sere hill. Otherwise, Favignana offers dusty roads curving among dry-stacked stone walls lining fields of tall yellow weeds and square hay bales. I never saw a goat. After a few slices of pizza at the port, unable to think of anything else to do, I rented a bicycle. Any direction you go you hit gorgeous dark rocky beaches and crystal clear water glittering in the bright sun. I would have enjoyed myself more had I not been given a bicycle several sizes too small—knees akimbo, I rode around Favignana like a circus clown on a tricycle. When I paid for my ferry ticket back, I still had no sense of why I had come at all: I had utterly run out of ideas. I missed June, missed waking up in my own bed, missed having normal days. A month into my travels, on a quest that at moments like this could seem preposterous, I wasn't anywhere I particularly wanted to be: I was merely not at home.

Yet what is travel if not the art of creative homelessness? On the hydrofoil trip back, I stopped resisting weariness and finally allowed it to overcome me. Exhausted from managing luggage, hotel needs, and food, gently massaged by the vibrating floor, soothed by the afternoon light diffused by windows so filmed by years of salt spray that passengers could barely see out, I let the ferry rumble me into a moment of demisleep, from which I calmly awoke into a moment of pure travel disconnection. Extended travel brings these moments of almost Zen accommodation to reality. Instead of planning ahead, you simply exist. Through filmy windows, nothing to see, so don't look; on a short passage, no reason to eat, so close your eyes and breathe. Anxiety will surely return soon enough: Where to next? How to get there? But for now, sit. On that ferry, for twenty minutes, I sat.

It worked. Refreshed by that brief snooze, I cheerfully got off where I had started, at the foot of Mount Eryx in Trapani, whose long, straight streets bristle with Renaissance churches and three- and four-story town houses from the seventeenth and eighteenth centuries. I filled a busy hour gathering tourist maps and bus schedules until the ocher limestone lining the west-pointing streets glowed yellow as the sun sank into the Mediterranean, off the far western tip of Italy. I returned to the Pensione Messina, buzzed twice, and read about the land of the Cyclopes.

IT WAS A DARK and foggy night. Odysseus actually tells this to the Phaeacians when he describes his arrival among the Cyclopes. With visibility so bad, the fleet doesn't even know it's approaching land until the ships gently beach on that goat island. The crews spend the next day feasting, and the following morning Odysseus leaves eleven ships and crews there as he and his own crew row to the land of the Cyclopes, near enough that "across the still bay water we could hear their voices and the bleating of their sheep and goats." Odysseus takes pains to note that the Cyclopes are rustics: Even so close to such a fertile and fabulous island, the Cyclopes have built no ships to take advantage of its fecundity. In fact, they have no trappings of civilization at all: They "neither plow nor plant," he says, and "they have no assemblies for counsel and no established laws, but live on high mountain peaks in echoing caves, and each is sole master of his own children and wives. None of them cares anything at all about his neighbors." Eventually, this last turns out to be a good thing for Odysseus.

When the boat lands, the crew sees a huge cave just off the beach, set up with walls as a sheepfold. Odysseus tells most of his men to stay with the ship, taking a dozen of the best fighters with him to find out who these Cyclopes are. He impulsively takes along a goatskin of the "dark, sweet wine" given to him in thanks by Maron, priest of Apollo back among the Cicones, whom Odysseus had spared out of reverence. He brings the wine, he says, "for in my stout heart I already suspected that soon I would meet a man both powerful and wild, a savage utterly without regard for customs or decrees." Good call. In the cave they find an orderly shepherding operation, with crates of cheeses, milking buckets, and pens of lambs and kids. His men—perhaps having learned a lesson from the Cicones—urge him to grab what they can and take off, but Odysseus, thinking more about the laws of hospitality, instead orders them to have some cheese, sit down in the cave, and hope that when its occupant returns he's friendly.

He's not. He turns out to be the giant Cyclops Polyphemus. He drives his sheep and goats into the cave, blocks the entrance with a huge boulder, and tidies up. When he starts a fire for his dinner, he notices his thirteen visitors and asks whether they are traders or pirates. Odysseus speaks for the terrified crew: They are soldiers returning from Troy, driven off course. He then asks for the guest-friendship of *xenia*: we "have come to your knees in hope of warm hospitality, or some gift, perhaps, some customary gift to strangers," he says. "Remember that we are your suppliants, for Zeus is the god of strangers, the avenger of suppliants, the guardian, I say, of sacred strangers."

The Cyclops laughs: "We care nothing at all for aegis-bearing Zeus, nor for any of the blessed gods." Then, weary of pleasantries, he grabs up two of the men "as if they were puppies and dashed them down at his feet where their brains ran out on the ground." He eats them and goes to sleep.

Odysseus resists killing the sleeping ogre "since we could not have budged that tremendous rock he used for a door." The next morning the Cyclops eats two more crewmen and herds out his flocks, replacing the boulder behind him. Odysseus then thinks up what is, besides the Trojan Horse, probably his most famous scheme.

From an olive trunk, Odysseus cuts a pole, sharpens the end, and hides it beneath the piles of manure in the cave. When the Cyclops returns, he eats two more men, after which Odysseus approaches him with a bowl of Maron's wine. Men drink the wine deeply diluted with water, but the Cyclops gets it straight. The Cyclops drinks it and asks for more, promising that if Odysseus tells the Cyclops his name he will finally give him a guest-gift. Odysseus keeps the wine flowing, giving this name:

No-Man, he says—they call me No-Man, "my mother, my father, and all the rest of my friends." The Cyclops then tells Odysseus what his guest-gift will be: to eat No-Man last of all, after he's watched the Cyclops eat his friends. Then, overcome by the wine, the Cyclops passes out, so drunk that he vomits gobbets of human flesh. Odysseus and his men heat the point of the olive pole in the fire; then, Odysseus shouting encouragement, they drive it into the Cyclops's eye, turning it as though drilling. The Cyclops shrieks, the men withdraw, and the Cyclops tears away the stake, leaping about the cave bellowing. The other Cyclopes call from outside the cave, asking what all the noise is about. Polyphemus cries out that No-Man is killing him. His neighbors draw the obvious conclusion: "If you are alone and nobody is hurting you," they say, "you must be sick, and sickness you cannot escape since it comes from almighty Zeus. You had better pray to Poseidon, our lordly father." And they leave.

In the morning, the blinded Cyclops moves the boulder so his flocks can leave the cave to feed, but he stands in the doorway, groping the backs of the sheep to make sure his captives aren't riding them out. Cleverly, Odysseus ropes his men beneath the sheep; the Cyclops doesn't think to feel below them, so the men escape, Odysseus last of all, clinging to the woolly underside of the largest ram. Here Polyphemus has the soliloquy I remembered from the film I saw in ninth grade, though in my translation there wasn't quite so much orating. He mostly tells the ram about that no-good No-Man who has ruined everything, then lets the ram go. Far enough from the cave, Odysseus scrambles to his feet and frees his men, and they go bounding for the beach, driving the sheep before them onto their boat, which they launch.

Then, still within shouting distance, Odysseus crowns his greatest triumph by doing the stupidest thing he's ever done: He begins taunting Polyphemus about how clever this No-Man turned out to be. The Cyclops, further enraged, pulls off the top of a mountain and flings it at the sound of Odysseus's voice, where it splashes ahead of the ship, the backwash driving the ship back to the beach. Odysseus pushes off again, and despite his men begging him to shut up, he shouts again: "Cyclops, if anyone ever asks you about the disgraceful blinding of your eye, say that Odysseus, sacker of cities, put it out with a pole—I, the son of Laertes, from Ithaca!" He doesn't include his e-mail or Social Security number, but he's provided more than enough information to assist anyone seeking revenge on him.

Like, say, maybe the Olympian father of anybody he had recently blinded. Polyphemus, remembering aloud a prophecy he once heard that he was destined to be blinded by someone named Odysseus, groans that he always assumed Odysseus would be somebody larger. He then prays for vengeance to his father, the sea god Poseidon, asking that Odysseus "never get home. But if it should be his fate to reach his own land . . . then may his coming be late and hard, after losing all of his comrades. Let him come, O god, in somebody else's ship, and may he find troubles enough at home." Odysseus and his crews lament their lost companions, eat some more goat, and then sail off.

IT'S ONE OF THE LONGEST EPISODES on Odysseus's journey, some 450 lines, and by far the most memorable. As I planned my trip, that cave of Polyphemus loomed as large in my imagination as it did in *The Odyssey*. If I found no other site on my trip, I wanted to find that cave.

When nobody at the Trapani tourist information office had heard of any cave I remained placid—Butler's book included a sketchy map of the Trapani area, locating the cave near Pizzolungo, on the Tyrrhenian Sea a few miles north of town. Bus schedules the tourist office did provide, and in an Internet café the European version of MapQuest showed me I could walk a kilometer or so south of the little city of Bonagia, just past Pizzolungo, with good hope of finding my cave—in any case, rife with such street names as Via Omero, Via Penelope, and Via Nestore, Bonagia certainly seemed like the place to start. The next morning just past Pizzolungo the bus swung around a bend in Route 20, no more than a half hour out of Trapani, and in the striated limestone mountains a gaping cavern hove into view. I leaped out at the next stop.

The people in the little hardware stores and beach outfitters of Bonagia met my questions about *"il Ciclope"* or *"la grotta"* with puzzled looks, but with the notes from my Internet search, I confidently tramped south, dodging semitrucks on the asphalt. The utterly calm Tyrrhenian gleamed on my right, and before long the cave yawned again above me, a deep cleft in the yellow and gray rock, stained with leaking red—iron oxide, of course, but forgive a fellow for fantasizing. I ended up in a tiny two-street neighborhood surrounded by fields. The cave opened directly at the end of a street called Via del Ciclope, up a long set of switchbacking wooden stairs. Had I remained unsure exactly which Cyclops this cave belonged to, for good measure the other street was called Via Polifeme. I climbed the stairs.

Fringed by laurels, the cave has a long, arcing roof that makes it look from the outside like an open mouth, slightly frowning. It even slavers lightly, water dripping off dozens of stalactites. A broad plateau in front of the cave overlooks the descent to the Tyrrhenian, no more than a mile or so down the slope. A low wall of dry-stacked rock runs across the cave mouth, with wooden gates at the openings and plenty of animal pellets inside—this cave plainly serves still as an animal pen. Soot coated the ceiling among the stalagmites, evidence of countless fires within. Probably thirty feet deep or more and a good fifty feet wide, the cave provided plenty of space for Odysseus and his dozen crewmen to hide—and plenty of places for me to sit and eat the oranges and cheese and crackers I had packed up as lunch. The description and photos from Butler's book left no doubt: I had found the very cave long identified with the Cyclops Polyphemus.

I can scarcely describe my disappointment.

BECAUSE, OKAY, here you are: now what? You've actually found a place you can identify as one of the sites on your pilgrimage. You've reached the Cyclops's cave! The thing is, once there, what do you do? I found the jawbone of some animal in the cave; was I supposed to try to conjure there the menace of some fearsome carnivore? Did I expect an actual Cyclops to show up? Joyce, in *Ulysses,* sets his Cyclops episode in a bar, where a one-eyed bigot berates the protagonist Bloom, eventually throwing not a mountaintop but an empty biscuit tin at him as Bloom smart-mouths from a departing carriage. So in my pilgrimage to the cave, would I have been happy had, say, some Bonagia store owner proved in some way threatening so I could cleverly escape? The proprietor of my Trapani pensione seemed a little crazy—had he actually been dangerous, and in moving to more normal lodgings I perhaps terribly clever? (Not really—I gathered my luggage the next morning and said *"Ciao, grazie!"* Handing over my passport, he pleasantly nodded.)

I spent a lot of time in that cave—probably close to two hours. I reread the episode and thought about where in this particular cave the monster and the crewmen might have stood, what the episode meant, and what the hell I was doing sweating in a cave full of goat shit north of Trapani, Sicily, while five thousand miles away my wife gestated alone.

On the surface, the meaning of the episode seems almost too easy. For one thing, it's the oldest story in the book—almost literally. A clever little guy gets into trouble with—but then gets the better of—a big ogre who wants to eat him, defeating him not by brute force but by his wits. That's Jack and the Beanstalk. It's David and Goliath. It's the fundamental horror show format in which some monster says to the protagonist, "I must have you over . . . for dinner! Bwa-ha-ha-ha-ha!" Philologists, who look into this kind of thing, find the clever-guy-tricks-the-man-eating-giant story in every culture from Iceland to Arabia, from Korea to Africa, and they confidently agree among themselves that what they find is evidence not that Homer's story has spread far and wide but that the episode from Homer is just the best-known version of a story so fundamentally human that it shows up in every culture there is. A German book written in 1904 compared 221 versions of the story, broken into three groups: the blinding of the giant; the false-name trick; and those (like *The Odyssey*) combining the two. Additional versions continually surface, but the point is made: It's the ur-story of a species comforting itself in a dark, scary world. Yes, there are big scary monsters out there, and we're not much for claws or teeth. But we've got it all in the smarts department, so we can eventually overcome. And certainly, about halfway through your life, this sounds not only comforting but true. We've all been held captive by giant man-eating corporations, or bullies, or governments; but we begin to think we've gathered a little experience, and that just maybe, with a little craftiness, that might pay off. Just the same, the big guy is big, and you probably shouldn't expect to get out without paying a high price. Simple enough.

But then maybe not so simple: Odysseus has shown several other things here, too. For one thing, he talks about going home, but here Odysseus chooses to do anything but. Stopping on an island with plentiful food and water, instead of loading up and continuing on, Odysseus decides to have a look around. Then, finding a cave full of easily portable booty, he again dismisses the safe course. It doesn't work out too well for him (and it goes especially poorly for six of his crewmen). If Odysseus looked like a bad boss when he lost control of his crew among the Cicones, how bad does he look here, when he leads them into an enclosed space, dismisses their urging to leave as quickly as possible, and then watches six of them die horrible deaths? Sure, he recovers and gets the survivors out of the cave, but you still have to figure none of them will nominate him for manager of the month.

After his first three adventures, Odysseus hasn't done anything more admirable than save a party of his men from a mess he dragged them into in the first place. Odysseus, the mastermind of Troy, still doesn't know enough not to lead his troops into a room with only one way in or out and wait around to see if anybody gets eaten alive. Then, when they do, he gets to mastermind a glorious escape. He's like the guy in the fraternity who always gets everyone else in the car arrested. He's missed something most of us learned in the third grade—with big bullies, the thing is to *not* get their attention.

That's the complexity of the seemingly simple episode. Is Odysseus the clever rascal who gets his men out of the tight jam? Or is he the pigheaded moron who gets them into it? Is he the husband and father desperate to get home to his wife, or is he the insatiably curious explorer who just needs to know, since we're here, who are those guys? The arrogant adolescent who shouts his name, literally, to the heavens? Or the near Zen master who denies his own name in order to evade attention?

* * *

OF COURSE, he's all of the above. The power of that name, No-Man, finally dawned on me, sitting in that dripping cave. Sure, Odysseus is sneaky—but we already know that. He solved the riddle of Helen's suitors, he sneaked into Troy in disguise, he invented the Trojan Horse. To see him outclever the big dumb Cyclops is cool, but hardly surprising. What he does in the cave that's new, though, is unname himself. "I'm No-Man," he tells the Cyclops.

That's not an easy thing, denying his own name. This is, after all, a hero's journey, and Odysseus faces all the things heroes face: women and men, gods and monsters. And for the ancients, heroism was all about fame: To be a hero, you make a name for yourself. In *The Hero with a Thousand Faces,* Joseph Campbell conflates all the myths in the world into a series of steps along the vast, general mythological journey, and Odysseus takes most of them. A hero must resist the call to adventure (as Odysseus does by trying to avoid shipping out for Troy), must face many tests and enemies, must have supernatural aid, must overcome a supreme ordeal, must return with what he's gained on his journeys.

But a central element of this journey is, counterintuitively, withdrawal from the real world. Odysseus has a lot more journey ahead—and plenty of withdrawals, figurative and literal, remain. But by taking this false name for the first time he at least symbolically vanishes. He takes himself—anyway, his name—out of the picture and does what's necessary. If you really want to get in charge, Odysseus figures out here, master not your enemy but your ego. By becoming No-Man Odysseus does that, literally saying: It's not all about me. It's about getting the job done.

And from the moment he undertakes that strategy, everything goes right. Before that he and his crew sit passively in the cave being eaten. Then Odysseus becomes No-Man. Suddenly, they attack the Cyclops: no losses. They escape from the cave: no losses. Steal the sheep: no losses. Then they sail away with no losses—until Odysseus abandons his anonymity and tells the Cyclops who he is, at which point his entire crew almost dies. In fact, if you take the long view, the crew does die: Polyphemus, after all, prays that Odysseus returns home "after losing all his comrades," which we know from the proem he eventually does.

In denying his name, Odysseus does something powerful, especially for a hero. For at least a moment, he says, "The hell with fame or riches or anything: Let's just get out of here," and he does. Of course, he then immediately screws it up. He lets go of his identity just long enough to save his life, then immediately reasserts his ego, dooming himself to another nine years of wandering. That is, with a wife and a child at home, after ten years of war, Odysseus is still acting like a cocky young man. He shows a glimmer of selfless wisdom, but just that quick it's gone. Odysseus still has a lot to learn.

SINCE NAMES ARE AT ITS CORE, the Cyclops episode got me thinking about names in another way, too. Over and over when I talked about *The Odyssey,* people remembered the same phrase, "rosy-fingered dawn," a phrase that has put to sleep generations of weary junior high schoolers. In this episode many days pass, and each begins with the return of those rosy fingers: They're the Homeric epithet reliably indicating the passing of time. Epithets have a lot of jobs in the poem. For one thing, they help fill up the rhythmically complicated lines that Homer wrote—some characters have several epithets, showing up depending on rhythmic needs. Menelaus, for example, can be referred to by his red hair, by his loud war cry, or by his father's name, among others. Some, like rosy-fingered dawn, are simply formalized language, probably developed to help the poet—or subsequent orators—compose dactylic hexameter in performance.

But those epithets attach to each character specific words that remind the listener of his or her identity, often in some way commenting on it. Calypso was the goddess "with braided hair," her lovely tresses failing to win the heart of Odysseus; in *The Iliad,* powerful Achilles is "swift-footed," both descriptive and ironic, given that he spends most of the poem sitting on his butt sulking (and eventually dies from a wound to his heel).

Odysseus, of course, has such epithets. In the first line of the poem he's called the man "of many turns," though most often he's called the man "of many devices" or "of many designs," since his legendary cleverness defines him. In this episode he calls himself "No-Man," and then at the end, when he cries out his real name and is trying to make himself sound like a big deal, he chooses the formal "sacker of cities." It's a fun thing to keep track of as you read Homer, and after a while you can't help wondering about yourself in those terms. I began to wonder: What would my epithets be? "Dependable refiller of copy paper," perhaps, or "possessor of once-solid credit rating." How about "maintainer of adequately tidy garage workspace."

I didn't like it, and when I thought about it in Trapani I realized that those epithets addressed not just my sense of myself but exactly what I was looking for in that cave: the point of making a pilgrimage anyhow. I don't want any more epithets involving competence with office equipment or responsible financial planning. By going to Sicily, Turkey, Tunisia, I got out of my chair, if nothing else. Once you've skittered around the planet a bit, even when you find yourself a captive in some indirectly lit office cave of gray-carpeted surfaces, toner, and machines with little fans inside them, people won't just refer to the quantity of little toys by your computer; instead, they'll talk about your big trip. "He's traveled some," they'll say. Which is something. Thus, when some future poet sings my name, instead of declaiming that I refinanced at a good interest rate, maybe he can praise me as a traveler. "Retracer of steps," he can say, "man of many guidebooks," or perhaps "he who could order cheap food in many languages."

Maybe; if I'm sung by poets, I'll leave it to them. But it was Odysseus's name, No-Man, that stuck with me. In the translation that June gave me, Odysseus calls himself "Nobody" (in Greek it's *outis*—nobody, or no one). But I had heard a classics professor speak once, and she quoted Odysseus calling himself "No-Man," and I loved its sound. So I began pulling out other translations: Nobody, Nohbdy, all kinds of variation on Odysseus's trick appear, in all kinds of wonderful translations. Then finally, like John Keats, I looked into Chapman's Homer (published in 1614–1616, George Chapman's *Odysses* was the first reliable English translation, inspiring Keats's famous poem "On First Looking into Chapman's Homer"). Chapman uses that chilling name: "No-Man! I'le eate thee last of all thy friends," Polyphemus says to Odysseus. And in that burlap-bound Classics Club edition familiar to so many penny-pinching undergraduates, my Trapani pal Samuel

Butler makes the same choice, only without the hyphen: Noman. I couldn't explain why that name captured me so—then I murmured it within that cave and I heard how satisfactorily its nasal *m*'s and *n*'s and sonorous vowels echoed within a hollow cave. I walked around the cave saying it. "No-Man," I intoned, feeling the reverberations.

YOU CAN GET LOST in that kind of thinking, so thank goodness for the goats. Annoyed by the occasional low rush of traffic and the constant banging from repairmen working on a house on Via del Ciclope, I had tuned out any sounds as I explored, ate, and lost myself in thought. Then, somehow, above the hammering and the traffic, I noticed a light hollow clanking, at first intermittent enough that I thought I was imagining it, eventually so frequent that I stood at the cave mouth and scanned the surrounding promontories. Finally, I saw them—one ridge over, a mixed flock of sheep and goats, making their scattered way along the fences at the edge of the developments; hollow bells of wood emitted a sonorous gong, metal ones adding a treble clank.

Goats and sheep—driven by a single shepherd shouting, "Heyy! He-eey!" and helped along by his dog. The herd made its way along the fencing, passing directly below me at the base of the stairs as I stood in the sun and watched them pass, watching them make their slow way to the next ridge, and the next, until their soft gonging and rattling was lost.

The hair stood up on the back of my neck. While I thought about the Cyclops, about his cave among the sheepy crags, it felt magical to be wakened from my reverie in the cave by sheep among the crags. The Mediterranean is a place of sheep and goats and mountains; Odysseus found it so, and so did I, and I confess to a moment of pure thrill. I had left home to see what Odysseus saw and feel what he felt, and if even for a tiny moment, I did.

ON THE WAY DOWN Via del Ciclope I met an old couple who seemed interested in where I was going; I signaled that I was interested in that cave up there. The woman shook her head vigorously: *"Chiuso!*

Chiuso!" she said sharply—Closed! Closed! She made a tumbling motion. The cave was closed because the stairs were unsafe? Something dangerous might knock me down up there? Instead of spelunking, I ought to consider gymnastics? Fortunately, I was already headed down. I waved and, frowning, she watched me go. Maybe it's no more complex than that: Explore first, ask questions later, but above all leave before anybody can give you any trouble. I got the lesson a lot easier than Odysseus did.

Chapter 8

"Help! I Need Somebody!":

The Hospitality of the Wind King

Next we came to the floating Aeolian island, home of Aeolus . . . When I, in my turn, asked him if I might continue my journey with assistance from him, he did all he could to help me. He gave me a leather bag, made from the hide of an ox of nine years, and in it he bound the winds, howling in all directions, for Zeus had made him their keeper, able to still or stir up whichever one he wishes.

—*The Odyssey*, Book X

EXTENDED TRAVEL reminds you that you are an animal. You spend a lot of time outdoors, sniffing the air, redolent of sage or salt; you watch the sun arc through the day, the moon grow full, then slight; you feel the predominant local wind kick up at dusk or dawn. Your bag gets heavy, your muscles tired. Forgetting to fill your belly before restaurants close for the afternoon can cause despondence; just the same, stumbling across a street vendor selling sausage or soda pop can take you instantly from misery to euphoria. You get blisters, windburn, mysterious stomach ailments. That is, you exist physically, all day long, in ways that during most of your everyday life you never notice.

Hyperaware of your body and its physical needs, you attend especially to three constantly nagging questions: Where shall I eat? Where shall I sleep? And where shall I next use the toilet? If you know the answer to all three, you feel cheerful and light, capering down some foreign street, local currency in your pocket, wondering at the miraculous path that led you so far from home. Know the answer to two and you feel good, in no terrible hurry to answer the next. Know only one, though, and you can't quite get comfortable—eating from a street vendor with no facilities, the backpack at your feet reminding you that you still don't have a hotel room, a meal can be satisfactory but rarely pleasant. Or race into the restroom upon getting off a bus and you feel better, but with no room and no food you can still find yourself out on the streets, nervous, hitting that weepy-crashy low-blood-sugar state in which no museum, ruin, or beach in the world could hold interest.

The Odyssey, a travel book among its other guises, never ignores this reality. "Nothing is more dog-shameless than the hateful belly," says Odysseus himself on the island of the Phaeacians, almost at the end of his journey. "Even so is my heart heavy with grief, but my belly continues its usual demands for food and for drink." Thus, before seeking to climb the peak, visit the garden, explore the cave, the traveler develops the skill to get to town and solve those primary demands. This shows up routinely in *The Odyssey,* which for all its metaphor and magic never loses sight of Odysseus as a man out in the world. Homer forever depicts him and his men beaching their boats and immediately eating or sleeping before even considering whether to explore their surroundings. I barely noticed those descriptions when reading at home, but on the road I loved them, and the "Travel True!" designation I used when Homer emphasizes those vital travel details filled the margins of my copy.

Consider the isle of Aeolus. Odysseus actually lands on that island twice, and when he describes his second landing he says, "There we went ashore, and after renewing our water supply my comrades took their meal beside the swift ships." The men eat and drink—it's hardly worth mentioning, yet in place after place, when the ships land, Odysseus points out that the men eat, drink, and sleep. I took great comfort from Homer's constant reminders that Odysseus, no less than I, was arriving in unfamiliar places where nobody was looking out for him, and he had to solve those immediate problems before setting out to learn what he could of the locals. Then I arrived at my own isle of Aeolus, and for the first time I feared I would not be able to solve them.

* * *

FROM THE LAND OF THE CYCLOPS, Odysseus tells the Phaeacians, he and his men "sailed on." He continues, "Next we came to the floating Aeolian island," and that's all he has to say about the path between the two. If you're marking the sites of this journey on a map, these directions give less information than you might hope for. Plus, once an island is floating, it's going to be hard to keep track of anyhow.

On the other hand, just north of eastern Sicily lay seven tiny islands: the Aeolian chain, which Thucydides mentions by this name as early as the fifth century BC. By the first century AD, Strabo was referring to Aeolus as a historical person, a man "called lord of the winds and regarded as their king" who lived in the Aeolians and taught sailors how to navigate the tricky waters around Sicily; Strabo's source for this matter is another historian, Polybius. Various sources place Aeolus on various specific islands among the seven in the chain, but Lipari (the largest; the chain is now sometimes called the Liparis), Vulcano (the closest to Sicily), and Stromboli (dominated by an active volcano) are the three most commonly cited.

Not to say that geographers haven't come up with other ideas. Some note that floating islands suggest icebergs, either in northern Europe or in the Black Sea; others suggest the floating pumice that follows volcanic eruptions. And since in the episode Odysseus leaves the island and sails on a west wind, almost reaching home before catastrophe strikes, some geographers have suggested other islands—like Malta— with a more direct easterly route to Ithaca. Interesting enough in a literal way, but unless you are desperate to complicate your life, if you're looking for Aeolus, you'll search among the Aeolians.

Odysseus says that around Aeolus's island "runs a wall of unbreakable bronze, to which the rock rises straight from the sea." He and his crews land there, and Aeolus and his incestuous family—six sons married to six daughters—invite the travelers to stay in their palace and join their constant feasting. After a month of answering questions about the Trojan War and the heroes' returns, Odysseus finally gets a chance to raise a question of his own and asks for help getting home.

Aeolus happily obliges, locking all the winds but one into an oxhide bag, and sending "the West Wind forth, that it might blow and bear us and our ships on our course"; once he's safely home, Odysseus can simply open the bag and release the contrary winds. For nine days, that zephyr does bear Odysseus toward home—Odysseus, anxious, stays awake the whole time, minding the tiller himself. Within sight of the fires of Ithaca, though, he slips into exhausted sleep. His crew, jealously assuming that the bag contains treasure Odysseus doesn't mean to share, opens the bag to see the loot. The resulting windstorm blows the ships right back to Aeolus, who determines, rightly, that Odysseus must be cursed by the gods and refuses to entertain him again. Odysseus, in despair, resists suicide, and the crews row sadly off to their next adventure.

AS A SOLITARY TRAVELER, with a backpack and no set plans, you place your trust in help—from other travelers, from locals, from the gods. "It doesn't matter," you say to yourself. "There's always room for one more—no matter how busy the town, how crowded the resort, how inauspicious the time of year, how late or unexpected my arrival, there will always be one more room for me, and I will always manage to find it." If you think about it, you are also saying, "The room will cost a price I am willing to pay and will be in an area I consider at least minimally safe." You probably make several dozen other presumptions, growing increasingly specific, and if you thought it through, the prospect of finding an acceptable room might turn daunting. Thus, you don't think it through—you show up, with your backpack and your guidebooks; you walk the streets and hope to find the tourist office; you discuss the destination with your fellow travelers aboard train and bus and ferry. Above all, you trust: There's always room for one more. And usually there is.

So when I took the train from Trapani it didn't worry me that I hadn't lined up a place to stay. In fact, I had not yet even chosen which island to visit, so my research inconclusively filled a couple hours as the north coast of Sicily slid by the train windows: cedars, apartments, blue and white fishing boats pulled up on rocky shores, and an occasional smattering of palm umbrellas. By the time I started seeing the Aeolians offshore I was still considering the archipelago, weighing various options; I had made no decision when I got off the train in Milazzo, the port city on the northeast Sicilian shore, visited almost exclusively by people catching ferries.

The train dumped me into a madhouse of red-faced, shouting Italians pulling huge suitcases behind them and carrying snorkeling gear. This was July, high season. Like most Europeans, Italians take their vacation time seriously, and island beaches are just as attractive to them as to anyone else. Even Mediterraneans like a Mediterranean vacation.

Different companies sell tickets out of different offices to different ferries, which depart for different islands from different piers, according to sometimes-accurate schedules that are sometimes posted in sometimes easily viewed places in offices that are always about to close. Thus, when I tumbled off the train, I joined a noisy throng, fighting for positions on shuttle buses, from there rushing to the waterfront en masse, crashing like waves against the doors of various ferry offices, some of which closed for lunch in our faces. The time for choice had arrived, and in the crush I made it fast.

I chose the first ferry out.

I emerged from the madness with a ticket to the closest island, and after an hour aboard a hydrofoil arrived on the tiny quay of Vulcano, just after noon on a Saturday in late July. I was again surrounded by tourists, squinting into the sun, dragging their luggage and scanning for signs for their hotels. Vulcano, an island of less than eight square miles with an offseason population of fewer than five hundred, has only a few hotels. My guidebook was straightforward: "Room prices erupt in July and August, when tourists storm in. . . . Reservations for this period should be made no later than May." In May I hadn't even known I was taking a trip, much less where or when—and here I was, blowing in with the storm of tourists, without a reservation. So I didn't waste time.

No luck. Trudging around carrying my backpack, I tried every hotel and guesthouse mentioned in my guidebook—nothing. I went to the place where the book assured me there would be a tourist office—nothing. I plodded over to an agency that could supposedly hook up a traveler with an *affittacamera*—a rented room in a private home—but it was closed. Listed phone numbers yielded no answers. I returned to the *affittacamera* agency an hour after it was supposed to reopen after lunch. It hadn't—a commonplace in the Mediterranean, where hours of operation, if they're even posted, are never more than estimates. I sat on a low stone wall in the sun and considered my situation: I was hot, I was tired, I was hungry, and I was homeless. The island, basically a smoldering volcano in the middle of the sea, has little shade and smells like sulfur. There are ideal circumstances for travel. These are not them.

THEN I THOUGHT ABOUT ODYSSEUS. The wall I sat upon girded a little sparsely trafficked circle, in the middle of which was a low, dark statue—of Aeolus, represented drawing the winds around him like a cloak. Great: I had found Aeolus, but I still had no place to sleep. Considering what came next, this could not have been more appropriate.

People traditionally interpret the Aeolus episode as just one more example of Odysseus as bad boss—unable to delegate, he exhausts himself and then, at exactly the wrong moment, succumbs to slumber. Since he's neglected even to tell his crew what's in the bag Aeolus gave him, blame for the resulting catastrophe rests on his shoulders. That is, this episode basically teaches Odysseus not to go to sleep when the game is on the line. But first, how dumb do you have to be if you don't know that? Second, we learn a couple of books later that Odysseus finds this lesson unlearnable: You have to sleep sometime, and if trouble has targeted you, that's when it'll find you. This episode isn't about sleeping at all. This episode is about asking for help.

So far Odysseus has been away from Troy barely a month—a couple of weeks dithering around leaving Troy, a week or so getting blown across the Mediterranean, a couple of days apiece with the Cyclops and Cicones, an afternoon with the Lotus-eaters. And in that month he has managed not only to annoy, with the rest of the Greeks, his patron goddess, Athena, but to massively offend her even more powerful uncle, Poseidon. This is not a strong start toward getting home. Then he shows up on the island of Aeolus, and a wonderful thing happens: First, he and his men just stay put for a breather, feasting and enjoying the party. Much more important, he does something men—heroes perhaps most of all—hate to do.

He asks for directions.

Okay, maybe not directions—but he comes close. He asks Aeolus for help. He humbles himself, just like he did by becoming No-Man with the Cyclops. Instead of the arrogant young sacker of cities, he's just a guy looking to get home, and he says so. And guess what? It works again. "Trying to get home, eh?" Aeolus says. "Well, sure! Here's unlimited power to take you exactly where you want to go, plus I've conveniently captured all negative influences right here in this bag, which is locked, and I'll place it in your very own care. Just don't do anything monstrously stupid, and home you go. It's yours to screw up, my friend." Odysseus, of course, is up to the challenge.

I hoped I could do better. A ferry to another island seemed a mistake; not only would I have to go through ferry hell once again, but I would lose a couple of hours making the passage, with no reason to believe Lipari or Salina would be less crowded. So I took a deep breath, shouldered my pack, and began another slog down a baking asphalt road.

Heading toward a beach camping area that I thought might provide at least some shade and perhaps a public toilet, I passed a wooden post outside a little tiki hut shop that rented scooters and bicycles. On it I saw the little white *i* on a blue field that is the international symbol for information, and the words "English! Deutsch! Francais!" all with happy little exclamation points. It was, literally, a sign. Sweating, miserable, and at wit's end, I followed Odysseus's model. I walked in, dropped my pack in front of the table that served as a counter, and spoke a single word: "Help."

A small woman with long dark hair, a deep tan, and a bikini top broke into a wide smile. "Help!" she sang. "I need somebody. Help! Not just anybody . . . Help!"

When you ask for help and they begin singing Beatles songs to you in your own language, this is a good thing. Then she stopped singing but kept smiling.

"I'm not really looking for a scooter," I said. "Just a room for the night."

She brightened. "Oh! Like a bed-and-breakfast!" she said. "Would that be okay?"

Before I could so much as nod, she pulled from behind some bushes another lovely woman in a bikini, whose name turned out to be Rosie. The way attractive, scantily clad women kept popping up from behind, things felt like the opening sequence of *Petticoat Junction*. Bikini number one smiled, pointing at Rosie. "She runs a bed-and-breakfast," she said. Did Rosie have a room available? She did. Was it expensive? It was not. Would I follow her? I did, humping along with my pack as she rode a block ahead on her scooter, then waited until I caught up, then rode another block. And so on to the Casa Schmidt, at the end of a long narrow road it would never have crossed my mind to wander, where she put me in a clean room with screenless windows (I was not to mind the geckos, which Rosie charmingly pronounced "jeckoes") and access to a tiled private breezeway where I later enjoyed, in the cool of the evening, one of life's greatest pleasures: an outdoor shower.

This asking for help is powerful stuff.

THE HOURS ON VULCANO thereafter passed magically. Vulcano is a snoozing volcanic island, so your easy walks around lead you to a beach with natural Jacuzzi bubbles, lightly radioactive mud baths, and steaming fissures you can easily investigate; one small beach on the west of the island had black volcanic sand. I rented a bicycle from my friends at the tiki hut and explored the rest of the island, lolled around the beaches—black, radioactive, and otherwise—and ate food. Late in the day the hot air rising from the island created a pleasant onshore breeze. Interested in the wind, I began years ago to travel always with a tiny, pocket-sized kite. There, on the island of the wind king, I actually flew it.

Another kind of wind impressed itself on me the next morning, when I climbed the Gran Cratere, Vulcano's large sleeping volcano. Because the rim of the crater has, of course, no shade, visitors are adjured to climb the steep cone and circle the crater either early in the morning or late in the afternoon (and, by the way, not to sit down, since the dense toxic gases jetting from the fumaroles collect near the ground). Arising at 6 a.m., I thus crested the rim of the volcano just as the crepuscular rays of the sun poked through the fumaroles' undulating mists; yellow sulfur formations bewhisker the mouths of the holes like hoarfrost, and the creeping fog made this rim of the earth feel otherworldly, magical. As the sun rose the environment resolved itself into little more than the brown, sandy edge of a nearly dead crater, though the misty fumes still rose. But I remembered up there Aristotle's theory that wind originated not from moving air but as emanations from the earth. I always thought that was ridiculous and rather quaint until I stood over those hissing fumaroles and it suddenly made perfect sense: Down in there somewhere was the wind factory, and out of these holes came, obviously, wind, visible for all to see in the mists jetting from the ground. Stromboli, the only live volcano in the Aeolians and the northernmost island of the chain, is still sometimes called "the weather glass of the Mediterranean" for the way its constant steam shows wind direction.

From the tour of the Gran Cratere I returned to one of the great breakfasts of my life, a breakfast so satisfactory I stood on my chair to look down and take a picture of it. Espresso, with cream and sugar; plums and other fruits; a madeleine; and a huge chocolate croissant with a dusting of cocoa, all arranged on a floral tablecloth by the bikini-clad Rosie, on a table under the tiled breezeway. Odysseus may have received better hospitality during his month with Aeolus, but I couldn't see how. All you have to do in this world is ask for help—and then, when it's offered, not blow it.

Fair enough. My work on Aeolus done, I steeled myself for reentry into ferry hell; I had a long way to go. I didn't expect to get all the way within sight of my next destination only to be blown back to Vulcano, but I had plenty of other issues.

I PASSED FOUR HOURS aboard the local train between Milazzo and Palermo, Sicily, in a state of exquisitely painful and utterly useless anxiety. Desperate to catch a midnight ferry out of Trapani, I desired nothing more than the train's forward motion. Yet in seemingly every station in every tiny town along Sicily's north coast, the train pulled over and idled interminably, as intercities and expresses, all hopelessly late and off-schedule, whooshed by. Fishing boats swayed in the Tyrrhenian; rows of satellite dishes atop homes made little villages look like fields of sunflowers or nests of baby birds, mouths agape; the sun sank behind picturesque ruins ancient and modern. Yet I enjoyed none of it; as the afternoon lengthened to evening, the midnight departure time for the ferry neared, and my level of anxiety rose until I could barely sit. At one point a nice old Italian woman actually reached over and patted me on the leg, nodding and closing her eyes: "Shush, now, it'll be fine; there, there," or its Italian equivalent. It didn't help.

The *Tao Te Ching* famously says, "A good traveler has no fixed plans and is not intent upon arriving." The *Tao Te Ching*, however, did not have a once-weekly ferry to catch, an island away, and less than half a day to do it. As the train stood motionless on yet another small-town siding, as the evening deepened and the clock ticked inexorably toward midnight, I had plenty of time to reflect on how I had gotten into this mess.

I hoped to catch the weekly ferry from Trapani to Cagliari, the southern port of Sardinia; if I missed the midnight ferry, I had either a week to kill in Trapani, where I had already spent as much time as I cared to in the Cyclops's cave, or a journey the long way around: a train up the boot of Italy past Rome, and a ferry from there to the north of Sardinia. Since I was trying to follow Odysseus and not circumvent his struggles, I wanted very much to catch that ferry.

From my room on Vulcano I could walk to the 1 p.m. *aliscafo,* or hydrofoil, back to Milazzo. From Milazzo I could catch the train to Palermo, where I had to get a bus to Trapani, where I could catch that overnight ferry to Cagliari. From there I'd have to make my way north to eventually find a ferry between the northern tip of Sardinia and the southern tip of Corsica, where I would finally reach the port town of Bonifacio, widely identified with the city of the Laestrygonians, Odysseus's next stop after Aeolus.

The aliscafo was a mob scene as usual, but I wisely went first thing in the morning and thus emerged after only a half hour or so among the shouting masses. Just after the hydrofoil pulled out of Vulcano, two English-speaking ladies scurried to the door. "Was that Vulcano?" they cried. "We needed to get off!" And they proceeded to display such an agony of whining, finger pulling, and wrist flapping that the ferry turned around and deposited them. Five minutes after the second departure another pair—a man and a woman this time—performed the same trick. This time the staff gave only disgusted stares.

I was plenty glad to find myself ashore at Milazzo, not terribly late. The train, though, was not so simple. The express from Rome, which left leeway for the ferry, was several hours late—the express from Rome is always hours, sometimes days, late. I found instead a local train to Palermo, which though it arrived in early evening still looked like it would leave me enough time to get a bus to Trapani that should get me on the ferry. I bought a ticket and passed a couple agreeable hours eating station-café panini with Vicki and Katie, two American exchange students who gave me advice on Italian pronunciation (the advice later turned out to be poor). The local originated in Milazzo, so it left on time, but aware of the unpredictable nature of Italian trains and overcome by that desperate hope of catching the ferry, I agonized as it trundled to Palermo, impervious to the comforts of even nice ladies. The man who misses the train dies but once; the man who takes the local wishes to die a thousand times.

Suffering or no, it arrived on time, of course—secret travel hint: locals almost always do. The next bus for Trapani, scheduled to arrive more than an hour before the ferry departed, left in only a few minutes, with me aboard. As the bus lurched into gear I took my first deep breath since leaving the tile breezeway on Vulcano—and recognized what a terrible blunder the whole day had been.

As we ground through the Palermo evening, every street we passed bustled with people out for their evening *passeggiata*—the ritual Mediterranean walk during which everyone in the community gets a coffee or gelato, window-shops, sees and is seen. Perhaps they ponder philosophical questions, like why Italian men of a certain age really do stroll along in sunglasses, expensive loafers, and sport coats draped over their shoulders—and why that works. The piazzas, arches, and colonnades of the Palermo streets glowed, strings of electric bulbs crisscrossing major thoroughfares. The entire city looked like a street party, and there I was, zipping through because Palermo wasn't on my *Odyssey* tour plans, and I felt like a fool. I had spent more than a week on Sicily, and I had failed to see its most famous city. On one hand, this fit: On his fierce quest to get home, what did Odysseus pass that with more time he might have liked to stop and see? On the other hand, I was a pilgrim, not Odysseus, and I promised myself: Henceforth, *Odyssey* or not, I would whoosh through no more major cities, ignore nothing more that I would later regret I had ignored. I called this the Palermo Principle.

The bus reached Trapani before 10:30. After a brief walk to the dock, I learned that not only had the ship just begun boarding, but the line at the ticket booth was sufficiently short that I could for 30 euros easily upgrade the ticket I had bought for one of the uncomfortable *poltroni*—airplane-style armchairs arranged in rows in uncomfortable, stuffy, closed-in salons—to a bunk in a private, if tiny, inside cabin, which promised to vastly improve my overnight passage. I still had time for pizza and soda pop at one of the dockside restaurants. I bought an extra piece to eat aboard ship.

IF YOU'VE EVER TAKEN A CRUISE SHIP, think of a Mediterranean ferry as the exact opposite. The *Oxford English Dictionary* recognizes a difference between a "voyage," which can have the connotation of a return to the point of departure, and a "passage," which lightly implies a one-way trip. E. M. Forster, consider, wrote of a passage to India, not a voyage: India was the destination, not a place to visit. On the ferry *Emilia,* then, I took a passage to Sardinia, one of the great travel experiences life has to offer. A straightforward passage by sea is everything air travel is not. It's human, respectful, ennobling: It's travel.

A cruise ship feels like a carousel—it tries way too hard to entertain you, it assaults you with gaudy colors and oddly arranged music, and it basically goes in a circle. Though a working ferry has many of the same amenities—plenty of cabins, bars, and restaurants, even a movie theater—it in every way radiates work, not play. Backed to the Trapani quay, the *Emilia* quietly vibrated as workers loaded not just passengers and cars but shipped goods, produce, trucks; it had the job of bringing stuff to Sardinia. Some of that stuff was people, and the *Emilia* provided things for those people to do during the trip, but nothing about the thick white and blue paint on the steel stairs and decks bespoke the fake or the fancy. A real working ship going about its business: Thrilled beyond measure—the *Emilia* felt to me like a ship out of the 1930s or 1940s—I flung my backpack into my tiny cabin and raced to the deck for departure.

I trolled for English speakers to share my excitement but utterly failed; even more thrilling: I was among the locals. We all stood on deck—the departure has moment, and somehow you don't want to miss it. Without so much as a blast from the horn—again, compare with the paroxysm of horns and firecrackers that accompanies the departure of a cruise ship—the *Emilia* slowly raised its loading ramp, kicked up its engines, and agitated the water astern as it toiled away from Trapani. Teenage girls shouted *"Ciao! Ciao!"* between the deck and the quay as long as voices could be heard; the yellow lights, illuminated domes, and streets of Trapani's porto district began to recede, the ship heading into the blackness of the open nighttime sea. The deck vibrated with the effort of it, and standing there you couldn't fail to marvel at the enterprise, the undertaking, the magnificence of the endeavor. A huge ship, filled with people and everything people make, leaving one shore, bound for another in the darkness. It's courageous and beautiful and heartbreakingly sad, for so much of our undertaking fails, or worse. But in each departure a hope, a miraculous hope. For a moment, as a spectacular orange half-moon descended to our west, the act of traveling seemed beautiful and noble.

Then back to my cabin. Mindful of the movie *Cast Away* (another story of a lost man desperate to get home) in which the lonely Tom Hanks converses with a volleyball called Wilson, I at some point conceived that since my only constant companion was my big green backpack, I ought to name it. I decided on "Spaulding," as a play on "Wilson" with a satisfyingly Groucho Marxian touch, though I spoke the name only once. My journal reminds me that in that cabin as I lifted the pack, by then filling with pamphlets and mementos of my visits, I grunted, "Spaulding, you're putting on weight." When I did so I felt like such a fool that I never thereafter thought of the pack as anything but an amalgamation of zippers and ballistic nylon, filled with underwear and travel guides.

In my cabin—A private sink! An extra bunk to spread out my stuff!—I washed socks and enjoyed my provisions, then slept like a child. The peremptory rapping at my door that woke me an hour before arrival again reminded me: Working boat here, buddy; we take on new passengers real soon, and we need you out of here. By the time I got on deck, cappuccino in hand, we had reached the dock. A long gangway, impossibly narrow, reached like a tendril from amidships to the quay, passengers filing down like ants. I could imagine nothing more romantic than such an arrival and went back down into the bowels of the ship, looking for that egress. I emerged, naturally, at the bottom deck, and came out the same way I had gone in: on the loading ramp, with the vegetables and the mattresses and the idling trucks.

I HAD NO BUSINESS IN CAGLIARI—I was headed to the north of Sardinia, from which I could approach the land of the Laestrygonians. Yet as I set out for the train station I paused in the Piazza Matteotti, the leafy square by the docks of this neat, pleasant-looking town, and I remembered: the Palermo Principle. So instead of leaving I turned and headed up the hill into town. I found a room in about five minutes, then spent the day exploring. The streets by the harbor are lined with sidewalk cafés along an arched loggia of nineteenth-century storefronts; above them the thirteenth-century fortified Castello district looms. There I visited the cathedral at its center, with its tiled dome and gold mosaics; the Torre dell'Elefante (a fourteenth-century tower erected by the Pisans sporting a lovely sculpted elephant); and the vice-regent's palace, in which I saw on one ceiling a painted allegory of, no kidding, administration and architecture, in which naked cherubs cavort with pen and ink and the tools of drawing—perhaps the same cherubs, freelancing, who had been doing archaeology in Schliemann's home in Athens.

I walked the city from end to end, visiting the obligatory Roman theater and finally ending up in the Orto Botanico, a beautiful shady garden managed by the University of Cagliari, where the highlight was not just the gravel walks among cactuses and other indigenous plants but the ticket stub, a lovely four-color print that was itself worth the 2-euro admission—though it just became another addition to that increasing weight of my backpack. I had a pizza in a restaurant where the man at the counter made suggestions for my walks around Cagliari and became excited about my trip: "Heyyy!" he shouted to his wife, through the bead curtain into the kitchen. "*Quest'uomo sta facendo un viaggio come quello di Ulisse!*" She came out, eyebrows raised: "Hmmm." Back to the kitchen. At a flea market in the Piazza del Carmine I bought a dish towel to replace a bandanna I had lost, and when I stumbled upon the tourist office I learned that a bus directly to the north of the island left at 5:30 the next morning.

At 5:30 there I was, and there it was, and I got on. As we pulled away from town I had no Palermo-style misgivings as the bus filled with Sardinian pop music, cretinous *American Idol*–style orchestrated vocal stylings. I watched the sun come up over the island's central mountain range. At the first stop the air was chilly, and the bus driver and I shared a smile. Perhaps I was in the care of Hermes, god of travelers. How would I know if Hermes had taken human form as a bus driver? What characteristics would the perfect bus driver have? Another long strip of asphalt between some damn where and some damn where else; rolling fields dotted with spiral hay bales alternated with unmown fields, waving gold in the misty dawn. I closed my eyes.

Chapter 9

Run Away! Run Away!:

Catastrophe in the Land of the Laestrygonians

So for six days and six nights we journeyed, till on the seventh we came to the towering town of King Lamus, the Laestrygonian citadel of Telepylus. . . . When we reached the fine harbor, about which high reefs of sheer rock run out on both sides while opposing headlands jut in at the narrow mouth, all the others steered their curving ships into this hollow haven and moored them together. . . . Only I tied up outside of that excellent harbor, making my black ship fast to a rock on the headland.

—The Odyssey, Book X

IF ODYSSEUS HAS a most famous adventure, it probably occurs in the Cyclops's cave. Other episodes—the choice between Scylla and Charybdis, the song of the Sirens—have made their way into our everyday language. But the simplest episode from *The Odyssey* has to be the visit to the land of the Laestrygonians. When I returned to *The Odyssey,* I don't believe I had ever heard of the Laestrygonians, yet in its straightforward way this episode approaches a kind of perfection. It sings the value of nothing more complex than sheer, shrieking terror. The Laestrygonians teach Odysseus this: Run for your life! Every man for himself! *Run!*

Homer's description of the entire episode lasts only fifty-three lines. Turned away at their return to the keeper of the winds, Odysseus and his men naturally have "no breath of breeze to help us on our way," so they row for six days and nights, coming on the seventh day to the citadel of Telepylus—"far gate" in Greek. This is a place where "twilight and dawn come so close together that there a man who could go without sleeping might earn double wages" by doing two herding jobs during the long days, leading many geographical interpreters to believe that Homer referred to the midnight sun of northern Europe or even Iceland or the Arctic.

But another geographical detail stands out even more. Telepylus is a harbor around which "high reefs of sheer rock run out on both sides while opposing headlands jut in at the narrow mouth"—a perfect natural harbor, where even in the worst weather "the water is never rough, no waves at all, but everywhere bright calm." Again, geographers imagine traces of Norwegian fjords here.

Eleven of the ships moor in that lovely harbor; Odysseus, canny, decides to tie up just outside it. Climbing the headland and looking around, Odysseus sees no buildings or fields but does see smoke rising from fires, so he sends three crewmen to check things out. They meet a young girl drawing water and say, basically, "Take me to your leader." She points out the palace of her father, King Antiphates. He's away, but in the palace the crewmen see Mrs. Antiphates, "huge as the peak of a mountain, repulsive and horrifying." The three emissaries, not too many weeks past the visit to the Cyclops, don't need much more information to know it's time to go. But before they can, the queen calls to Antiphates, who instantly strides home, grabs an emissary, and prepares him for dinner. The other two run back to the ships—I imagine their arms waving over their heads like Gilligan: "Skipperrrrrr!"—but it's too late. Antiphates has given the shout, and the "monstrous Laestrygonians—more giants than men" crowd in around the cliffs, hurling boulders down onto the trapped ships; "spearing the dead like so many fish, they carried them home for a loathsome supper." No lotus flowers, no wine, no cheese, no sheep, not even a single word—Antiphates' daughter doesn't even answer the emissaries when they ask who's in charge: Like a creepy child from a horror movie, she simply points, silently, to her father's castle. The emissaries go there, and things go completely south.

It's a rout—panic, ships splintering, men screaming as they're slaughtered and consumed. And so, mid-battle, with the situation hopeless and out of control, Homer's spotlight finds our hero. "Now while they were slaughtering those within the deep cove," Odysseus says, "I drew my sharp sword from my hip and slashed"—what? What does the magnificent Odysseus, sacker of cities, king of Ithaca, hero of Troy, man of many devices, slash with that sword?

"I drew my sharp sword from my hip," he tells us, "and slashed the hawsers of my dark-prowed ship, urgently bidding my comrades row, that we might escape this danger." If you missed that, I'll translate: "Row, you guys, row! Get us out of here! The hell with the others, row for your lives!" Which they do, and escape, but from twelve ships leaving Troy, Odysseus is now down to the one ship beneath his own sorry butt.

It's brilliant—it's perfect. And it stands out as a landmark along Odysseus's path toward awakening.

In this episode we learn a truly important thing about Odysseus: that is, he's educable. So far on this trip he's done almost everything wrong that you possibly can. He lost control of his crew at Ismarus. He led them into danger, ignored their warnings, and watched them get eaten alive in the cave of the Cyclops. On the journey from the isle of Aeolus he at the worst possible time fell asleep at the wheel. He's beginning to look like a lost cause.

Then here we come to a harbor, not unlike the cave of the Cyclops— a deep fastness with only one tiny exit. And Odysseus has the sense to say, "Well, I don't know about you, but I'm going to stay out here." He recently found himself in a big enclosed place with a single exit, and he didn't like how that worked out, so he tries something different this time. Though he's the leader, the others don't follow; they go inside. And before a single page is turned, they're all dead.

BEYOND WHAT IT TELLS US ABOUT ODYSSEUS, this episode makes a point about his crew that wasn't clear to me until my wife pointed it out: "They're red-shirts," she said once, listening to me yet again recount-ing and considering the episodes of *The Odyssey*. Red-shirts— referring, of course, to the seemingly endless supply of disposable crew members in *Star Trek* who had the job of going down to check out some new planet, only to be killed, thereby allowing Captain Kirk to defeat a bad guy and usually kiss a girl wearing harem pants.

Odysseus's crew members do the following things: They get drunk on the shore at Ismarus, causing death for six from each ship. They foolishly eat the lotus, thereupon needing to be dragged back to the ships. They bodily provide three meals for the Cyclops. They go behind Odysseus's back to open the bag of winds supplied by Aeolus, at the last moment preventing the fleet from reaching Ithaca. And then here, at Telepylus, unlike cautious Odysseus, they row right into a murderous trap, instantly reducing their number by eleven-twelfths. And don't forget, though there's only a single boatful left, they're not done—we know from the proem, the very first words of *The Odyssey,* that the remainder are going to cause their own deaths by slaughtering the cattle of the sun against direct orders.

If Odysseus seemed like a poor leader in those early episodes, you get a different perspective when you look at these adventures together. You have to figure: Sometimes it's not the coach; sometimes the team just stinks. Still, most important—and this is the key to the episode— when there's nothing for it but to run like hell, the thing to do is run like hell. Odysseus doesn't spend a moment thinking about the honor of leading his last boatful of men to certain death attempting to defend their helpless compatriots. These Laestrygonians are giants; they're smashing the fleet into kindling and spearing the crews like cocktail weenies. The thing to do is run, and Odysseus runs. It's great advice, advice I'd give a kid: When there's way more of them than you, when the battle has devolved into slaughter and there's no hope, then live to fight another day. Run—just run away.

SO YOU CAN FORGIVE ME if, when I set sail for Bonifacio, the medieval cliff city on the southernmost tip of the French island of Corsica, I was spoiling for something to run away from. I took the twenty-minute ride on the ferry *Bastia* from Santa Teresa, the beach town on the northernmost tip of Sardinia.

Bonifacio had been easy to choose. Thucydides located the Laestry-gonians, with the Cyclopes, on Sicily—an island, it seems, where almost everybody was liable to eat you up. The Romans placed them at Formia, a resort town south of Rome, near which Cicero was eventually killed—but then again, the pragmatic Romans placed everything near Rome. Both these places conspicuously lack anything like the protected, peaceful harbor Homer describes. But moderns—from Ernle Bradford, author of *Ulysses Found,* to Paul Theroux—almost universally identify the Laestrygonians with the harbor of Bonifacio. This is widely enough known that once, when my planned journey came up in conversation, a guy my stepsister was dating said, "Oh, you'll have to stop in Bonifacio, for the Laestrygonians." So I did that.

The only thing I found to run away from in Bonifacio was the methodical way the businesses there go about skinning tourists. Every menu seems like a bait-and-switch operation, every price tag somehow misleadingly low, every possible hotel room preposterously expensive. Which was why I ended up staying in the beach town of Santa Teresa on Sardinia, rather than spending a night or two on Corsica itself. This turned out really well, if for nothing more than the approach to Bonifacio by sea.

A SWELL OF PROBABLY ten feet or more rolled through the Strait of Bonifacio, so the twenty-minute ferry ride felt a bit like a motorboat trip across a lake on a windy day; it was by far the roughest ferry crossing of my journey, rising and falling enough to give that roller-coaster feeling to the stomach. Much more important, though, was what I could see, or could not see.

Sure, I could easily see even from the Sardinian shore the stratified limestone cliffs of Corsica. I could not, however, see anything that looked like a harbor. The farther across the strait we got, the more people crowded the deck of the *Bastia,* pointing to the striated wall of rock; not a shadow betrayed any kind of opening. When we got close enough to distinguish sails, you could see a few tiny boats clustered near the wall, but the ferry still seemed to sail straight toward an unbroken rock face. And then, the way one of those Magic Eye pictures in the newspaper in an instant resolves itself, the motion of the boat separated one wall from another and we could suddenly see the harbor entrance—almost as one, we gasped. A moment later the *Bastia* turned right, into the harbor—headlands pinched together, just as

Homer describes—and the swell vanished, the water utterly calm. Of course, there's a cliff for Odysseus to climb, and there's even a hollow just outside the headlands where Odysseus could have moored his ship.

Above all, though, are the cliffs. Vertical cliffs at least two hundred feet high entirely surround the harbor. I certainly didn't expect giants to throw boulders on the ferry, but as you looked up you could not fail to think: If the folks on top weren't feeling welcoming, this harbor would spell big trouble. The Bonifacio harbor perfectly fit the Homeric description, and I made the steep climb up road and stairs to the fortified town of Bonifacio, spread across the headland like frosting.

If you're looking for your prototypical medieval Mediterranean town, with the red tile roofs and the stone churches, the louvered shutters and the tiny balconies strung with laundry, the stucco walls and the narrow, curving cobblestone alleyways, go straight to Bonifacio. Buttresses arc across the Rue du Corps du Garde, remnants of an aqueduct system that once filled a central cistern with rainwater; the Eglise Sainte Marie Majeure looks just exactly how a twelfth-century church should look, with a stone loggia supporting a wood roof over a plaza of slate pavers that stays cool even on a hot July afternoon; little kids in striped shirts gambol in front of the wooden church door. The church's seven-story stone clock tower dominates the town.

I wandered the streets, turning this way and that, into little overpriced gift shops, eating tiny portions beneath umbrellas at overpriced sidewalk cafés, traversing flagstoned cross streets, peering up at the Juliet balconies, loitering in plazas choked with tourists just like me. The people at the visitors' center offered only quizzical looks when I asked about Odysseus, so I took the map delineating the five-street-by-six-street town and saw what there was to see.

There's a tiny museum on the picturesque city bastions; the Market Square where the marketables comprise mostly tchotchkes; the atmospheric Street of the Two Emperors (Napoléon and Charles V of Spain both stayed there at one time or another; Napoléon was born on Corsica, which shares the Mediterranean heritage of its sister islands like Sicily, Malta, and Sardinia, accosted over the years by the usual assortment of Phoenicians, Romans, Vandals, Byzantines, Saracens, Genoese,

Pisans, and popes). At the tip of the peninsula a peaceful necropolis is populated, like those in New Orleans, by aboveground vaults in little stone huts; some feel like crypts, behind wrought-iron gates, others like tiny churches, others like waiting rooms behind glass weatherproof storm doors. Lit candles burn serenely in many; "*Ici repose . . . ,*" says inscription after inscription, and in the quiet, far above the sea, you likely find a moment of repose there yourself. Bonifacio even has a fabulous stairway hacked directly into the southern cliffs, supposedly created in a single night in 1420 by soldiers of the king of Aragon, laying siege to Bonifacio. I paid a few euros to walk down and look at the strait.

But whatever direction you turn, you can't go far without running out of space, ending up on medieval city walls, leaning over a parapet or out a window, looking straight down at the sea, or straight across to Sardinia. Steep stone staircases, crenellated walls, and, everywhere, holes—to clear rainwater, to be sure, but also to drop things. Heavy things or hot things or slippery things, on those below who mean you ill. Odysseus's crews learned the hard way: It's good to be higher up than your enemies. And if they're higher up than you are, sometimes there's nothing for it but to just run off.

AFTER AN OVERPRICED DINNER, having found a paucity of the kind of cheap food and lodgings I relied on, I was ready to run, too. I stayed in Bonifacio long enough to see the lights come on in the evening, meant to be a lovely spectacle when seen from a departing ferry. True enough, but I remember from my idle hours in Bonifacio less what I saw up in the lovely medieval town than what I saw down below, on the docks. A modern port town full of restaurants and shops runs along the pleasant quay, and people loitered in the evening, eating ice cream, watching boats dock. Not the ferry, mind you, which docks way out by the mouth of the harbor—people watched yachts.

The *Kisses,* for example, from George Town, Grand Cayman, a four-story wedding cake with an Australian crew in uniforms. As it backed in, from its back emerged an automatic gangplank. I wondered: How rich would you have to be before an automatic gangplank got to the top of the list of things you needed? Tight smiles of envious satisfaction emerged among the onlookers as the crew wrestled for twenty minutes to get that automatic gangplank to touch the dock, then installed by hand ten separate pieces of railing. The huge ferries and hydrofoils of the hoi polloi back in, tie up, and throw down an aluminum gangway; by the time the *Kisses* was finally docked, the *Bastia* could have unloaded 150 passengers. The *Kisses* even had its own rug for underneath the dock end of the gangway, so it doesn't get scratched, I suppose. Two curving staircases arc down the yacht's stern, like some movie ballroom.

Next to the *Kisses* docked the *Nobody,* of London, a mere two stories to the *Kisses'* four. The crew trotted out some stuffed leopards, and the man who appeared to be the owner, in white pants and a pink shirt, lay talking on a cell phone—perhaps ordering an automatic gangplank. Given the name of his ship, I was about to request permission to step aboard when someone within flipped a switch and the *Nobody* began pumping the quay full of Sade-style orchestral jazz. The shouted conversation necessary to explain why the yachtsman ought to invite this dirty middle-aged vagrant aboard his yacht sounded ludicrous even to me, so I just moved along. I never saw anybody leave one of the yachts. I idly wondered in what way stepping off your yacht long enough for an expensive dinner in whatever port you found yourself constituted travel, but even I could identify sour grapes when I tasted them. I decided I'd seen enough.

On my way to the ferry I passed the *St. Elisabeth,* a wooden one-master with two oars; next to it the white-and-blue *Ajaccio* moored, covered with nets and floats. A working vessel, all open with the exception of a metal cabin for the captain. It looked beautiful and clean and real, seeming to have much more than the yachts in common with the fifty-person, single-masted ship, black with tar, that Odysseus would have sailed.

I was still romanticizing working boats as the ferry took me back to Sardinia and Santa Teresa, when I fell into conversation with a fellow named Carlo. I tried to wax eloquent on the feeling of a working ship, but Carlo, a native Mediterranean, wasn't buying. "It's just another dirty ship that smells like gas," he thought every time he got on a ferry. I had just visited the land of the Laestrygonians, which turned out to be a tourist town making its living by, if not eating its visitors, then certainly helping them to leave behind some of their life's blood in the form of international currency. I liked conflating the yacht people with the Bonifacians, so I conceived of this dirty ship that smelled like gas conveying me safely away from the Laestrygonians, and I tried to laugh Carlo off.

BUT IT WAS TOO LATE—Carlo made too good a point. My romanticized version of travel was no more real than the yachty version I sneered at. I wasn't sure what kind of trip I was on, but an adventure on the edge of civilization it was not, and I would probably do well to begin admitting that to myself. Start, perhaps, with French.

As helpful as my French had been in Tunis, it failed me in Bonifacio. This might be because Corsicans apparently speak a French barely recognizable even to mainland French (much like Sardinian Italian—in Cagliari I saw Italian-to-Sardinian phrase books, after which I gave up and spoke mostly English, slowly and hopefully). More likely it's because, to use a phrase a friend once turned, I speak French the way retired people drive: There's a lot of three easy right turns to avoid one scary left; things progress real, real slowly; and I often indicate something I don't mean at all. The problem was, everyone in Bonifacio, a nice international tourist town, had all the English they needed to help me with whatever I needed. Had I been Italian or German it would have been just the same. And stopping in a ritzy resort town might have its mild challenges, but Everest Base Camp it's not.

I wasn't wandering the world's unexplored places with a doughty crew and a questing spirit. Regarding the questing spirit, I did my best, but as for the strange and fantastic, no dice. I was traveling in high season in a region that has been catering to tourists for thousands of years. Yet in my self-conscious quest for adventure I had begun scowling at the developed places I visited as though their reality made them disappointing, or even somehow wrong. In Tunisia, I had managed to cast a jaundiced eye at watching young women smearing suntan lotion on their naked breasts, and I decided it was about time for that to stop: My romantic notion of my trip had to die. Leaving Bonifacio and the

Laestrygonians, I had to let go of my idiotic belief that in the Mediterranean of the twenty-first century I could somehow truly be lost. I pledged, back in Sardinia, to look about me with more equanimity.

NOT THAT I didn't have legitimate gripes. For example, I got on a ferry on Sardinia—in Italy—and landed on Corsica—in France—with no more ceremony than if I had got on a bus in Buffalo and got off in Ashtabula. Nobody looked at my passport, much less stamped it, and I didn't get a cool new kind of money to look at. This is just wrong, and I blame the European Union. People in Greece complain that switching to the euro has raised prices and hurt their tourist trade, and maybe so. But for me, the worst effect the EU has had on European travel is the cheapening of frontier crossing.

I emerged from the airport in Tunisia, for example, with a passport stamp in Arabic and a pocketful of strange and fascinating dinars; even crossing by bus from Turkey into Greece took an hour and yielded two new passport stamps (an exit and an entry) to gaze at, and new currency to fold, a pocket full of unusual coins, with unfamiliar weights and sizes, to fondle. Next would come experimentation: Which coin was worth a bus ride? Which a soda pop? Sadly, that currency was the euro, which remained with me for months. I deeply resented that I had come all the way to Greece yet would never have the chance to spend a drachma. The Greeks started using drachmas in the sixth century BC; the drachma spawned countless other currencies; and the Greeks returned to it a few years after the modern state emerged in 1827. But then Greece joined the European Union, so by the time I got there all I got was euros. The same euros that clattered in my pockets in Sicily, on Sardinia, and then on Corsica. The euro is the monetary equivalent of plane flight: another leveling agent, another destroyer of the details that make places different.

As for the passport stamp—at least in the last century, during which standardized passports have been the norm, in moments of difficulty travelers have been able to open their passports and turn for comfort to the burgeoning number of stamps they've collected, a sort of cosmic "Yes I can, I've done it before." More, visas, stamps, and annotations layer a passport, turning it from a soulless bureaucratic document into a treasure, a souvenir. What is a passport, after all, but a codified example of the guest-friendship of *xenia*? Our country warns you not to mess with this passport holder, but in return we promise safety to people who hold your passports. The stamps in your passport tell you who your guest-friends are, and whose you are.

And then you enter the EU, after which anywhere from Helsinki to Crete you can step off boat, bus, or train like you've been there all your life. There's something to be said for ceremony; something has been lost. Among the Laestrygonians, Odysseus lost most of his crew—what I lost was the last fragment of belief that my trip, in the modern Mediterranean, could be anything approaching real adventure.

ALWAYS ORDER A MEAL RIGHT after you get money. You can make this an actual travel rule and you won't regret it. If you buy a meal before you either cash a traveler's check or find an ATM, you're checking prices, husbanding unfamiliar coins, and you end up with some variation on a can of juice and piece of bread. But with fresh money in your pocket you feel expansive and, wherever you sit, you order whatever you want. A quest travels on its stomach, so you won't regret this strategy. I got money before my midmorning second breakfast under an umbrella in the main plaza of Santa Teresa, a sunny cobblestoned trapezoid surrounded by three- and four-story stucco buildings in pink, blue, yellow and white, all with green louvered shutters closed against the Mediterranean sun. The cappuccino, a few *cornetti,* juice, and fruit seemed like a feast.

If Bonifacio is a tourist town where people pay a lot of money to sit at undersized café tables, Santa Teresa is a beach town where people lie on the beach for free. In the evenings vendors fill the town center with tables selling the same hemp, recycled paper products, and jewelry as in every other tourist town on the planet. And people walk among them—and the art galleries, and the tourist shops, and the bars whose tables spill into that cobbled main square—and eat ice cream and panini and drink orange Fanta like God intended for vacationers to do.

On the beach you lie beneath umbrellas and watch people play paddleball and volleyball; the coconut guy walks by every hour or so, crying, *"Fresca, fresca, FREEEEEEEsca,"* using tongs from his blue bucket to pick slices of fresh coconut from between palm leaves in his basket. You can stare at the tiny waves lapping the shore long enough that for once you actually see the water itself. The closest layer is clear, but for a tiny shade of blue, as though someone had dropped in a tincture of food coloring; a silvery precipitate of suspended silicates sparkles like glitter in a snow globe. Then a pale lucent yellow-white, where the low ripples trough inches above the sand. Then a layer of the palest light pharmacy-bottle green. Then a swimming-pool aqua, then teal, then violet, and then finally, far out, that famous wine-dark, fish-full sea.

In Bonifacio I gave up on my idea of my trip as some kind of adventure, as a challenge, and recognized that I was really on a long Mediterranean vacation. And if I'm going to lie with my butt in the sand and my feet in the sea, I'm looking for a place like Santa Teresa. It felt like the Jersey Shore.

BUT THE JERSEY SHORE OF THE MEDITERRANEAN. In the mornings I lay in bed and heard the women splashing water on their front stoops, then sweeping and drying them with towels on the end of mop handles. In a room overlooking the sea and the rocks, the Hotel Bellavista served a breakfast that included not only an all-day cappuccino that kept my handwriting jerky well into the evening but a bun layered with Nutella and cherry jam that I called a Black Forest Cake Sandwich. The nice lady at the hotel lent me a beach umbrella and moved my luggage when my room flooded. When the next morning the faucet in my new room delivered no water at all and I hazarded a joke in Italian—*"Oggi, no aqua; ieri, aqua tutto!"*—the maid smiled in a way that made me think I might have come close to making sense. I spent an extra couple days in Santa Teresa enjoying the atmosphere and trying to think about where to go next; with each destination I had begun to outdistance my skimpy research, and the Laestrygonians had been the last episode for which I knew where I was heading. Thus Santa Teresa, where I at least had a place to stay and knew why I had come, felt like a haven.

The sunset hours, when I wandered the little town, drifting into and out of stores selling flip-flops, towels, and local wines, passed in a haze of peacefulness, between the heat of the days at the beach and the thumping of the discos that began around ten in the evening, when my day was ending. I found myself one night at the end of a road leading out onto a spit of rocks jutting north toward Corsica—the very tip of Sardinia. On the rocks below a solitary guy sat and played a bongo as the light faded.

An orange sun sank into the sea to the west, illuminating below me rocks on which that afternoon I had clambered, sitting alone for an hour or more, dangling my feet in the strait and gazing thoughtlessly at the Bonifacio cliffs. Up above at sunset, I sat near the Tower of Longonsardo, begun in the fourteenth century but built atop the remains of an ancient nuraghe tower. The nuraghe towers, found only on Sardinia, are conical stone structures built without mortar during the apex of the civilization that built them, around 1200–900 BC—the time of Odysseus or just after. Not much is known about that Bronze Age Sardinian society, but some seven thousand of the towers dot the island.

A little farther along the Strado Pedonale Panoramica stood a smooth, featureless, almost Brancusian statue of the Virgin Mary. When the sun continued down and the statue's spotlights came on, I couldn't help noticing that with its hooded head, gently spreading arms softened by a robe, and vertical gap in the robe, the statue looked alarmingly like part of a woman rarely seen represented that size. In my journal I called the statue "the Vagina of the Rocks," but it got me to thinking about that rocky strip of land at the end of Sardinia. Three millennia ago the nuraghe culture put a tower there, and merely decades ago practitioners of modern religions felt similarly inspired. This strait between two of the largest islands in the Mediterranean is just important—a place that draws people, from ancient civilizations to drum-circle castaways, and whether towers or statues, they leave traces behind.

And there again geography brings you back to *The Odyssey*. The places associated with *The Odyssey* tend to be the geographical pressure points of the Mediterranean: the Laestrygonians at the fortified city on the tiny strait between two important islands; the Cyclops at the western tip of Sicily, the largest island in the sea; Troy on the Dardanelles, key to the Black Sea; Scylla and Charybdis guarding the strait between Sicily and the mainland. It's no surprise that many different geographers have tried to bring the Strait of Gibraltar into the mix (commonly cited as the gate of hell, Gibraltar also sometimes surfaces as the home of Calypso or the path to the land of the Lotus-eaters). It only makes sense that a people exploring these places for the first time would find in them echoes of the key elements in their most important stories—or, of course, that echoes of those remarkable places made their way into the stories themselves.

What happens to Odysseus at the marvelous harbor has little to do with geography: He simply realizes that he's in over his head and makes a run for it. That could have happened anywhere, and the lesson would be just as valid. And certainly it's possible that Homer, looking for the perfect setting for Odysseus to demonstrate that he had learned something from the Cyclops, heard some Phoenician sailor talk about a perfect harbor in a faraway island, and there came the setting for the tale of the Laestrygonians. Or, of course, a later sailor familiar with the tales of Homer could see the harbor and say, "Here—it must have been here."

No matter: Whether or not the Strait of Bonifacio really was the home of the Laestrygonians, the place itself was one of those that had drawn visitors and monuments for millennia—a place that somehow just made sense to be. Since I didn't know quite where I was going next, that was a comforting thought. I wouldn't have another like it for a while.

Chapter 10

Bewitched, Bothered, and Bewildered:

In the Neighborhood of Circe

Circe . . . sat them on chairs . . . and fixed them a potion of Pramnian wine, in which she mixed . . . a dose of her miserable drugs. . . . When she had served them the potion and they had downed it, Circe, without more ado, smote them all with her wand and penned them up in pig-sties. And sure enough they had the heads and bodies, bristles and voices of swine. . . .

—*The Odyssey*, Book X

"E-MAIL ME, O MUSE, of the man, the man of twists and turns . . ." A friend of mine sent me a message with that subject line during the week or so I spent wandering the Italian coast southeast of Rome trying to make sense of my search for the witch Circe, and it gave me a rare moment of laughter during a frustrating time. I probably wrote more e-mails during that week of benighted peregrinations than in the rest of the trip combined, and they contained mostly childish whinings, to my friends and to my wife, complaining that I was lost. Having rushed out the door with less-than-thorough research, spurred by June's pregnancy, I finally found myself beyond even my skimpiest plans, with no idea where I was trying to go next, and I just kept showing up places and hoping something sensible would happen. Trains whipped me up and down the Italian coast, never quite getting me anyplace that made sense. My pockets filled with tiny slips of paper, tickets to local buses. It was a time of poor choices and cloudy thinking—of not hopping off or suddenly not getting on, of missing a bus or getting off at the wrong stop. My trip felt out of control and nonsensical, I was lonely and confused and didn't know what to do, and I e-mailed somebody and said so every day.

Those e-mails stabilized me. On my own and far from home, I appreciated that I could maintain contact with loved ones—especially June, with whom I loved to travel. Her patient heart and wry observations had calmed me during many a panicky train station moment, reminded me to breathe during interminable bus rides. This time, though, I was on my own. So another exhausting, fruitless day of hurried conversations or scattered bus connections would end with a trudge into some e-mail café, payment of a euro (and maybe a couple more for a Fanta and a chocolate bar), then a squeeze of backpack, floppy hat, and guidebooks in among the chic Italians before sitting down to whine to her for another page or so.

On the other hand, that e-mail comfort might have been counterproductive. After all, this may have been the most Odyssean segment of my trip: The essence of Odysseus's journey involved confused wandering, far from home and family. What if he had done the same—instead of being utterly separated from Penelope for two decades, what if he had e-mailed her day after day as his journey progressed further into the unimaginable? Clanking into some overpriced e-mail café, wearing a little leather skirt and a big sword like a character from the movie *Troy,* getting an Orangina or an espresso, rolling his eyes about how long it took Hotmail to download. Then: "P: War over—remember my horse idea? Worked! Other hand, that Agamemnon—what an asshole. More later. Stopping by Ismarus for supplies. Need anything? Home soon!—X, O." Then later: "Still on the road—you wouldn't believe it. Almost home, idiots in my boat open bag of winds. Lots more; long story. Short version: still out here. MapQuest no help. Doing what I can. How's little T? Tell him daddy misses him!" Then a reply: "O—Little T is 12 and needs his father. I appreciate your excuses, but Nestor got home two years ago. Whither my sacker of cities? You don't mention where you are now—no goddesses involved, right? RIGHT? Weaving, weaving, weaving. Oh yes—your father has moved into a hut in the bushes. Get your ass home. P." A funny thought during a week when every decision went wrong, every choice backfired. I was trying to find the place associated with the sorceress Circe. No wonder my trip felt bewitched.

THERE APPEAR TO BE RULES for the endless card game on the dock at San Felice Circeo, the tiny, ritzy town at the base of Monte Circeo, the seaside crag an hour or so south of Rome named for the witch with whom Odysseus spent a year feasting and having sex. From what I could tell, these are the rules.

1. There must always be three men playing cards beneath the little tent on the dock, near the *Noleggio Barche* (Boats for Rent) sign. Two of the men must be shirtless and one must be bald.

2. If you come up to inquire about boat rental, they are not allowed to answer or acknowledge your presence until at least forty-five seconds have passed. If they do acknowledge your presence, please interpret a hostile squint as the phrase "Greetings friend! And how may we be of service to you?"

3. Two of the men must speak exactly no English and must completely ignore your forays into Italian. The third must have enough English to clearly understand your goal—to rent a boat so you can take a quick jaunt to the cave, reachable only from the sea, called "La Grotta della Maga Circea," the cave of the witch Circe.

4. The English speaker, now playing the role of good cop, must attempt to convince the others that since every one of their boats sits idle—boat rental, even during high season, at San Felice apparently an evening affair undertaken by groups of rich people— a quick one-hour rental for 40 euros or so is a good idea. The business, after all, being to rent boats.

5. The others energetically shake their heads. Certainly not! Well, okay, maybe for . . . 100 euros.

6. At some point the bald man, whichever role he happens to be playing, must without comment go to a faucet on the dock, stick his head under, turn on the tap full blast—ahh! much better!—then

return and take up where he left off, whether it be at cards, negotiation, or aloofness.

7. A hundred euros manifestly preposterous. Okay, then. "You come back later—maybe we have group." Maybe not, though.

I had this interaction three separate times, with variations. Given that Homer describes Circe living in a house, and the only cave Odysseus describes is the one he and his men use to store the rigging of their ship, my continued interest in the boat ride to the cave may seem odd. But since I could think of nothing to do near Monte Circeo to complete my pilgrimage, the seeker after Odysseus may be forgiven for seizing on something, anything, more.

Monte Circeo, a lone peak on a spit of land poking into the Tyrrhenian, is named for Circe, so taking the train (and then the bus, and then another bus) to San Felice seemed like a no-brainer. And since the first thing Odysseus does at Circe's island of Aeaea is climb a hill and look around, trudging up the road to the mountaintop didn't demand much brainwork, either. At the top of Monte Circeo, though, are a couple of nature trails, some Cyclopean walls, a lovely view of the Tyrrhenian, a bar that doesn't open until dinnertime, and about a dozen broadcast antennae.

I was looking for Circe, and that scarcely satisfied. I was alone and far from home and uncertain of what to do next, so an assault on the sea cave named for her, down by the ritzy docks of San Felice, looked like a reasonable move. Bewitched, indeed.

FROM THE CATASTROPHE at the hands of the Laestrygonians Odysseus and his single remaining ship and crew sail to Aeaea, the island home of Circe the witch, where first off they throw themselves down on the shore and devote two days to sleeping and grieving for their devoured crewmates. Then Odysseus grabs his spear and climbs to the highest point to get a look around; from there he sees smoke rising from the forest. He decides to return to the ships, feed his men, and send out a group to investigate. On his way down he kills a huge stag, flinging it in front of his men and encouraging them that they'll all feel better with a bite to eat—"travel true," of course. That takes up the rest of their day.

On day four Odysseus admits they're utterly lost ("we're ignorant of east and west alike," he tells the crew) but says he's seen smoke rising from the forest. Mindful of their recent encounters with man-eaters of one variety or another the men instantly panic, but Odysseus points out that panicking accomplishes nothing. He splits them into two groups; he takes charge of one and puts the other under the command of Eurylochus. They draw lots to see which group goes to investigate, so Eurylochus "and twenty-two weeping comrades" thus set out.

At the clearing, they find a stone palace surrounded by wolves and lions, though the animals fawn on the men and wag their tails like dogs. Inside the palace stands the lovely Circe, weaving a vast tapestry, singing. The men call to her and she quickly opens her doors, through which all the men except the suspicious Eurylochus go and gladly drink of a mixture of wine, honey, barley, and magical drugs that she gives them. Circe then gives a whack with her magic wand and turns them all into pigs. The terrified Eurylochus runs back to the ships and tells the tale, begging Odysseus to take the remaining men and flee.

No chance. Odysseus grabs his spear and heads toward the palace. On the way there he meets Hermes, who thoughtfully supplies him with not only a magical herb, called moly, that will protect him from Circe's potion, but also specific instructions on how to vanquish the witch. Then Hermes zips back to Olympus and Odysseus continues to the castle.

It unfolds exactly as Hermes has said it would. Circe offers the cup, Odysseus drinks, Circe makes with the wand: no effect. Odysseus, as Hermes instructed, threatens Circe with his sword, at which point she throws herself at his knees, recognizing that he must be Odysseus, the man of many turnings—Hermes has always told her he'd eventually drop by. She suggests that he sheathe his sword and follow her to bed. Again as Hermes suggested, Odysseus demands she swear an oath by the gods that she will do him no further harm. She swears, and so to bed. Meanwhile, Circe's four palace nymphs prepare food, drink, and a bath, and Circe then bathes Odysseus. Then she leads him to the dinner table, but he sulks, asking how any decent man could be expected to eat when his men have been turned into pigs. (I didn't write "travel true" here, but "man true" seems to apply: Sex? I'm in! A bath at the hands of a goddess? Bring it on! But something as pedestrian as lunchtime? Suddenly greathearted Odysseus thinks only of his crew.) Circe quickly undoes her magic, with the men returning as younger, handsomer, and even taller versions of themselves. Talk about the healing properties of mud.

Circe sends Odysseus back to the beach to store the ship and supplies and bring back the crew. Off he goes, telling the story to the men, who are delighted and ready to troop off, though Eurylochus reminds them that Odysseus is the same man who led a group into the cave of the Cyclops. Odysseus lets the crew talk him out of beheading Eurylochus, noting that he is "by marriage a near kinsman of mine," a little detail that explains a lot: he's the dopey brother-in-law, and Odysseus's hands are tied (even so, he later has cause to regret his mercy).

The joyous reunion of the men at Circe's palace lasts an entire year, at which point the men come to Odysseus, clearing their throats to suggest that it might be time to head for home. It makes sense— Odysseus is the one sleeping with the goddess, after all; even if the four nymphs are being nice to the crew (Homer doesn't say), the crew-to-nymph ratio is about eleven to one, so you can't like the odds. The men have a point, Odysseus admits, though he's not perfectly cheerful: "They wear my heart out with constant complaining, whenever you're not around," he mutters to Circe, but he says he's ready to go. True to her oath, Circe gladly helps—but instead of merely bidding farewell, she sends him on his next adventure: to the kingdom of the dead.

SO, ANYHOW, Odysseus spends a year sleeping with Circe. Add to that the seven years Odysseus spends with Calypso, and you get eight total years of a ten-year journey spent in sexual thralldom to goddesses. Tough life, right? The jokes my friends made about my trip were predictable: I was expected to leave for the Mediterranean and say to my wife, "I'll be home in a couple months—*probably*."

This episode contains other elements, too, of course. Just as Odysseus shows at the Laestrygonians that he learned from his experience with the Cyclops, here he shows that this learning continues. When Eurylochus tells him that it's time to cut and run, you can almost hear Odysseus thinking: "I've recently seen what cut and run looks like, and this isn't it. A lady with a magic wand—I've seen worse. There's no immediate menace; I'll investigate, then decide." Eurylochus can stay behind, "but I will go," Odysseus says, "since I very strongly feel that I must." That is, Odysseus finally feels a strong sense of responsibility toward the crew he has left, and here he demonstrates real leadership—my ship, my crew, my job: lemme at this witch. As boss, Odysseus has vastly improved.

But first, and centrally, with Circe, Odysseus has one of the adventures all men have: He faces a woman so powerful that around her men turn into animals.

PEER THROUGH THE VENEER OF FANTASY and *The Odyssey* is a book about stuff we know: girls and bad guys; jobs and responsibilities; friends, coworkers, and family; places and traveling between them; home and how to get there. Regarding girls, we've had a glimpse of Penelope, Odysseus's wife, who is so crafty and faithful that she becomes legendary for those characteristics; she's like the übermom. We've seen Helen, the cause of all this mess, cheerfully over it, at home feeding dinner and drugs to her guests, like a movie star whose highly publicized misadventures never seem to dim her glamour. And we've spent time with Calypso, who kept Odysseus occupied for seven years in highly comfortable lodgings, and then with some annoyance sent him on his way when told to—a petulant trust-fund girl with a place in the Caymans. Remarkable archetypes, but so far not much part of most of our daily lives. Thus when with Circe we meet a certified femme fatale, it's almost a comfort. Finally, someone male readers can relate to: the girl who bewitches you but doesn't have your best interests in mind.

A woman like this has been showing up in stories, of course, since the dawn of time. Gilgamesh, hero of the oldest piece of literature in the West (*The Epic of Gilgamesh* originated in modern-day Iraq at least a thousand years before *The Odyssey*), resists the attentions of the goddess Ishtar, who turns her ex-lovers into animals; a similar witch shows up in *The Arabian Nights*. In more modern times, how many men in cartoons turn into wolves when the pretty girl goes by? And did the cunning woman who brings out the beast in the men around her fail to appear in even a single Humphrey Bogart movie? Most important, any man cataloging his own history will remember encountering a woman like this by the time he got to the eighth grade.

Odysseus treats her just like Bogie did. He does his groundwork; once she springs her tricks he's prepared to get the upper hand. Charmed by his power, she pledges her loyalty; then he safely has his way with her.

I'm in awe. In my own experiences with such women, I have always danced along feeling like I was following the script left by Odysseus, only to come to my senses some months in, wearing a dog collar and a leash, happy to eventually get away however I can. I believe most men share my experience, and that's part of what makes Odysseus a hero. He's already smart enough to outwit the Cyclops (the ur–bad guy, just as Circe is the proto–bad girl) and wise enough to resist the easy temptation of the Lotus-eaters. He's learning lessons along the way, but here, finally, he shows us something we cannot fail to admire: Odysseus gets involved with a woman who is—literally—poison to him, and instead of ending up with an expensive divorce and a decade of therapy bills, he gets a yearlong vacation on a Mediterranean island filled with feasting and sex. Every man I know—and most women, too—has at some point entered into a relationship that's supposedly casual and time-limited, only to find himself trapped in a vortex of confusion and manipulation and guilt and madness. Not Odysseus. He tames the magical woman, saves his companions, and has things pretty much his own way for the next year. To say nothing, of course, of how instrumental Circe turns out to be in his upcoming adventure among the dead. If there's a place I can go to learn this lesson, I'll go.

THERE'S NOT. Or at least if there is, I never found it.

Odysseus gives the following description of his journey from the harbor of the Laestrygonians to the shore of Aeaea: "we sailed on." If the directions to the island of Aeolus were skimpy, these simply don't exist. In fact, in describing the crew's whereabouts when they reach Circe Odysseus even says, "We do not know where the light-giving sun goes down beneath the earth, nor where he rises." In *The Quest for Ulysses,* classicist J. V. Luce says of this description, "We should take the hint, and not try to locate [Aeaea] on the map." I came to that advice too late to follow it.

Strabo says that Circe lived in Italy (he describes Monte Circeo and notes that the locals will show travelers a bowl they claim belonged to Odysseus), but he notes that according to Homer Circe is the aunt of Medea, the witch-wife of Jason who eventually murdered their children. Jason's wanderings are universally placed in the Black Sea, so to account for the distance between aunt and niece Strabo says simply that Homer "invented a residence for both of them out by Oceanus"— thus even Strabo washes his hands of any real location for Aeaea. Moderns like to ignore Odysseus's description of the isle as lying "in a boundless crown of deep sea," accepting the tradition that has grown up surrounding Monte Circeo, in some cases going to considerable lengths to explain how the mountain used to be an island (a strait, over the years, filled in to become a marsh, and eventually a peninsula that led to today's dry land) or to note that if you come at it just so, from the sea, well, it *looks* like an island.

Fine by me. I made my way there.

AN OVERNIGHT FERRY left for Civitavecchia, north of Rome, at midnight from the airportlike concrete docks of Olbia in northern Sardinia. The moon glittered attractively in our wake, but perhaps my friend Carlo from Bonifacio had ruined ferries for me—I did, as he said, feel less like a 1930s movie star than like someone spending yet another night on a dirty ship that smelled of gas. It was humid and hot on deck, and I stayed out there until we left more out of obligation than because the deck was pleasant. People have the same compulsion to make last-second mobile telephone calls aboard ferries that they do aboard planes; others stood and smoked, and a madly yipping dog completed the scene. I thought, Hmm. How can I, standing at the rail of a ship, make a little dog stop barking and not start again? I decided to get a drink.

The *poltroni* for deck passage were crowded, and the public bar was filled with bedraggled, dirty-looking families with vacation's-over stares watching *McCloud* dubbed in Italian; with its bile-green walls the bar felt like being in a TV set with the color adjusted wrong. Kids circled and hollered. My tiny single cabin had no sink. Brushing teeth in the slopping public restroom in steerage on a Mediterranean ferry: contraindicated.

Next morning at disembarkation, not a single sign pointed from the dock to the train station, but we resourceful few found a trail, and before an hour had passed were on a train to Rome, where we emerged at Stazione Termini, among dozens and dozens of cheap hotels, where a *paninoteca* for a cheap warm sandwich and a soda pop is never more than two steps away, and where the omnipresent *nasone* fountains (it means "big nose," describing the hooked dispensing pipe) provide endless water bottle refills for travelers thirsty and penurious. Rome is easy. That may explain why I had such trouble staying away from it.

My entire knowledge of Monte Circeo came from a picture I had seen in a book written in French. I knew Monte Circeo was eighty miles or so southeast of Rome, though neither of my Italy travel guides had a word to say about it. (I carried the Michelin green guide—great for cultural stuff, but hardly inclusive; and the *Let's Go,* which spent so much time regaling its presumably college-age travelers on the dangers of virtually any public place that I began calling it the "Let's Not.") I found online a few brief descriptions of the Monte Circeo national park and San Felice Circeo, the city at the base of the mountain, but to get a clear sense of where I was going I finally just bought a big driving map, which at least helped me locate the mountain just south of the city of Latina. The people at the Rome tourist information agency told me to catch a bus from there to the park; an easy day trip, they said.

True enough, if three hours each way is easy, and thus my wanderings began. The Latina train station is in the middle of nowhere; I got on the only bus I could find and asked if it went to San Felice; the driver told me to get off in Latina. Since in Rome I had got on a train to Latina, and got off at the stop marked Latina, I was nonplussed, but soon enough the driver signaled for me to disembark, sweeping his arm in the general direction of the street on which he dropped me. I obediently walked up that street, asking passersby about the *stazione d'autobus,* which I eventually found, and there I did find a bus to San Felice. A smallish and not especially attractive beach town at sea level, San Felice becomes ritzy around the corner in the *centro storico,* up on the mountain itself: a medieval-looking hill village with stucco buildings about which I never did learn much except that it had very expensive cafés. From its green little square dotted with orange trees, I found the road that switchbacked through the conifers to the top of the mountain, and I marched up there and sat for a while, looking at the sea, then walking the nature trails for a bit. No smoke from stone houses implied the location of the local witch, so I headed back down. My road map indicated "La Grotta della Maga Circe," and that seemed like a good idea. Hence my eventual familiarity with the unusual traditions among the cardplayers on the dock, and my inability to visit the cave.

Stymied, I bought some grapes and cheese and orange soda and thought for a while. Since the men on the dock had specifically told me to come back the next day, I regretted having treated my adventure as a day trip from Rome. Just the same I idly looked for a guesthouse or hotel, finding only highly expensive options and giving up. I waded in the Tyrrhenian near the docks, then made my way back to my bus and back to the train to Rome.

For my next trip I found a direct bus from Rome, causing me once again to imagine I was taking a nice day trip to San Felice, where I would enjoy a satisfying boat ride; with no connections to make, I even slept on the bus out.

Again with the attempted boat rental; again with the madness on the dock; again with the grapes and cheese and disconsolate wading. Again with an unsuccessful search for a cheap hotel, this time augmented by a failed attempt to get help from the San Felice tourist information office—closed all afternoon, of course. On this trip back, though, just after making its first stop in the tiny town of Sabaudia, the bus drove through a cool, deep green forest of pines and oaks, which my map showed me was called the Selva del Circea—"the forest of Circe." I watched it go by from the windows with regret.

*   *   *

THE BEACH, A FEW DAYS LATER: With heavy knapsack, hot boots, travel guide, and scowl, I crunch along through the sand along the Mediterranean shore. Not for me the comfortable chairs, the beach umbrellas, the bath-warm waters of the shimmering sea. No, I'm in search of the witch Circe, and goddamn it, I'm going to find her whether she likes it or not, and whether or not I like it.

It starts again in Rome. The idea of a third trip to San Felice to take a walk in the woods struck me for some reason as dispiriting, so I made yet another foray with a couple tourist information desks—and got a sudden new piece of information. *"Ulisse?"* a nice woman asked, brightening. "There's a place—some statues," she said, though she couldn't quite remember what it was all about. She had a suggestion, though: the Istituto Archeologico Germanico di Roma—someone there knew something about it, she was sure.

It being the first day of August, of course, the institute was closed; even the reception desk was in the process of closing for the remainder of the summer, and I was assured that nobody could help me. As I turned glumly to leave, though, a largish, stern, but gentle-seeming man asked in German-accented English what I was looking for. Well, I told him, um . . . Circe. I was following Odysseus, and I was looking for Circe. He frowned, then gestured impatiently for me to follow him to his office. He was about to leave for the month, of course, so he had only a moment; as we walked, he said over his shoulder, "You should have called ahead."

How do you say "Long story" in Italian? He suggested a couple of English-language libraries in Rome; I tried to make him understand that I wasn't reading about Odysseus, I was following him, but I don't think it took. With a discontented sigh he found a scrap of paper from his desk and wrote down two names: Sperlonga and Baia. He suggested I not miss those. Then he smiled at me as if I were a slow child and bid me farewell. I went to find a train to the town of Fondi, whence I could get a bus to Sperlonga. I checked my big bag at the train station but carried a change of clothes. This time I wanted to be ready for anything.

*   *   *

TACITUS AND SUETONIUS, Roman historians of the first century AD, speak of a place called Spelunca, a country house of the emperor Tiberius near a large seaside cave; the cave supposedly collapsed on him during a dinner party, killing many guests but not him. Tiberius loved his Homer, famously quizzing his dinner companions about the name Achilles used while posing as a woman or the nature of the song the Sirens sang. (Collapsing roofs and tableside pop quizzes: Yay! Let's go to Tiberius's for dinner!) Through the centuries people lost track of the cave and the house, though they had resurfaced by the seventeenth century, when grand tour travelers described visiting the cave at Sperlonga. In 1957, a classically minded engineer in charge of building a nearby road took the time to search the cave—and discovered, in the grotto, thousands of sculpture fragments. By the time the archaeologists were done they had found the foundations of Tiberius's house and pieced together a model of the cave itself, which had apparently held several larger-than-life sculptural groups: Odysseus and his men blinding the Cyclops, the crew sailing past Scylla, and other Homeric scenes. The partially re-created sculptures now have their own museum, next to the cave.

The group of Odysseus and his men blinding the Cyclops sat at the deepest point of the grotto and has its own room in the modern, airy museum—the giant Polyphemus lies back, drunk, while life-sized statues of Odysseus and his companions position the pole for his blinding. The head of Odysseus, with his tousled beard, fierce expression, and the cone-shaped traveler's hat (called a *pilos*) he is commonly depicted wearing, is probably the most widely known sculpture of Odysseus. The scene of the men sailing past Scylla that probably sat in the middle of the grotto takes up most of another room, with Scylla's six heads grabbing terrified men, and smaller groups fill the rest of the open, sunlit museum, along with displays of vases and other artifacts found among the ruins. I took photographs and wandered the museum, which I had almost entirely to myself. I was glad enough the Istituto guy had sent me, but it didn't bring me any closer to Circe.

And then I curled around a corner in the cool museum, and

suddenly—there she was: a three-quarter-size marble figure of a woman, with little pigs gamboling at her feet. She's lovely—something like a Roman Marie Antoinette, with a little Princess Leia thing going on in the hairdo: At last, a sculpture of Circe, and there I stood, face-to-face with her. It felt like the moment in *Planet of the Apes* when Charlton Heston stumbles across the stuffed body of his crewmate.

Archaeologists aren't entirely sure the sculpture represents Circe, but so close to Monte Circeo, in a cave full of sculptures of other Homeric scenes, with those cavorting piggies, the evidence is strong. It was certainly strong enough to complete my quest for Circe. I looked at the statue for a long while, trying to work up a sense of threatening magical powers, but no luck. Perhaps I was just tired.

From the people at the desk I learned the time of the bus back to the train station, and during the hour I had to wait I wandered down to the seaside and into the grotto itself. A yawning cave almost exactly the size and shape of the one at the end of Via del Ciclope on Sicily, this grotto didn't have Circe's name, but in it I could easily imagine the sculpture groups set up, making a kind of shrine: "a marble Odyssey," the booklet I bought at the museum called it. I couldn't imagine enjoying a dinner with Tiberius, what with the falling rocks and the trick questions, but even without that the cave demonstrated the centrality of the Homeric stories, at a point when they were already older to the Romans than Shakespeare's plays are to us. Yet instead of feeling old and distant, these stories—the foundation myths of another people—remained so immediate that Tiberius dedicated his country estate to them. Much the way the Julians claimed descent from the Trojan Aeneas, Tiberius liked to claim descent from Telegonus, a son that according to post-Homeric legend Odysseus fathered with Circe, so the Odyssey stories meant even more to him. In the first century, these stories still formed the base of Roman culture. Already people were looking back to think about the example Odysseus set regarding bad guys they might have to neutralize, monsters that might eat their companions—and dangerous women with other than their best interests in mind.

* * *

I THOUGHT ABOUT all that for a while and then went up to miss the bus back to the Fondi train station. It might have been that I thought the ladies in the museum said twenty after when they had said twenty till; they may have actually said the bus came in twenty minutes; or it may have just been a final quick enchantment from a witch who had finally shown herself and wanted me to remember that I was not a pig only by luck. Fair enough, but in the end I sat in the midday heat by the side of the road long enough that I got sick of it, eventually making that long, irritating trek up the beach from the grotto into the little town of Sperlonga itself, where I knew at least some bus would come eventually. As I went I passed beachgoers inert in chaises and beneath umbrellas and I thought about the Palermo Principle—after all, I had completed my search for Circe; perhaps this was the time to relax. Yet, no. I learned that from Sperlonga I could find a bus not simply east to the train but instead north a few miles—I was thinking about that cool forest I had bused through several times near Sabaudia. Perhaps now I could get off and have a walk there. Plus, now that I thought of it, the bus stopped in San Felice. Perhaps my luck had changed; maybe I could finally get that boat ride.

Sure I could. I'll spare the details. Say only that by the time I had suffered my final dockside humiliation and was finally back on a bus north, I lacked the spirit to get off near the witch's forest. The bus drove through the long, cool forest of oaks and pines. Huge spreading trees looked almost like an orchard, with tall trunks and armatures spreading like umbrellas, the late-afternoon sun glinting down onto the needles and brown grass. I closed my eyes.

I ended up in Latina, staying in the big ugly Excelsior across from the train station. On the main street there I stumbled upon a pizzeria where I had the best pizza of my life. I would get a piece of the Napolitano—anchovies, olives, tomatoes, cheese, capers—and another of anything else. They had pizza with ham, with pineapple, with hard-boiled eggs, with salad. Then I would have another slice of Napolitano, then another, until the couple behind the counter grew friendly and we had the usual chat about Ulisse and my quest. They gave me a free orange Fanta. If their restaurant had a name, I never noticed it. But if you ever find yourself in Latina, southeast of Rome, walk due south from the train station on the main street until you find the restaurant on the left where everybody from the neighborhood goes with their kids. Try the Napolitano.

ONLY WHEN I LOOKED BACK could I see how thoroughly my own experience seeking Circe followed Odysseus's. Circe completes the circle of women in *The Odyssey*—we have Penelope the chaste, Calypso the party girl, Nausicaa the gamine, and finally Circe, the whore to Penelope's Madonna. The point is less that you have to resist a woman—Odysseus comes across every archetype there is; the idea is to respond appropriately. Circe is only dangerous until Odysseus responds appropriately; after that, she's more than hospitable, helpful in every imaginable way. Helpful enough that Odysseus gets so comfortable that his men have to snap him out of it.

That is, in the larger picture, I don't think Circe is necessarily a woman—she's not necessarily even a person. She's just something—anything—that makes you lose track of what you're doing. I was following Odysseus, thinking about his episodes, and then I focused so heavily on finding the exact Circe that I lost track of the big picture entirely. Just so Odysseus: He faces the challenge Circe presents and then, so satisfied with his excellent performance, takes his eye off the ball for an entire year. I spent only a mixed-up week, but that was plenty.

And one more thing. In this episode Hermes simply walks up to Odysseus and gives him a magical herb and specific directions—just like my friend from the Istituto. Odysseus learns here, as I did, to trust those helpers. With Circe, Odysseus shows he has learned the secret about dealing with scary, powerful forces: Don't try to do it alone. This is a goddess, a witch, a magical woman. Odysseus could be the greatest hero in the world—actually, he is—but if he drinks that potion on his own, he's going to be a pig. Instead, he gets help from a nearby god and a secret drug. With Hermes, Odysseus demonstrates he's learned something from his experience with Aeolus as well: When good advice comes your way, don't just listen—make sure you follow it.

A good lesson to learn, because for his next adventure, Circe has some important advice for him, too. She sends him to hell—and explains how he can come back.

Chapter 11

Regarding the Journey to Hell, and How upon Arriving There I Found It Closed

On our way to the ship, I spoke these words to my men: "You think, I know, that you're going to your own dear country, but Circe decrees quite another journey for us—this one to the halls of Hades and dread Persephone, to hear the truth from Theban Tiresias." At this their spirits collapsed, and right there they sat down, weeping and tearing their hair.

—*The Odyssey*, Book X

"BEFORE I SEND YOU HOME, there's another journey you must make, to the halls of Hades," Circe tells Odysseus. The Theban seer Tiresias has a prophecy Odysseus should hear about his return home; Tiresias being inconveniently dead, Odysseus must consult him in the underworld. Circe's directions are straightforward, if magical: "Don't trouble yourself for a pilot," she says, "but set up the mast, spread the white sail, and sit down, while the North Wind carries you on." That is, the ship will find its way to the house of Hades on its own (though, powered by a northerly wind, one can presume it heads somewhere to the south). Circe also mentions that Odysseus will cross Oceanus, which the Greeks of Homer's time believed was the circling stream that surrounded all the lands of the world. She tells him that he'll find a grove where "the River of Flaming Fire and the River of Wailing, a branch of the River Styx, meet around a rock and go thundering on into the waters of Acheron."

Odysseus tells the Phaeacians he sailed for a single day, then came to

Oceanus, "where the gloomy Cimmerians live enveloped in fog . . . dreadful night is endless for the wretches there." And from these clues, geographers have concluded that the kingdom of the dead is anywhere from the South Pole to Naples, whose surrounding volcanic fields, stinking of sulfur, were considered by the Romans passages to the underworld; from the northwestern shores of the Greek mainland (where two rivers actually do join together at a rock; an ancient *neky-manteion*—a place where pilgrims went to speak with the dead— stood there, mentioned by Pausanias) to the Black Sea (Herodotus tells of a people called Cimmerians living there)—to say nothing of the somewhat common attempt to place the entrance to the house of Hades at the Strait of Gibraltar, since there you do encounter the ocean, though it's hardly the circular flowing stream the Greeks imagined. Still, no place I went was likely to truly make me feel as though I had reached the land of the dead, and among the dead, disregarding any geographic consideration, is where Odysseus goes in the episode that constitutes the entire Book XI.

So for my own journey, the kingdom of the dead finally gave me a chance to ignore the geographers entirely, something of a relief after my experience with Circe. As I organized my Odyssean trip, friends asked how I would know I was visiting the right places. At first I told them about the centuries of geography and argumentation that surrounded Odysseus's journey, about how I chose from different sources to make a path that looked and felt sensible—and, not incidentally, travelable using modern methods and limited funds. But the kingdom of the dead brought to the fore the unavoidable arbitrariness of the entire undertaking; even if there are ways to convince yourself that you have found the correct location of the Lotus-eaters or the Cyclops's cave or the isle of Aeolus, fictional places all, once you try to find the geographical location of hell you have officially sailed beyond reason.

So I eventually started telling my friends this: "If I tell you that I went to the kingdom of the dead, and I come back, I'm telling you a fib—because from what I know that's a one-way ticket." Just the same, although the visit to the land of the dead is not the most commonly talked about of Odysseus's travels, it forms perhaps their central episode, connecting Odysseus with mythical heroes worldwide and providing him with the moment of awareness that completely changes him and his journey. Everyone from Gilgamesh to Jesus to Buffy the Vampire Slayer has gone to—and made an unlikely return from—the land of the dead, so if there's anything without which the hero's journey remains fundamentally incomplete, that's it. My reading of this passage certainly changed me. So I needed to find a place to visit to signify the house of Hades, but justifying its placement on a map seemed almost pointless. Which meant I got to go wherever I wished. And for once on this trip, I knew just where that was.

TO GET TO THE INTERESTING PARTS of the Chiesa di Santa Maria della Concezione (the Church of the Immaculate Conception) in central Rome, you go down instead of up. That is, instead of walking into the sanctuary of the Renaissance church, up stone steps off the Via Vittorio Veneto, you go down, below the steps, into a kind of side door. There, in a small anteroom with a few racks of postcards on a stone floor, a man in a brown robe—a Capuchin monk (we get the word *cappuccino* from the color of those robes)—will take your small admission donation with a friendly smile and point the way into a long hallway, off which are crypts. If you take out a camera, which you'll immediately want to do, he'll make sure you understand that photography is not allowed, whether by murmuring a few halting words of English or by shaking his head and waving his arms. You'll get the idea.

So I never put that intermediary of a camera up to my face: Instead, I looked right at the crypts, filled with the bones of Capuchin monks. Thousands of bones, arranged in patterns and tableaux as lovely as anything else you'll see in Rome—certainly as lovely as anything else dead in Rome, and Rome is pretty much filled with displays of dead people. In Rome, skeletons with scythes and sweeping robes point to hourglasses and remind you of your mortality everywhere you look, from Saint Peter's to the smallest cemetery. Fragments of saints under glass grace countless churches, and monuments to the remembered dead fill the city—yet there is nothing else like the Capuchin cemetery in the Church of the Immaculate Conception. If you're looking to commune with the dead, I'm convinced it's the best place on earth.

The day I was there the monk was a shortish, thin fellow with a white beard and a gentle smile. He took my donation and ushered me into the long hallway, where my life changed.

Above me, an artist had decorated the plaster ceiling with human bones the way a toddler pastes pieces of macaroni onto a paper plate. A large triangle made up entirely of what turned out to be jawbones enclosed a gossamer, meandering floral pattern made of gently curving human ribs, from which dangled little vertebrae florets.

Off the long hall are five crypts, each filled with artwork made of human bones—delicate traceries of pelvises and vertebrae; nicely proportioned thighbone archways beneath rows of human skulls; ceiling rosettes made of scapulae, collarbones, phalanges. In many crypts, bones—the bones of an estimated four thousand or more Capuchin monks—create niches in which stand, or recline, complete monk skeletons, clothed in those hooded coffee-brown robes.

Decorative art covers the walls and ceilings like the plaster filigree in a Renaissance palace—only it's all made from bones, all with a focus on the brevity of earthly life. It's breathtaking. Clock designs—Roman numerals of phalanges, often without clock hands—imply that mortal time is swift but eternity long; so do hourglasses, with shoulder blades arranged as wings: *tempus fugit,* indeed. In some places skulls, too, have graceful scapula wings, and there are several full skeletons of children, empty eyes seeming to implore you not to kid yourself: Nobody is spared the fate we all share.

I believe I closed my mouth after twenty minutes.

Few other tourists found the crypt while I was there, but those who did seemed to follow a pattern. Two or three gaily chattering people would enter; voices would quiet as they made donations and would hush to a whisper as they pointed out to one another the bones, then the skeletons. Then a moment or two in front of each crypt; a thwarted attempt at photography; then the purchase of a couple of postcards or a brochure from the monk; then, within fifteen minutes, exit.

I stayed a good hour and a half. The place was mesmerizing—I had never before seen such a loving acceptance, even a celebration, of the inescapable end of life. After a very few moments during which the grinning skulls, the winged skeletons, seemed ghastly, even ghoulish, the crypts became instead a respite from the bustle of travel, a place for contemplation, just as they were surely designed to be when in 1631 the monks moved in, bringing with them "the mortal remains of their·brethren" from their previous friary (near the Trevi Fountain). It's fair to conclude that the monks thought about death, and thought about it plenty. They made special places where you could go and do the same, and could sit real close and get to know it. They thought that was good for you.

When I was in college an art history professor, encouraging us to seek to understand the values that motivated the artists we studied, urged us to address those central issues: "You'll want to think about this between now and your deathbed," he regularly said. That professor crosses my mind occasionally, but in the crypts he came to mind especially when I looked at two of the full skeletons in their brown robes; each held a sign. Said one, in English, "As you are now, we once were"; said the other, "As we are now, you soon will be." Same message: You've got a short vacation there on Earth, but soon you'll be dead—and you'll be dead a long time.

The most moving piece in the entire cemetery, for me, graced the ceiling of the crypt called the Crypt of Three Skeletons. There, in the center of the vault, in a graceful oval described by four discrete layers of vertebrae, was the entire skeleton of a child, holding in one hand a balancing scale, like the scales of justice (made, it appeared, of a thighbone crossbeam, with the two pans made of pelvic bones; even the chains appeared to be phalanges), and in the other a scythe, the blade made of scapulae. The full skeleton, its large child's head heartbreakingly out of proportion with its body, yet radiated a kind of calm, a simplicity of message. Me, too, it said—and you. And everybody.

When I finally left the crypts, I stopped in the anteroom, picking up and putting down postcards as I sought to regain my equilibrium. Certainly I ought to buy some, but what: One of each crypt? Just one to remember the place by? The whole little guidebook? I lingered for a few minutes before I realized that the monk was watching me, smiling. I showed him a couple of postcards I planned to buy so that he wouldn't think I was swiping anything, but he just smiled, indicating the hallway to the crypts. He spoke no words, just raised his eyebrows: Yes?

"*Sì, molto bella,*" I said, making the prayer gesture that always seems to accompany that phrase when you're telling someone, in any language, that you think their country is beautiful. He pointed to his watch, to me, to the crypts, and once I understood that he wasn't trying to tell me that the place was shutting down, I realized he was noticing that I had spent quite some time back there. "*Molto pensaro,*" I said, trying to indicate that they had made me think. I probably had said "many of thinkingness" if I had said anything at all, but I pointed to my skull and I think he got it.

He got a lot, it turned out. We stood together, a deep warmth between us, chatting with my few words of Italian and his scattered English and a plethora of hand gestures, for a good five minutes. I managed to convey—I think—that I was traveling on my own and had been deeply moved by the cemetery of his order. He managed to convey that few people stay a long while in the crypts, and that he had visited Canada very briefly once. "*Ehh, nord-americano,*" we said together, raising our arms as though we, or someone, had scored a point—in any case, we had found a connection. It was a sweet and peaceful moment, but soon it became clear that no matter how much we wanted to converse—about the spirit, about art, about peace, about the connection (and the difference) between the living and the dead—we had reached our linguistic limit. So with a sigh we turned to the counter and I handed him my three postcards. As he rang them up he handed them back, but I noticed there were four—I took the fourth, a painting, and shook my head: No, this one wasn't mine, trying to hand it back. He shook his head, too, pushing it back toward me. Perplexed, I still resisted, until I looked closely at the extra card.

A close-up—from the Sistine Chapel: Michelangelo's representation of God reaching out to Adam, their fingers all but touching. The moment when God gave life to mankind. Looking into my eyes, the monk took the card back, held it against his heart, and then offered it again to me, both palms upward. A gift—he was giving me this card as a gift.

In this place of death, of skeletons and warning and dust, of reminders that death is necessary and all around us, he gave me the most beautiful picture we know of the creation of life. I didn't cry, but

I held that card to my chest, I said *"Grazie, grazie, oh, molto grazie,"* and we shook one another's hands time and time again, and then I walked out into the gray skies, the traffic, the honking horns, and the chattering tourists of the Via Veneto.

Death in life, life in death; the dead speaking to me in plain voices, giving me straightforward advice to help me live the remainder of my life, help me be the man I wish to be. What's more, only after I embraced the dead, accepted the underground crypt for all its macabre beauty and truth, did life—in the form of a postcard from the hand of a monk who didn't speak my language—wake me up and remind me, in a moment that lacked only a crashing D-sharp chord from a church organ, that it's especially when surrounded by the dead that you can finally, truly appreciate the gift of life. It's one of the most unforgettable moments of my life.

And from my perspective now, the only problem is it happened five years before my *Odyssey* trip.

SO, QUICK CUT. Instead of inside the crypt, the hair standing up on the back of my neck, my spirit merging with the greater universal oneness as I commune with the dead themselves, I am outside the church. Darkness is falling, and as buses and taxis grind around the curve of the Via Veneto as it climbs a hill, I stand outside the pointed iron fence, the gates locked with a padlock. I am shouting into the plastic speaker of a cheap intercom. A sign beyond says, "Closed for renovation," in English and Italian, and I press the button on a little buzzer that ostensibly raises the monks inside the church. Trying to outshout the traffic, I read from a piece of paper a helpful woman at a tourist agency has made for me: *"Per favore,"* I holler (that part I knew already). *"Posso visitare la chiesa per un attimo?"* A moment, just a moment: *"Un attimo, solo un attimo . . . per favore, per favore . . ."* Pedestrians, tourists, and people waiting at the bus stop cast dismissive glances. The monk who answers lapses occasionally into Italian but tells me mostly in rather understandable English that he would love to help me but he just cannot, that he is alone caring for another monk who is very sick; no, I cannot come back another day; no, though he understands I am on a journey he cannot help me; the church should be open sometime next year, and perhaps I can come back. *"Mi dispiaci, mi dispiaci"*—he is sorry, he is very sorry.

The sun continues going down. And I, too, am *molto dispiaci.* I trudge, in the noisy, humid darkness, across town, back to my crappy hotel room near the train station.

MY ORIGINAL VISIT TO THE CAPUCHINS had occurred five years before, when I took a trip across Asia and Europe, ending in Rome. It happened exactly as I've described it, and that Michelangelo postcard is still with me, taped to the wall above my desk. So when I planned my Odyssean adventure and considered where to visit the land of the dead, the Capuchin cemetery came naturally to mind.

In fact, the whole issue of the land of the dead stood at the center of what I was trying to do. When I finally read *The Odyssey,* and then began rereading it, I had been utterly unfamiliar with the episode of Odysseus's journey among the dead, yet it was that episode that shocked me into awareness of the power of what I was reading.

Though his crewmen weep and tear their hair at their destination (Odysseus did the same when Circe first told him), to the land of the dead they go, bringing along a couple of sheep Circe has thoughtfully provided as sacrifice—the dead who drink the blood can "speak the truth" to Odysseus; the others must simply continue their formless existence, gibbering like bats. When Tiresias arrives, he drinks of the blood and says Odysseus can, in fact, make his way home, so long as his men do not touch the cattle of the sun god, "to whom all sights and sounds are known." If they fail in this and eat the cattle, Tiresias prophesies "destruction for your ship and crew, and should you yourself escape, your return will be lonely, late, and unhappy, for you will come home without friends in a ship not your own to a house full of trouble"—exactly as Polyphemus had prayed to his father, Poseidon. Tiresias also tells Odysseus that even then his arrival home will not signal his journey's end: He'll have one more trip, on which he must carry an oar inland until he finds people so unfamiliar with the sea that they have no salt for their food and misidentify his oar, asking him why he's traveling with a winnowing fan. There he must plant the oar, making a sacrifice to Poseidon. After that, Tiresias tells him, he will live happily until to him "will come an easy death from the sea, a peaceful death in your comfortable calm old age." Whether "from the sea" in this case means "far from the sea" or "caused by the sea" depends on which translation you read, with subsequent myths providing room for interpretation.

Readers already know from the proem that the crewmen are doomed to eat the cattle—it's also plain from the fact that Odysseus is alone with Calypso when we meet him—but Tiresias's prophecy is something of a red herring in this episode anyway. It's good enough advice, though as we'll see Circe gives Odysseus much more detailed and practical advice when he returns to her island. But much more important than the prophecy is what else happens to Odysseus among the dead.

The first person he meets is Elpenor, the youngest of his crewmen ("not any too brave or bright," Odysseus describes him), who the night before had gone to sleep drunk on Circe's roof. Waking up and forgetting he was on the roof, he fell and broke his neck. Odysseus and his men left him unburied in their grim focus on their journey to the underworld (apparently they never even missed him), but as a shade he beat them there. Elpenor asks Odysseus to please give him a decent burial when they return to Circe's island. Odysseus agrees.

Odysseus also converses with his own mother, Anticleia, who he is stunned to learn has died of longing during her son's long absence. She tells him that Penelope remains faithful and Telemachus is safe (this all happens, of course, around seven years before his return, so the ruinous suitors have not yet beset Odysseus's home); on the other hand, she tells him, Odysseus's father has withdrawn from the palace and lives like a slave out in the country. Shaken by the news of her death, Odysseus tries to embrace his mother three times, extending his arms; but she "thrice flitted through them like a shadow or a dream." To his cries of despair, his mother pragmatically tells Odysseus: This is how it is when you're dead.

A long passage follows during which Odysseus sees a parade of famous dead women, but this is much like my thumbing the postcard racks after seeing the crypts: just downtime to let you process what's happened. Odysseus has gone to hell to meet a prophet—and while there, he bumps into his mother. Who has died, no less, from grief because of his absence. It's the first—and best—guilt-inducing mother joke of all time. You think your mother laid it on? Meet Anticleia: "Sure, you have to blind your Cyclops, of course, you're a big shot; but would it be so hard to write once in a while? No, you go out and have fun, sleep with your goddesses, I'll just stay here AND DIE!" For a guy who's spent the last year idling with an enchantress, this has to be a shaky moment: "While I've been living the good life, my mother *died*." Ninety-plus percent of his crew has been killed on his way home, but Odysseus still has no trouble enjoying Circe's hospitality. Then, suddenly, it's not some nameless crew member, it's his mom, dead—because of him. Actions have consequences in a big way here, and Odysseus notices.

Then something even bigger happens. After the women finish parading by, here come the men. Agamemnon first, of course, and he tells Odysseus his own sordid tale of homecoming, which readers recall because both Nestor and Menelaus told it to Telemachus: Agamemnon's faithless wife, Clytemnestra, and her lover, Aegisthus, murdered him upon his return. His son subsequently evened the score, but Agamemnon shares a piece of advice with Odysseus: not to tell his wife all he knows, but to keep secrets from her. If there's anybody on the planet who doesn't need advice to be dishonest it's Odysseus, but nonetheless, there it is. And then comes the pivotal moment in *The Odyssey*.

The ghost of Achilles steps forward.

ACHILLES, OF COURSE, is the hero of *The Iliad,* the center of that tale as Odysseus is the center of this. Achilles' withdrawal from the fighting when he feels mistreated by Agamemnon, and its fatal consequences, form the core of that poem.

Achilles is the greatest fighter among the Greeks, rendered nearly invincible by his mother, Thetis. Much more important, Thetis is also a seer, and she knows that Achilles faces a choice: He can live an unexceptional life at home, with wife and family, or he can fight at Troy, where he will win great glory but surely die. Though Thetis tries to protect him from the war by hiding him, Achilles chooses the short, glorious life described in *The Iliad*.

Here in the underworld, when Odysseus sees him, Odysseus refers to that chosen glory. Having secured greater honor than any other man when alive, Achilles now has similar status among the dead: "Your rule is mighty among the missing," Odysseus says. "Then do not sorrow so that you are dead, Achilles."

Achilles, the world's greatest-ever example of the love of honor and glory, rolls his eyes in disgust. "Do not try to make me welcome death," he responds. "I would rather live on earth as a hireling of one who was but poor himself than to be king of all the ghosts there are! But come, tell me what you know of my son . . . ? And what have you heard of [my father], noble Peleus?"

I don't think I even noticed this the first couple times I read *The Odyssey*—I was just making my way through, getting the story: "Okay, he's in the underworld, here's Achilles and so forth. Next come the Sirens, then on to Scylla and Charybdis . . ." But somewhere on my third or fourth reading, when I had time to dawdle over this conversation, I realized that I was reading something almost heretical. Achilles, the most celebrated hero of all, whose love of honor and glory defined him, tells Odysseus that he made the wrong choice. "Honor?" he seems to say. "Glory? For the birds. But your son? Your family? That's worth your time." It's pure advice, the tiny kernel of awareness distilled from the fury of his life—and it's the exact opposite of what you would have expected.

Imagine the ghost of Obi-Wan Kenobi appearing to Luke Skywalker, only instead of telling him to seek help from Yoda to save the universe, he said, "Look, all this Force business? Totally not worth it: Go home, have a couple kids, and just try to enjoy your life." It's the Gipper saying, "Hey, win, lose, who freaking cares? It's all a game—just be careful out there."

Odysseus here shows the backstory behind his seemingly blithe decision with Calypso, turning down immortality for the chance to return to his loved ones. He hears from the most immortally famous of the heroes with whom he fought that the immortality of fame and honor don't stack up well when compared to the pleasures of family life. Here, clearly, is genuine advice for Odysseus.

And for a middle-aged man reading *The Odyssey,* that piece of advice set up a harmonic resonance that vibrates to this day. The truth that most powerfully characterizes the dawning awareness of middle age, possibly unlearnable except through experience, is that whatever your work is, however much you value it, at some point you realize that your people are more important. *Way* more important. Nobody ever said on their deathbed that they wished they'd spent more time at the office, we tell each other, as if it's something new. And here's Achilles telling it to Odysseus in the oldest story we have.

A look at Odysseus's journey before and after his visit to the underworld demonstrates the power of this advice. Beforehand, Odysseus stops at Ismarus to pick a fight; chooses to not only investigate the Cyclops's cave but to hang around until the owner gets back to wreak havoc; loiters a month or so with Aeolus; then spends a year lying contentedly in Circe's arms. Odysseus wants to get home, but he's not exactly running the yellow lights.

Then he visits the halls of Hades. He sees that his absence has killed his mother and hears from Achilles that wandering the planet seeking fame and glory is a waste of time. More, Achilles reminds him that he's got a son waiting somewhere—when Odysseus gives a good report of Achilles' son, Achilles "stalk[s] joyfully away through the field of asphodel" in the land of the dead.

Odysseus sees this joy. Another parade of the famous dead follows—this time men—but Odysseus clearly knows he's got what he came for, and it's a lot more than Tiresias's advice not to kill the cattle of the sun god. He loads up the men and back they go to Circe.

THE LAND OF THE DEAD is the center, the tipping point of *The Odyssey.* It contains the moment where Odysseus finally turns toward home like he means it. Naturally, my choice of where to visit to commemorate this important moment meant a lot to me—especially since I felt that I knew the exact right place to go; that in Rome I was right there at it; and that when I had gone there before, I had taken away the exact lesson that Odysseus learns. That life is short, that glory is a phantom, that the unknowable but ultimately human reality of love carries far more weight than such chimera as honor and glory.

So my inability to return to the Capuchin crypts made me desperate.

I spent several days, in essence, running around screaming: I asked for help from travel agencies. I pleaded with tourist offices official and unofficial. I made friends with the cultural affairs assistant at the American embassy. I even contacted the Vatican—all without luck. And when the U.S. government and the Holy See can't get you in to see the dead monks, you're just not going to see the dead monks. I had to think of somewhere else to go to commune with the dead.

I went from church to church surveying saint parts; I visited the tiny Museo delle Anime del Purgatorio, on the west shore of the Tiber, dedicated specifically to communications from the dead (the dead specialize, it seems, in burning handprints, usually into printed matter but sometimes on linen; their message, presumably: "Ouch, damn it!"). I looked at dead people hither and yon without satisfaction until— d'oh!—I finally drew an obvious conclusion. If you're looking for the dead, Rome has one famous destination that will put you in close contact with a good half million of them. So I went to the south of town and waited for the bus that would take me to the catacombs.

THE CATACOMBS, several underground graveyards filled with early Christians, line the Via Appia Antica—the Appian Way, the famous ancient thoroughfare leading south from Rome. Before the second century AD, Christians could not legally bury their dead in Rome—and the aboveground tombs seen along the Appian Way were expensive. Families with Christian sympathies offered land, and Christians began digging catacombs—long galleries below the ground, lined with niches in which bodies were placed. When one level filled up, gravediggers just dug below and made another. The rock beneath the ground south of Rome is called tufa—made of volcanic ash, it's easy to dig through but hardens once exposed to the air, which made it perfect for creating a labyrinthine underground necropolis on the fly. I visited the Catacombs of San Callisto, filled not only with average

Christians but with popes, saints, and martyrs as well. On the bus there I fell into conversation with Asli, a willowy young Turk studying art history, and we walked together to the pleasant lawn, lined with cypresses, surrounding the small aboveground entry to the tombs.

A priest named Father Rocco gave the tour, leading us down into the cool passageways, pointing out barrel-vaulted family crypts dug into the earth, Byzantine frescoes, and statues of martyrs. Periodically, little holes in the walls formed niches for oil lamps, used when relatives visited the tombs. In the twenty-minute tour we never left the second level of the four-level catacomb and walked only a fraction of the twelve miles of galleries. Father Rocco chatted amiably about the importance of regularly looking hard at death: "Our eyes have gotten out of the habit," he told us. "We look too much at things. So the human being becomes a thing among the others." Achilles surely would have agreed.

But vision wasn't the sense that overpowered Asli and me. The moment we turned the corner at the base of the stairs and left the light of the sun behind, Asli turned to me, her eyes wide: "The smell!" she said. "I love it!" What people call the dust of centuries—in those catacombs, you could smell it. And the funny thing—all that death, it didn't smell bad. It didn't stink of putrefaction; it smelled cool and quiet. Damp, to be sure, but long, and above all peaceful. There was something stately about our gentle passage along the cool paths among so many dead. At first it seemed like the wrong lesson—Achilles tells Odysseus to despise death, I thought. But rereading yet again I realized: Achilles tells Odysseus rather to love his life, love those with whom he spends it, not waste his time on foolish pursuits. To be sure, my chase after Odysseus could seem like a foolish pursuit, but I was nearing its end, nearing the moment when I would return to June, and eventually to the baby who would join us. What's more, it was for just such moments of recognition that I left home—and that I kept rereading *The Odyssey*. Among the dead Odysseus learned not to despise death but to be aware of it, and to let its certainty inform his life. I learned that once among the Capuchin crypts, and the lesson, patient, waited again here beneath the ground.

When we emerged from the Catacombs of San Callisto into the pleasant green lawn and cypress trees, Asli and I felt thrilled, overwhelmed. Like Odysseus, we had come back from the dead. At that moment, above ground, the golden sun filtering through the trees, the world felt like a miracle—a living miracle. I hadn't gotten back into the Capuchin crypts, but I had been there before, and I felt that I understood the lesson—leaving the catacombs, in fact, I found myself suddenly delighted with the progress of my travels. Like Odysseus, I was ready to continue on, and this time I imagined that my eyes burned with the fierceness of my desire to get moving. I made a train reservation toward my next destination—Naples, from which I planned to visit the islands of the Sirens—and looked forward to a peaceful evening on my own wandering the Eternal City.

SO NATURALLY Asli and I complicated that evening with ill-conceived and poorly executed plans to meet for dinner, which led to one of those endless wanders through the streets of an unfamiliar city during which acquaintances, each too polite to seize control of the plan, bounce along failing to do what they set out to—in this case, find a cheap dinner and eat it on the steps of some monument. Directions raised and countered, likely restaurants suggested and vetoed as hunger and frustration grew. Finally, Asli remembered a place she had eaten days before—she was sure it would be open, and off we went.

It was a chain—a harshly lit, garish, fast-food pizzeria, where the cheap pizza cost twice what a handmade sandwich cost in any of the dozens of *paninoteca* around the train station. I wanted to say to her, "What? We've dithered all over Rome for an hour and now we're going to a chain restaurant?" But anything I would have said rang in my ears like the noises of a species of blasé traveler called Lonely Planetoids, and I didn't want to sound like that.

On a trip, once, my wife and I found ourselves telling two threadbare, smoking British backpackers that we were leaving our Bangkok guesthouse for Chiang Mai in the north of Thailand. Their eyes rolled: Touristy, ruined, you had to be there ten years ago. Unable to change our train reservations, we glumly went ahead—and returned, thrilled, a week later, having hiked among hill tribes, eaten street-vendor pad thai from banana-leaf bowls, and tried opium. The scornful two remained in the lobby, almost exactly where we had left them, still talking about places they were too cool to go. With a new friend we called them Lonely Planetoids and resolved never to become them. In Rome, in that awful pizzeria, with Asli, I kept my resolution. We had spent an afternoon together, and if Father Rocco and the dead—and the Capuchins, and Achilles—had anything to share it's that time is precious, and people are, too, and an afternoon was worthy of respect.

We chatted peaceably while waiting for our crappy chain pizza with its cotton crust and its soupy topping, and as by the time it arrived we were enormously hungry we gorged on it and kept smiles on our faces. In the end we parted cheerfully, and from Asli's hotel door I walked at night in a city where they speak a foreign language along a busy street to a vast plaza with a fountain, thence to the train station where I loaded up on local junk food, and then back to a cheap hotel room where I read books about where I might go next. I had no complaints.

I had more destinations, and somehow—though I didn't know quite where they were—I knew I would make my way and then I would return to my wife, and I felt comfortable and at peace. At peace; my visit to the catacombs had brought me that. From the dead, what more can you ask?

Chapter 12

Hold Me Back!:

The Island of the Sirens

First you'll come to the Sirens, enchanters of men. Whoever in ignorance comes near them and hears their song, never again returns to rejoice at home with a welcoming wife and small children.

—*The Odyssey*, Book XII

ODYSSEUS EMERGES from the land of the dead a changed man, and reading the episode enlightened me, too. As Achilles spills his truth about the hollowness of glory *The Odyssey* springs to life and I realized: The reason the ninth-graders down whose throats we tend to stuff *The Odyssey* usually hate it is that it's not written for them. What ninth-grader contemplates mortality? Most ninth-graders I know—and the ninth-grader I was—share a lot more with the arrogant scorn of Achilles in *The Iliad* than the weary "Oh, for pity's sake, what next?" endurance of Odysseus. In fact, I later discovered that the abridgments of *The Odyssey* read by many ninth-graders didn't even include this utterly central episode. No, *The Odyssey* is not for them; *The Odyssey* is written for me—for middle-aged people, experienced in life's complexities, who can savor its counterintuitive turnings, find subtle undertastes in its cloudy wine. Returning from the land of the dead, Odysseus almost officially starts the second half of his life—a middle-aged moment if there ever was one. Clear-eyed and finally certain of his goal, Odysseus returns to Circe.

* * *

THERE HE BEGINS DOING SOMETHING NEW: actually trying to get home, traveling like he means it. So did I—in the days following the confusion surrounding Circe and the land of the dead, I traveled with better luck and more satisfactory outcome than during any other period on my travels. In this, as in most things, I had it far easier than Odysseus.

Circe slyly tells Odysseus that he's now a special case—everybody else dies only once, but Odysseus, back from the dead, will die twice. She then encourages the crew to spend a day in feasting and reminds them to bury young Elpenor, which they do. During the feast she leads Odysseus off and debriefs him about his journey to the Underworld. Then, unbidden, she gives Odysseus specific directions for his next three episodes: the island of the Sirens; the choices represented by Scylla and Charybdis; and the island of Thrinacia, on which graze the cattle owned by Helios, the sun god. She repeats the warning of Tiresias that the men must under no circumstances touch those cattle. If they leave the cattle unmolested, they might make it back to Ithaca; if not, as the Cyclops prayed and as Tiresias warned, Odysseus can expect to return "lonely, late, and unhappy."

The first obstacle Odysseus will now face, Circe says, is "the Sirens, enchanters of men." They sit on an island, "in a meadow mid the moldering bones of men, great heaps of them"—the remains of those who have heard the Sirens' enchanting song, gone to listen, and never returned. But just as Hermes had a plan to deal with Circe, Circe has a plan to deal with the Sirens: Odysseus must stop the ears of his crewmen with wax, so they cannot hear the song. Odysseus, of course, will want to listen, so Circe tells him to force the crew to tie him to the mast, allowing him to hear the Sirens' song but not act on the foolish impulses the song will inspire. He must further instruct his men that when he pleads for release, they should "just tie you still tighter with even more ropes."

That's exactly what happens. Odysseus shares Circe's counsel with his men—a wiser choice than keeping the advice secret, as he had after leaving Aeolus with the bag of wind. As the ship gets going, he plugs their ears, and they bind him. When the ship nears the island,

the Sirens begin singing, enticing Odysseus to sail to their rock, promising that all who hear them enjoy what they hear "and go on all the
wiser." They know all about the war at Troy, they tell Odysseus, all
about his suffering—"and we know all that will happen on the boun-
tiful earth." Useful stuff—Odysseus naturally orders his men to stop,
but Circe's plan works. When he pleads, the sailors only tie him more
tightly and row on until they're out of earshot. A simple episode, no
less powerful for its brevity.

IN THE BARDO MUSEUM, in Tunis, hangs a tile mosaic of Odysseus, tied
to the mast, gazing at the Sirens, women with the bodies of birds—
while the sailors concentrate on their rowing. I love that image of
Odysseus: Looking where others don't look might be a good epithet
for him. Much more important in that mosaic, though, is how the
Sirens look: half woman, half bird.

That is, for Odysseus, the Sirens might have been many things, but
they would not have been sexy. Some myths say they were turned into
birds when they failed to save the goddess Demeter's kidnapped
daughter Persephone, who became part-time queen of the underworld; the Muses are said to have defeated them in a singing contest,
after which the Muses plucked Siren feathers for crowns to celebrate
their victory. Post-Homeric myth said that if anyone sailed past them
without capitulating to their charms the Sirens would kill themselves,
though Jason and the Argonauts sailed by them before Odysseus, and
the Sirens seemed to survive that (in that case, the poet Orpheus sang
loud enough to drown them out). Anyhow, the three tiny Italian
islands now identified with them are said to be the rocky form the
Sirens took after Odysseus's passage caused their death (though they
supposedly turned up in other places, too, of course; one Siren, named
Parthenope, supposedly washed up on the shore at Naples, originally
named for her). Some mythographers collate the Sirens with other bird
demons, like the Harpies. The point is, there was nothing charming or
sexy about the Sirens. Not for Odysseus.

Almost ever since, though, the Sirens have been portrayed as beautiful women (think of the sexy women at the baptism in *O Brother*,

Where Art Thou? or of the terrifyingly sexual women in the crooked house in *Cold Mountain*); often, as in the Starbucks logo, they are portrayed as mermaids, though none of this comes from Homer or even from the myths of Homer's time. In *The Odyssey,* the Sirens tempt, to be sure, but they do not offer pleasure; they offer information.

It makes sense: Odysseus has just left a year of sex and feasting with a goddess; surely more of that wouldn't tempt him. But information? Crafty Odysseus always wants that, especially now that he's regained his focus on getting home. (Though more than one modern interpreter sees Odysseus tempted less by information about the future than by the Sirens' knowledge of the past. In two books, *Achilles in Vietnam* and *Odysseus in America,* psychiatrist Jonathan Shay interprets *The Iliad* as describing the madness of war and *The Odyssey* as representing the steps a warrior takes to return from that place of madness. The Sirens represent the temptation to lose interest in rejoining the world, simply sitting around reliving war experiences.)

ANYHOW, THE SIRENS: Pretty or not, bird or woman, sex or information, sailing landmark or fantasy land, none of it matters. The Sirens represented something to be passed by, resisted, and they had a specific location: the Li Galli islands somewhere near Sorrento, just south of Naples, a couple hundred miles south of Rome. I was in Rome; I headed south.

Regarding the Sirens' islands—and the next several destinations, all described by Circe—geographers from Strabo on down generally agree: Circe's comments fit suspiciously well with ancient sailing instructions, the magical creatures corresponding to the hazards or landmarks sailors face, sailing south from Monte Circeo. Strabo described the islands of the Sirens with detail: "a sort of elbow . . . juts out, long and narrow, from the territory of Surrentum [modern Sorrento] to the Strait of Caprea [Capri], with the sanctuary of the Sirens on one side of the hilly headland, while on the other side, looking towards the Gulf of Poseidonia [the Gulf of Salerno], lie three uninhabited rocky little islands, called the Sirens." For centuries called the Sirenuse, after the Sirens, they are now called the Li Gallis, and sailor Ernle Bradford, who thought of Odysseus as a historical personage and used wind patterns and sea currents to document a painstaking search for the geographical sites along Odysseus's path, notes that the Li Gallis constitute the last islands off the west coast of Italy and the natural point to turn south toward Sicily. "If I were instructing a sailor with neither chart nor compass how to get down to Sicily from Cape Circeo," he says, "I would be inclined to say: 'Keep coasting . . . until you come to a small group of islands at the head of a Gulf. There are three of them close together. At this point, take your departure from the coast, and sail south . . . until you sight the volcano Stromboli. . . . [There] you have two alternatives: either follow the islands westward . . . or take the shorter route and carry on southward . . . through the Messina Strait." Since Circe tells Odysseus to sail past the Sirens, then choose between either the dangerous Wandering Rocks (Circe describes them as noisy and smoky, like a volcano) or the equally dangerous passage between Scylla and Charybdis, identified with the Strait of Messina since time out of mind, it's hard to disagree. Look at any map—it works.

So identifying the islands of the Sirens thus presented no problem; actually finding them, and the way to them, proved somewhat more difficult. Leaving home, I knew only that I was heading eventually for the Gulf of Salerno, but whether that meant I would be wise to stay in Salerno itself, or the famously Anglophone Sorrento, or the expensive isle of Capri, or somewhere else, I had no idea. I consulted map after tourist map, but the three tiny islands never showed up. Only when I bought a plain-old driving map did I finally find them straightforwardly identified: Just south of the Sorrentine Peninsula, which forms the southern end of the Gulf of Naples, there they were. Since all kinds of dotted lines indicating ferry routes skirted the area, I thought my best bet was to set up camp in Naples, take a ferry to Capri, and from Capri look for a ferry to Positano, which, following the route on the map, looked like it would do everything but scrape its hull on the islands.

THEY SAY THAT when tropical termites are ready to build a nest, they all scurry around aimlessly piling up stones. When two nearby piles grow high, then lean together and form an arch, an electric awareness apparently jolts the group and suddenly the termites shift into a different gear and go on to build their giant nest and pursue the rest of their termite lives. An arch sets termites in motion. Mediterranean tourist towns are filled with arches—church doors, alleys, gateways all funnel crowds through arches, which manifest the difference between termites and humans.

Because if termites were like humans, the minute that first arch was built, two termites would stand exactly underneath the arch and one termite would take out the tourist map and say to the other one, "Can you tell where we are?" and then they'd have an argument, while all the other termites trying to get through the arch bunched up behind them, grumbling. Or else three termites pulling wheeled luggage would stop beneath the arch, asking a fourth termite to take their picture, causing several termites behind them to miss their ferry. Or a single termite would stop beneath the arch to make a call on a mobile telephone.

Welcome to high season. July in the Mediterranean is the play-offs; August, when Europeans shut down their whole continent and rush to the Mediterranean to get in each other's way near the beaches, is the championship. Every train fills to bursting, passengers lining the aisles beside the compartments; room prices, already nearly double the off-season rate in July, blithely rise by another 15 percent or more; boarding a ferry, scarcely humane at the best of times, resembles the Oklahoma land rush: A stuffy hydrofoil vibrating over choppy seas is bad enough sitting down—faced with the prospect of standing, even the mildest-mannered family will sharpen elbows near the gangway. Seventeen miles off the coast of Naples, connected by numerous ferries to Naples and Sorrento, the rocky, cloud-topped island of Capri has been one of the Mediterranean's chief tourist spots since Augustus showed up in 29 BC; our old pal Tiberius lived the last years of his life there, engaged mostly in lechery. So, the busiest tourist month and one of the busiest tourist spots: You do the math.

I got up early and caught a hydrofoil from Naples before 6 a.m., sailing beneath a rising sun already venomous, blinding, vicious—a sun that all but made sarcastic comments while stinging retinas into orange blindness and floating blobs of green afterimages. I caught a glimpse of the cone of Vesuvius, south of Naples, and within an hour we approached Capri, a green, mountainous little island veiled in fog. I quickly purchased a ticket for Positano. Perhaps because things seemed too easy, I worried that the ferry might pass between the Li Gallis and the coast, thus putting me on the wrong side of the islands—Odysseus, after all, would surely have kept to the seaward side of the Sirens. The saleswoman reassured me, and I used the hour before departure to climb the steep, winding stairs to the city of Capri, at the top of the mountain above the harbor. The cobblestone stairs meandered past tiny houses carved into the cliffs, looking over fenced patios, commonly passing through tunnels of bougainvillea, the morning sun filtering through the purple flowers, rendering the walled alleys almost ridiculously lovely. At the top, among Capri's famous little squares surrounded by palms, cacti, magnolia, and expensive shops (and filled with a crush of English-speaking tourists), you can lean on stone walls and look out over the island, the sea, and the harbor—where boat after boat disgorges further packs of tourists. Capri's warren of curving stone streets, white walls, and surprising squares reminded me of Tunis, I thought, or perhaps Jerba, or maybe Istanbul—and for the first time I thought not "What a treasure of memories" but "Man, for the foreseeable future, I am going to sound like an asshole." I made my way down and was one of the first on the ferry to Positano—the first direct ferry from Capri to Positano, I was told, of the season. We passed cliffy coastline, arched bridges connecting little outcroppings to the main cliffs—the ferry made a peaceful, almost stately trip along what is called the Amalfi Coast.

I sat in the bow, near Dawn, a nice woman from Florida, and her two preteen children, Veronica and Charlie. Charlie, covered lips to crown in zinc, wore a floppy denim hat fringed in red. When he removed his sunglasses, the pale circles of skin beneath them gave him raccoon eyes. As map in hand I peered over the gunwale, sketchbook at the ready, we naturally got to talking, and when I reached an ecstasy of excitement as the islands hove into view and I made ready with my sketchbook, they occasionally grabbed up blowing map or snagged backpack, making sure nothing flew overboard. I peered into the wheelhouse over the shoulder of the captain and saw the Li Gallis outlined by purple on his chart—a no-go zone, not for fear of Sirens, but because the islands are part of a protected natural area. The islands grew closer, and as they emerged I leaned over the rail and sketched.

Three little islands, mostly rocky, each covered with a little toupee of greenery, thrust themselves out of the sea—one looked almost exactly like the nose of a surfacing submarine; another, the largest, had the ruins of a foursquare stone tower and two or three nice buildings, with arched doors and windows and Art Deco–looking crenellations along the roofline. I madly sketched as the islands loomed closer, then seemed to hesitate as we drew alongside, then began receding. I drew a last few lines, gazed a moment, then snapped shut my sketchbook and returned to my seat, with Dawn and Veronica and Charlie: I had successfully sailed past the islands of the Sirens, and it wasn't even noon. This was the stuff—I was thrilled. When the boat docked in Positano we all stepped off, watched the boat take on passengers and leave, and then turned to explore—except we turned out to be in Amalfi, one unutterably charming Mediterranean hill town to the south of where we had planned to be.

Dawn, with a lunch reservation to keep, was frustrated and annoyed with herself; I was somewhat philosophical. We bought tickets marked "Positano," got on the direct boat for Positano, and when it stopped we got off. What more could we have done? It's the Mediterranean, the ferries do what they will, and you cope. Positano was far closer to the Li Gallis, so even though I'd made my sketches, I preferred to spend my afternoon there rather than in Amalfi. Young Veronica was the least concerned, casting our misstep as a scene in the television show *The Amazing Race:* "This could have been a fatal misstep for team America," she intoned. "Three teams are tied for last place—*can* they catch up?" They could—the next ferry for Positano left in a few moments, and we climbed aboard. "A lot of people not getting up," Dawn noted when the ferry pulled up to the dock. "Those are the people traveling on to Positano who know what they're doing."

Positano looks almost exactly like Amalfi, and like Capri—white, yellow, and pink stucco houses with red roofs carved into the steep hillside, twisting cobbled alleyways leading generally uphill, fragrant purple bougainvillea everywhere; restaurants and stores line a comfortable beachfront and pop up among the little squares and alleys, becoming ritzier the higher you climb. It's the picture-postcard Mediterranean seaside hill town, and one of the most famous. Odysseus may have sailed right by, but Picasso, John Steinbeck, and Jean Cocteau hung out, especially during its *La Dolce Vita* years in the mid–twentieth century, when Liz Taylor and Richard Burton failed to resist temptation there. Dancer Rudolf Nureyev actually bought the Li Galli islands and lived there until his death.

In no rush to return to Naples, I first foraged for a little sandwich, eating a peaceful meal on the shingle beach, looking out at the Li Gallis not far offshore. On the beach I couldn't help noticing a little table beneath an umbrella, and a sign that read "Noleggio Barche"—boat rental. I hesitated for a while, and then I thought, Well, why not, and I approached. The woman reading a book beneath the umbrella had enough English to tell me that they actually ran little tours out to the Li Gallis each morning and afternoon. The morning tour was canceled for lack of interest, and things didn't look much better for the afternoon, but why didn't I come back in a couple hours and we'd see what we could work out? I wandered the ritziest streets—the balcony of the hotel Le Sirenuse (a mermaid emblem, of course) has a spectacular view of the city, especially the multicolored tile mosaic dome of the city's lovely little cathedral. I suggested to the concierge that Positano might be pretty. He did not contradict me. Clouds rolled in, cooling the day with a gentle drizzle.

AT TWO O'CLOCK the still-pleasant lady on the beach told me nobody else wanted to visit the Li Gallis, but before I could shrug and wander off she made a suggestion: It would take probably an hour and a half to make the trip—would I care to rent a boat for the regular 40 euros, and she would supply a sailor at no charge? Note to San Felice Dockside Cardplayers' Union: This is how you rent a freaking boat. She spoke into her cell phone and a moment or two later a grinning, rotund man in a red Speedo pulled up to the beach in a little yellow twenty-three-foot open boat. He beckoned with a smile and I hopped aboard.

He had very little English, so in my fractured Italian I explained about my journey as he expertly guided our little boat over the wakes of passing pleasure craft and we putted toward the Li Gallis. He may have understood me—in any case, he kept smiling, and he seemed to find it perfectly reasonable for an American in a dirty white canvas hat to wish to be conveyed to the Li Gallis in the rain and there perch in the bow, making sketches. I tried to make clear to him as we traveled around and among the islands that I would see more here than Odysseus had; he nodded and smiled. He looked like the Happy Buddha. It wasn't until we arrived at the islands that I had a moment of recognition, not about the islands but about our boat. The copy of *The Odyssey* my wife had given me those many months before had on its cover a featureless, wavy blue sea broken by nothing but a tiny yellow boat—and here I was, on a wavy blue sea in a tiny yellow boat. I grinned to think of it, and the Happy Buddha grinned back as though he shared the joke.

He piloted us between the three islands, timing the currents and swells. One island bears the remains of an old fortification from the twelfth-century days of the Maritime Republic of Amalfi, and on the largest—called il Gallo Lungo—are those beautiful stucco houses; I never learned whether Nureyev built them, though I suppose he did. The Buddha pointed out some caves and a couple goats cavorting amid some stone ruins, but the swell made being too close to the islands a bit dodgy. Plus the rain was increasing, so we headed back. The Buddha pointed out the scar of a recent landslide on the mainland, and then he showed me how to use the boat cushions to keep the rain off.

I found a ferry from Positano that went directly back to Naples.

NAPLES. IF I HAD MISSED PALERMO, at least I visited Naples, which is sort of the Palermo of the mainland: noisy, chaotic, and perfectly, madly, Italian. You emerge from the train station into the maelstrom of the Piazza Garibaldi, filled with buses, cabs, and scooters, and the contiguous Piazza Mancini, surrounded by crumbling buildings and filled with an all-day surging crowd of market tables, cheats, and pickpockets: a whirling mixture of grit and glamorous young Neapolitans on scooters and in black clothing, with their parents and grandparents mixed into the crowd. It's hard to reconcile: These breathtaking girls in makeup and tight skirts must somehow end up as those barrel-shaped old women carrying shopping bags; the young men with tattoos and wraparound shades, shirt collars open a button, must become these grinning white-haired old men with thick fingers, their shirts open two buttons at the top, three at the bottom. No matter how unlikely, it's the only explanation.

On the Palermo Principle, I touristed Naples for a day, roving the streets of its *centro antico,* consuming piece after piece of its fabulous, cheap pizza. You can read every guidebook, but save yourself some time: It doesn't matter where you stop, it's all beyond perfect. Just get one piece at a time, and you can try them all. You might say the same thing for the churches and museums; according to my guidebook UNESCO has called Naples's ancient center one of the most architecturally varied spots in the world. Founded by Greek colonists in the seventh century BC, captured by the Romans in the fourth and subsequently by the Byzantines and almost every medieval and subsequent species of dynasty, Naples has three main streets that have run the same routes for twenty-five hundred years—especially fueled by all that pizza, you can stop almost anyplace along its dirty thoroughfares and expect rewards, whether a tiny, catty-corner piazza, dry fountain, or sixteenth-century church. The fourteenth-century Duomo, for example, offers more than the obligatory frescoes and sculptures (as well as the blood of a saint supposed to liquefy twice per year)—it has spread to engulf previous chapels, thus comprising fourth-century floors and fifth-century mosaics. An archaeological dig off the north apse even takes you belowground to ruins of ancient Roman structures and Greek-era streets.

Trying to see Naples in a day is like trying to see Europe in a day, so my hours passed like a cinema montage: portals in medieval city walls; tiny, dark churches with brooding Caravaggio panels or trompe l'oeil ceilings depicting saints in ghoulish haunted-mansion green; a turreted thirteenth-century castle overlooking the Gulf of Naples, alongside an eighteenth-century palace turned art museum, alongside the Galleria Umberto, a three-story nineteenth-century arcade, with long glass barrel-vaulted ceilings and a glass dome at its center.

And most amazing, the Angevin cloister of the Chiesa di Santa Chiara. The Palermo Principle often lands you directionless in some city center you didn't expect to be wandering. Exciting but tiring, so you might duck into a church just for a place to catch your breath, and there discover that you can pay extra to see the Chiostro Maiolicato, which, at 4 euros, must be worth seeing. Which was how I found myself beneath the bright-blue sky seated on a concrete bench covered by spectacular hand-painted majolica tiles, among a grid of sixty octagonal columns, each covered by those same tiles. The lightest breeze stirred the cypresses and pines that dotted the courtyard, crisscrossed by brick walkways and surrounded by the loggia of that thirteenth-century cloister. And then a student began practicing piano, the clear notes falling out a window seemingly one by one, and then the church bells started ringing, and I can be forgiven for not hurrying to get up, and maybe not wanting to ever. I tried to connect the music I heard to the Sirens, but then I thought, No—this is the music you hear after you're done with the Sirens.

THE SIRENS ARE ALWAYS PORTRAYED as the thing you want but shouldn't have, but I decided that misses the point. The Sirens tempt Odysseus with information, but once he's had a witch and a dead prophet lay out his exact future, complete with advice and driving instructions, it's hard to imagine Homer wants to imply that knowing stuff is bad.

No; know everything you can—Odysseus demonstrates that in his every waking hour. The Siren song itself isn't the message here; the message is the self-restraint. A famous series of *Peanuts* cartoons shows Linus, trying to give up his blanket, forcing Charlie Brown to promise to withhold the blanket, no matter how much Linus begs. But Charlie Brown, of course, time after time instantly yields. The Cowardly Lion does much the same after Dorothy's been captured, announcing all the terrible ways he'll wreak revenge and asking the Scarecrow and the Tin Woodsman for only one thing: "Talk me out of it." They don't.

Circe teaches the same lesson to Odysseus: The people around you can't stop you. Stop yourself. Don't expect the men to keep you off the rocks. Stop their ears and get yourself tied up; that's the only way you'll defeat temptation: You've got to take care of it yourself. Odysseus's choice here has entered the language even regarding mental health, where troubled patients, during lucid moments, can create advance directives giving doctors permission to take actions the patients may refuse in their shattered mental states. Psychiatrists call these "Ulysses contracts" and struggle with a role somewhere between that of the clever Circe, offering wise counsel, and Odysseus's crew, merely following instructions.

But if you have to look to the mental health system for an example of binding yourself to withstand temptation, you've gone way too far. Look at your hand—there on the third finger of your left. Which brings right back that old concept of the Sirens as enchanting women. I had rather hoped that during my time around the Li Gallis I'd have some delightful flirtation with a woman that I could symbolically resist in one way or the other, but as ever that kind of literalism eluded me. The thing is, of course, you don't really need to be that literal— traveling alone you meet dozens of people every day, some of them of the gender you happen to like, some of those friendly enough to get you thinking. The girl on the bus, whose eyes were so green; the Australian girl in Athens who met me for lunch, then left a note at my hotel. From Rym, my Tunisian escort of uncertain intentions, to Asli, my Turkish companion among the dead, I had no shortage of people with whom to imagine I was being tempted.

Because the lesson, of course, is that the specific people themselves don't really matter. Any moment you weaken, there's always some Siren around. She is the glance on the street, the long pat on the arm, the dangerous hug dance at someone else's wedding. She's out there, and if you need to hear her, she's singing. The inside job, the murmured stock tip, the whispered conversation between your rival and your boss. She's whatever calls to you, whatever you think you need when you think you need something. Sometime, like Odysseus, you have to make your accommodation to her song. And you know before you start: Sometimes what you don't do is as important as what you do.

But here's the thing: If you make sure your hands are tied, if you make sure other hands are on the tiller, if you make sure somebody's eyes are face front—you can listen. If you can learn to embrace the limitation itself—if you demand they bind you to the mast, if you abide by your professional oath, if you tie your own hands and heart with a circle of gold on your finger—you can hear the song, and you can keep off the rocks. And you can listen all you want.

A LOVELY LESSON, and one to take home. But to be honest, the moment of transcendence that I will always associate with the Sirens did not occur when I figured out that resisting temptation was good. It occurred aboard that little yellow rented boat with the Happy Buddha. As a little child, I used to wake up in the middle of the night, hearing cars swoosh by on the big street near our house. If I stood on the bed, I could get my chin on the windowsill and watch the little double cones of their headlights, rushing left, rushing right, pursuing their mysterious errands, and that comforted me. It was not just me, awake, alone in the night. Others were up, going places, doing things, certain in unknowable purposes of their own. I marveled at that certainty, unable to imagine who could be so sure, so aware of where they needed to be, that they could be out in those rushing cars in the night. That will, that motivating force, mystified me.

And then there I was, in a little yellow boat on the vast blue sea, with a smiling round Italian man at the helm, making a patient, certain way to the island home of the Sirens. From somewhere beyond the ken of my childish mind I had come upon that motivation, that certainty. The moment brought goose bumps, but I was still mystified by it.

And I still had a long way to go.

Chapter 13

The Truth About

Consequences:

The Choice Between Scylla and Charybdis

> On the other side are two cliffs, and the sharp peak of one is so high that it hits the wide sky, where a dark unmelting cloud surrounds it. . . . About halfway up is a cave, a gloomy cavern facing the West and Erebus. . . . In it lives Scylla, yelping terribly. . . . She has twelve feet in all, horribly dangling, and six necks, tremendously long, on each of which is a terrible head with teeth in triple tiers. . . . Now the other cliff, as you will see, Odysseus, is lower . . . beneath which the demon Charybdis sucks down the black water. Three times a day she belches it back and three times sucks it down, most horribly!
>
> —*The Odyssey*, Book XII

THE NIGHTTIME TRAIN RIDE SOUTH FROM NAPLES is like the disco scene from *Apocalypse Now*, a place of chaos, lawlessness, and surging crowds. Every cubic centimeter of space on the train is filled with overheated human flesh; narrowed eyes, feigned sleep, almost no conversation within compartments, overt hostility should you try to walk down an aisle. With no sleepers available I buy a first-class ticket, which at least guarantees me a seat. When I board at 9 p.m. for the six-hour ride, two Italian men and I find the compartment with our reserved seats occupied by intransigent Asians—two men and a woman, stretched out across all six seats. We produce, then translate, then fiercely brandish our tickets, but the occupying force remains recalcitrant. The train has long been moving, impasse unresolved, when the conductor comes by. He throws up his hands, exchanging a few words with the Italian men that are clear enough: He and one other conductor must cover the entire train; we're on our own. This stiffens our opponents' resolve, but a few minutes later, surprisingly, he returns, makes a show of checking tickets, and repeats to the invaders several times that they must take their unassigned second-class tickets back to second class. We sit, and they depart momentarily.

The conductor shrugs and leaves, and instantly they're back, with reinforcements; five of them occupy the three unreserved seats in our compartment. I tilt my head back and prepare to endure. I have complained that air travel infantilizes, but now I yearn for its comparative niceties—the principle of getting to sit in the chair you paid for without having to expend scarce resources on defense seems attractive. Sure, air travel renders you lamentably passive, but this night feels rather too active.

I drift in and out of sleep, facing the rear, occasionally awakening to see countryside rolling by backward in the dark; after nearly two months of constant travel, this feels simply normal. Where will I next sleep? Don't know. Look, the moon, a narrowing C, well past full; it was full on the last ferry, a week ago. How back to Rome later? Don't know and, bleary-eyed, don't care. A state of graceless grace, floating on the lake of uncertainty, the unknowableness of travel. Bodies in motion, hurtling through space in the night, squeezed in a compartment with the sweating, the snoring, and the sneering; I clasp my hand over June's ring on the string around my neck and try to breathe deeply. I'm glad when at 3:15 a.m. we roll into Messina, on the far eastern tip of Sicily, a tiny train-ferry hop across the Strait of Messina from Reggio di Calabria. Just north of Messina is the hook of land called Capo Peloro, in the sickle of which supposedly swirls the whirlpool Charybdis; back on the mainland, five minutes north of Reggio, lies Scilla, the cliff town that still bears a sea monster's name. But that's for tomorrow. Stumbling from the train, I instantly befriend a young French couple who emerge at the same time. We pool our guidebook resources and in fifteen minutes bid each other good night in the stairwell of the Hotel

Cairoli, two stars, where the television soothes me to sleep with dubbed *Star Trek*. Scotty appears not to have the accent in Italian.

A FERRY RUNS BETWEEN MESSINA AND REGGIO DI CALABRIA about every twenty minutes. It takes less than half an hour to cross, and you don't even buy passage for a specific journey. It costs a euro or so, the ticket comes out of a machine, and nobody asks you for it during your brief time aboard. And not only car and passenger ferries shuttle across the channel. Cruise ships, cargo ships, train shuttles, and countless other vessels pass between Sicily and the mainland constantly, several times an hour, twenty-four hours a day. Were ever two monsters so disrespected?

It didn't use to be so easy. Circe has told Odysseus that after he passes the Sirens he has a choice. He'll come to the Wandering Rocks, which clash together on any ship or creature that tries to pass between them; "not even wings are sufficient to pass them safely by," she says, then mentions the *Argo*, the famous ship of Jason on his quest for the Golden Fleece, the only vessel to have ever safely gone between, and that only with the help of the goddess Hera. In later descriptions, Jason's Wandering Rocks are represented as lying in the Dardanelles and Athena as his protector; some therefore claim that these represent a different pair of moving rocks, pairs of which perhaps dot the Mediterranean like novelty salt-and-pepper shakers. No matter, Circe's advice is clear. Wandering Rocks: not recommended.

The alternative to this certain death involves another choice: between Scylla and Charybdis. On one side of a passage so narrow "you could shoot an arrow from one [side] to the other" is a vast cliff. Facing westward, halfway up, is a cave, within which lies the terrible monster Scylla. With twelve feet, six long necks, and six mouths lined with triple rows of teeth, she fishes from her lair for dolphin and dogfish. And, of course, for men from passing ships: "with each of her heads she snaps up a man."

The other cliff is lower. Atop it stands a fig tree, but below, the whirlpool Charybdis sucks anything that passes several times a day. Circe speaks frankly: Choose Scylla, "for it's better to mourn for six of your men than to lose the whole crew." Odysseus wonders whether he might not at least arm himself and have a chance to fight off Scylla, but Circe rolls her eyes: "[Scylla's] evil is deathless, terrible, dire, and ferocious—truly invincible! . . . To flee her is bravest and best." If Odysseus hangs around fighting, she'll just have the chance to eat more of his men.

Circe is exactly right. After they pass the Sirens, the men catch sight of the Wandering Rocks, "smoke and great waves and . . . the roar and booming of surf," dropping their oars in panic. Odysseus encourages the crew, wisely guiding them away, toward Scylla. He urges them forward as they row, telling them to stay clear of Charybdis—but wisely making no mention of the monster, "since I didn't want my men too frightened to row." Despite Circe's advice, he arms himself and takes a position in the bow, scanning for Scylla. As the ship moves forward, Charybdis "suck[s] down the briny seawater, and whenever she belched it back she would be all boiling and foaming like a cauldron on a roaring fire." Odysseus and the men stare transfixed.

Naturally, that's when Scylla strikes, grabbing "the six best and strongest men I had. I looked back at the ship and my crew just in time to see their ascending feet and hands dangling above me. They shrieked out to me in their anguish, for the last time calling my name. . . . Then, in the mouth of her cave, she devoured them, screaming and reaching their hands toward me in their horrible throes." Then just that quickly the ship passes out of further danger, but the cost has been great: "Of all the sights I suffered while searching the sea-lanes," Odysseus says, "this was the most heart-rending." Odysseus made a hard choice. The right one, of course, but that doesn't make him feel any better. Because the obvious—and perfectly true—message here is simple: Choice is a bitch.

YOUR FRIEND IS DATING the worst person ever. Mean, irresponsible, two-faced, whatever. Your friend is in trouble but can't see it, and asks your advice.

The most common of all human situations, right? So you ask the most common question: "Do you want me to tell you what you want to hear? Or do you want my honest thoughts?" The friend begs: "Be straight with me, you're the only one I can trust." So you say what you think, and the friend, stunned, withdraws in pain and humiliation. Maybe years later the friendship returns, maybe not; either way, it's never the same. Or you smile supportively and say, "Don't worry," and when the situation inevitably explodes, the friend implores, "Why didn't you tell me? I counted on you!"

Ah, the choices of adulthood. Remember the choices of youth? "Hmm, college or the merchant marine?" Interesting, worth thinking about, but really, for most of us, an 80-20; not a hard call. "Hey, I'm engaged, but it's late, and I'm drunk, and you're kind of pretty . . . do you suppose it would be okay if . . ." Again—easy to understand, tempting to be sure, but in the end a no-brainer, 90-10 at least, for being smart.

And then comes adulthood, when the easy choices—the *easy* ones—are 51-49, and the hard ones make the Ouija board look scientific. Stay in the boring but stable job, supportive of family, surrounded by friends—or take the chance on the position with so much promise, yanking family up by the roots to new town, schools, friends? How about the same question, only put not to you, but to your spouse? Or say you've got that boss, and you've had all you can take of this cul-de-sac of a career path. The band is sure sounding good these days, and maybe this is the moment to just take the leap; on the other hand, health insurance is nice, and so is rent money. You can make all the legal-pad lists you like, but every one of these questions ends up a push—and by the time you're thirty-five or so, these are the only questions you face; the easy ones are long gone. In middle age, you face the stark truth: You gotta give something to get something, and what you give is always awfully valuable, and what you get neither guaranteed nor clear. Every dilemma comes down to a choice between not-secure-enough security and far-too-risky risk. Welcome to adulthood.

And then here we come sailing between Scylla and Charybdis: the terrible certainty that if we choose Scylla six men die—though the others will certainly live—versus the terrifying risk that in avoiding the sacrifice of those six we may all go down. This perfectly represents the decisions of adulthood, even before you add in that even getting to Scylla and Charybdis required the difficult decision about the Wandering Rocks. Odysseus chooses the painful but less-fatal option—Scylla—and has to watch the monster grab six of his men. It sounds hideous. Odysseus, who survived the bloodbath at Troy, who saw the Cyclops eat six of his mean alive, who saw eleven ships' worth snuffed out in an instant among the Laestrygonians—Odysseus calls watching six men die in Scylla's cave the worst thing he's seen on his travels.

Of course it was—Odysseus did the hard, adult thing, and made a terribly difficult choice. He managed his information sensibly. Everybody got to know about the Sirens and the Wandering Rocks, but no crew who knew about Scylla would row into her territory, so he kept that to himself. It worked, but the remembered cries of those who died as a result of your cleverness will probably keep you up nights. Anyhow, it will if you're willing to take responsibility for your decisions, and by this point that's Odysseus. It weighs on him. The kicker is that Odysseus later ends up having to face Charybdis anyway.

That accurately represents adult choices to me; that sounds like the world I live in. Homer described it perfectly almost three thousand years ago, and nobody's improved the description since then.

AS FOR WHERE TO FIND this awful choice, in the fifth century BC, Thucydides blithely described "the strait in question . . . between Rhegium [Reggio] and Messina . . . [as] the Charybdis through which the story makes Ulysses sail," and since then and probably even before there has been universal agreement that Homer here describes the narrow Strait of Messina. Every source from Thucydides to the most modern points out that though most places in the Mediterranean show limited tidal variation, the current in the Strait of Messina changes direction with each high and low tide; water from the Ionian, to the south, is colder and more saline (thus denser), causing all kinds of subversions, upwellings, and swirls when the waters slop back and forth four times a day, rendering it a complicated place for navigation. Homer merely misspoke, Strabo suggests, when he said Charybdis cycled only three times per day.

Regarding the sea monster, Strabo quotes Polybius on how much Homer's description of Scylla fishing for men as well as underwater prey ("as a fisherman out on a point of rock, with a long pole casting his baits for what he can catch . . . hooks a fish and flings it flapping ashore, so they were snatched up towards the cliff") fits the details of actual methods fishermen of this area still use to catch swordfish, dolphins, and dogfish, which Homer describes Scylla herself eating. "Homer attributed to Scylla that sort of fish-hunting which is most characteristic of Scyllaeum," Strabo says. Further quoting Polybius, Strabo notes that the alternating currents funnel large schools of fish into the narrow strait, where the largest predators thus enjoy constant and easy hunting, further connecting the strait to place of frenzied feeding. More modern interpreters opine that Scylla's many arms and legs fancifully represent the tentacles of a giant squid, the likes of which may surface here along those rising currents from the nearby depths of the Ionian; lines of suckers, of course, stand in for her rows of teeth.

Add in that the brief description of the Wandering Rocks could easily describe the smoky, noisy isle of Stromboli, farthest east of the Aeolians (some suggest the Wandering Rocks could even be, as others suggest of the island of Aeolus, the floating pumice that accompanies volcanic eruptions), and Scylla's location seems perfectly sure. As ever, why not? Perhaps Phoenician sailors brought tales of terror from these tricky waters to Greece; perhaps Greek colonists saw the waters and said, "Scylla and Charybdis!" Perhaps a real guy named Odysseus faced two monsters. In any case, since people have thought about it, the Strait of Messina has been home to the legend of one of the most terrifying sea passages in history.

And I crossed it, barely aware, at three in the morning. I woke up in Messina ready to make a better job of it in daylight.

THE PASSENGERS ON THE OVERFLOWING TRAINS SOUTH do not stop in Messina; they carry on to beaches and tourist towns throughout Sicily, ignoring what is basically a modern transportation hub. Thus, when my hotel gave me a breakfast voucher to a coffee bar around the corner, I sipped my cappuccino and ate my *cornetto* in peace, reading the *International Herald Tribune*. Messina is like Troy—a city that doesn't know when to quit. A mere forty miles or so north of the active volcano Mount Etna, Messina receives the same kind of shake-ups that Naples does (and that Troy does; the Mediterranean is riddled with faults) and so is routinely devastated by earthquakes—an especially bad one occurred in 1783; in 1908 one even worse completely destroyed the town (seventy thousand died), though Messinians set their jaws and once again rebuilt. Plus, the town's situation on a major harbor on a major strait on a major trade route has brought it more than its share of conquest, of course—a few varieties of Greeks and Romans were followed by the Goths, the Byzantines, the Arabs, the Angevins, the Aragonese, and the Bourbons until, finally, Messina became part of the emerging Italian state. Shelling during World War II, unfortunately, significantly destroyed landmarks rebuilt after the 1908 quake.

And yet hard-luck Messinians are tremendously tough—they rebuilt again, and today Messina is a modern town of wide streets and leafy parks, and after my cappuccino I went to investigate. At the dockside I instantly found what I was looking for: a fountain made by the sculptor Giovanni Angelo Montorsoli in 1557, all brilliant white, of three figures: Poseidon (called by his Romanized name of Neptune); Charybdis, hideous maw open, chained at his left; and Scylla chained at his right, dog snouts girding her around the middle. (Traditional representations of Scylla made her rather human, with a woman's torso and head and six extra dog heads coming from her waist; she's described that way by Ovid, who says she was turned into such a beast by none other than Circe, angry as the result of a love pentangle including, if you can believe it, the Cyclops Polyphemus.) Poseidon now faces the sea, holding his famous trident, though the sculpture was designed to stand on the shore with Poseidon's back to the sea, so his outstretched hand conveys less the act of calming the waters than of claiming the town as his own. Odysseus certainly wouldn't have disagreed.

The bright-white fountain is filled with seahorses and serpents, jetting pleasing arcs of water into various bowls, the whole thing shimmering beneath a bright sun on a lovely partly cloudy day. I watched the fountain for ten or fifteen minutes. Then I walked to the Stazione Marittima and hopped on a ferry. And then a half hour later I stood on the shore at Reggio. I had spent the night with Charybdis, already crossed between the two monsters twice, and it was barely noon. I found a ticket for the train to Scilla. Ten minutes later there I stood, on a stony little beach beneath the famous cliff, which a nice man told me the locals called the Scolio Ulisse—the cliff of Ulysses. At its top a castle got its start in the ninth century, continually improved and fortified—though wrecked by the occasional earthquake—ever since. I promised myself a visit, but I had other priorities, because I saw an important sign on the beach.

NOLEGGIO CANOE: canoe rental. One more chance to hire a boat in Italy; how could I resist? The two fellows beneath the umbrella initially suggested that since nobody else wanted to take a tour of the strait at the moment, perhaps I would come back tomorrow. I wasn't buying; not that old game. They could rent me a boat or not, but I was about finished with coming back later. They shrugged—moto or kayak? My eyes widened, and we made an exchange: I gave them my knapsack and documents to keep dry and 5 euros, and they gave me a blue fiberglass kayak and a paddle. And thus alone, in a tiny little boat under my own steam, I paddled out between Scylla and Charybdis.

I can't say I felt any dangerous currents, and I can't claim to have heard any whimpering from Scylla (she supposedly makes a hideous yelping noise, "no stronger than that of a puppy just born"). And I doubt I made it actually through the entire crossing—once you've paddled for half an hour or so and find yourself in the middle of a channel, with monstrous containerships churning along in the center and ferries passing closer by, a kayak starts to feel like a mighty small boat. Of course, I never got anywhere near the main channel, and I buzzed happily over the mostly limpid surface of the strait. I did have to orient the wobbly kayak into the wakes of those containerships, and when I was tardy, water slopped in. I spent the rest of the day slightly damp, appreciative that the men under the umbrella had insisted I leave my knapsack with them. When I got far enough from shore that I couldn't recognize my particular beach, I felt insecure, so I paddled out only until I could reassure myself that, facing south, to my left I could see Scilla and to my right see the hook north of Messina. I floated there peaceably for a while, absurdly thrilled: I was, quite literally, between Scylla and Charybdis, and all signs pointed toward living to tell the tale. I saw no cave in the cliff, of course, and felt no whirling tug on my paddle, but I was happy. After my troubled weeks chasing Circe and the kingdom of the dead, my visits to the Sirens and Scylla and Charybdis had gone extremely smoothly. I sat there cheerfully, rocking in what I can describe only as a gentle current, then paddled back to the beach.

After returning the boat, I sat down with the two men beneath the umbrella, pulling out a loaf of bread and some grapes I had brought for a snack, and we shared the food and a genial hour of conversation in a pastiche of Italian, French, German, and the few words of English they had. They approved of my quest and couldn't remember the last time they had rented a kayak to someone similarly engaged; we discussed the leaders of our countries (*"Boosh—pazzo, sì?"* followed by searching looks); and when we reached the crumbling fringes of our language skills we laughed and bid genuinely fond farewells. I walked up steep streets to the little town of Scilla itself, in a saddle at the base of the rock outcropping that formed the cliff. I lingered alone in a tiny plaza outside a little *pasticceria* for a couple pieces of pizza and an orange soda and then sat inside for some kind of delicious creamy pastry. Nearby, a wall-mounted bas-relief sculpture of "Scilla Mitologica" dispensed drinking water; she looked like a mermaid. I went inside the castle, now a museum, and there I saw nice terra-cotta representations of Scylla and Charybdis and maps showing where the dangerous whirlpool was supposed to be.

On the ferry back, I kept an eye out for any of the telltale upwellings or swirlings that so many other sources describe rendering the strait dangerous, but I saw no indication of anything like a complex current. I watched the ferry captain pull the ferry into the Messina harbor with no more attention than a mom pulling her minivan into a commodious garage. I tried to look over his shoulder at his charts, and he engaged me in conversation. I was a little sheepish, but I asked: This business about Charybdis . . . a whirlpool, dangerous currents, you know . . . all that. Was any of that . . . you know . . . for real?

Once when I was perhaps twelve or thirteen—anyhow, too old for it—I was in a national park in one of the states where the jackalope postcard shows up in gift shops and forms part of the tour guide rap. After a tour, I hung around the guide and finally asked him: The whole jackalope thing, that was . . . that was just made up, right? I mean, right? I'll never forget the look on his face—the dropped chin, the twitch of a sneer; the disappointment that a child so old should still be so stupid. A dentist must direct this expression at an adolescent who asks about the tooth fairy. "What do you think?" the ranger asked me with a hint of actual disgust. I had hoped that would be the last time I ever saw that expression.

Then that ferry captain looked at me for several seconds. Then he inhaled, and he spoke. "No," he said. "No, no, no. Never, never, never." Then he gave me a tight smile, raised an eyebrow—Anything else, you idiot?—and excused himself. I went back to my hotel, my shorts still lightly damp from the waters of the strait.

AFTER THE 1908 EARTHQUAKE, Messinians created a museum that the brochure describes as a sort of Noah's ark for what they recovered from previous museums as well as art from—and fragments of—the city's collapsed churches and ruined public buildings. In one sense it makes a sad exhibit, conjuring a beautiful city, lost over and over again. Just the same, freed from their spots of distant honor in apse and nave, spectacular mosaics of cobalt and gilt gaze at you from eye-level niches three feet away; it's like having a front-row seat to the moment the Middle Ages turned into the Renaissance. Majolica tiles cover reconstructed columns no farther away than the end of your nose. You will probably get a better—and closer—look at a Caravaggio (The Raising of Lazarus) at the Museo Regionale di Messina than anywhere else in the world. Outside the museum are strewn architectural details—columns, fractured statuary, friezes—from tumbled Messinian buildings, and again you can't help but think of Troy: What might you be able to find at Troy if like this they had treasured the remains of what came before rather than, as they naturally did, reusing them?

But Messina is at its best with what remains standing. Two-tone Byzantine arches mark the twelfth-century church of the Annunziata dei Catalani (built atop the remains of an ancient temple to Neptune), and though a vast staircase into the hillside is about all that's left of the seventeenth-century church atop Monte di Pietà, the view of the city and the strait is worth the hot climb.

From there you can see the city's highlight—the cathedral, its clock tower, and the Piazza Immacolata, which contains another spectacular fountain by Montorsoli, this one featuring Orion. Inside the cathedral, completely rebuilt since 1908, and again after 1943, the lofty timbered ceiling covered in paintings and mosaics is worth a half hour of gazing on its own. And outside the church is that clock tower. Built in the 1500s, it was struck by lightning in 1588; damaged in the earthquake of 1783; and utterly destroyed in 1908. Rebuilt in the manner of its predecessors, it now contains what Messinians claim is the world's largest animated clock, a thing of clattering gilded mechanical horses and chariots, moving cathedrals, trumpeting angels, and even a mechanical golden skeletal angel of death with a scythe, though none of them do much more than rattle in a little arc, out one stone portal and toward another. Cocks crow, lions roar, and the tower eventually blares the "Ave Maria"—the whole noontime show lasts a good ten minutes. In the side of the tower is a large orrery along with a phase-of-the-moon globe, a calendar, and a year indicator. When I was there all were wrong except the year (though I couldn't really tell about the planets). Maybe it needed oiling—I'm sure the Messinians will get to it.

FOR TRAVEL BEYOND Scylla and Charybdis, Circe gave Odysseus only one piece of advice: Whatever you do, avoid the cattle belonging to the sun god, Helios. Naturally, that's the next place the crew goes—and delightfully, that place is associated with the city of Taormina, about an hour south of Messina by train. That meant I could stay in my hotel another night, making three in the Cairoli, nearly a record for my trip.

Luxury.

Chapter 14

Everyone Loves a Hero:

The Cattle of the Sun

Next you will reach the island Thrinacia. There you'll find grazing the cattle and wooly fat sheep of Helios, seven herds of cattle and seven fair flocks of sheep. . . . If one hair you harm, I foretell utter destruction for your ship and crew, and should you yourself escape, your return will be lonely, late, and unhappy.

—*The Odyssey*, Book XII

THE TRAIN TO TAORMINA travels the Circumetna Line, so on the ride of less than an hour from Messina I gazed up to my right at the black cone of the volcano, smoke running down its side like a stream in the coolish morning air. I found greater amazement, however, at the view to my left as we trundled south. Most of the way down we could look across the widening Strait of Messina at the tip of the mainland. Then suddenly, just before the stop for Taormina, the opposite coast veered sharply east and vanished—we had reached the bottom of the boot of Italy. Ithaca lay far to the east, off the Greek coast—and here, at Taormina, for the first time you could turn east without a great big hunk of Europe in the way. If you were trying to get to Ithaca from Messina, you'd go down to Taormina and turn left. Once you're on the general western Mediterranean route of *The Odyssey*, geographically, at least, Taormina fits the travels perfectly.

It doesn't fit anything else, but there's no reason why it should. The ancients are completely silent on the location of the island of the sun god, and moderns seem to adopt Taormina for the same reason I did:

It's convenient, and it fits. Still, the name *Thrinacia* that Homer gives the sun god's island does sound similar to *Trinacria,* the name used by Greeks and Romans for Sicily: It means triangular, which Sicily manifestly is. Regarding cattle, Taormina, dug into almost vertical cliffs above the sea at the foot of Monte Tauro, takes for its symbol a woman with the legs and torso of a bull. Of course, Homer also describes the island as small, able to support only the magical flocks of the sun god and little other animal life, which is the exact opposite of Sicily. Whatever; Taormina was, literally, close enough—an hour from Messina— and it would do. A trip there couldn't possibly do any worse for me than it had for Odysseus.

THE ONLY REASON HOMER SENDS ODYSSEUS to the island of the sun god is to get rid of the rest of his crew so that his journey can, as any transformational journey must, leave him finally, utterly, alone. If he learns a lesson there it's nearly as simple as the one he found among the Laestrygonians: Sometimes, you just can't win for losing.

Tiresias, in the halls of Hades, told Odysseus: Whatever you do, don't eat the cattle of the sun god. Circe told him the same thing, her last piece of excellent advice: Under no circumstances may you touch even a hair on the hide of these cattle. Eat the cattle, the crew dies. So as soon as they're past Scylla and Charybdis, and Helios's nice-looking island of Thrinacia appears, Odysseus tells the crew what Tiresias and Circe had told him: "there . . . lies the worst of all evils for us! So come now, and row on out from this island and leave it astern."

Remember, please, that since the debacle of the Laestrygonians— itself definitely not his fault—Odysseus is on a winning streak. He got Circe to return his crew from swine to human form and got them a yearlong rest in the bargain; then he successfully led his men to hell and back. He kept them from certain death near the Sirens and led them away from the Wandering Rocks. In the terrible strait between Scylla and Charybdis he lost only six men, a pretty good deaths-per-affected-crewmen-per-monster ratio—his best, actually, on the trip. After all this, he mentions to them that though the next island they come to looks nice, he has been told by two different supernatural beings—the shade of Tiresias and the sorceress Circe—that this island is the one place in the entire world they should avoid, for it holds the cattle owned by the sun god Helios, and if the men touch a single hair on one of those cattle the entire crew will die.

So naturally the men want to land there.

Odysseus's old pal Eurylochus—the man so frightened of Circe, the annoying guy somehow related to Odysseus by marriage—talks back. "It seems you're made of iron," Eurylochus says, "since you won't allow your friends, exhausted with toil and lack of sleep, to set foot ashore on this sea-girt island, where we might enjoy a good meal." He raises the specter of terrible winds in the night, asking that they stop at least until morning. The crew backs Eurylochus, and Odysseus caves. "I'm one against many," he says, a universal truth: Without the support of your crew, you're worse than alone.

The crew's mutiny should surprise nobody—what group since the dawn of time hasn't taken the first opportunity to turn away from the only one who can save it? You can't help but compare this moment to the land of the Cicones, where Odysseus failed to control his crew. Odysseus has learned something since then, for even in his belief that "a god was plotting some evil against us," before he beaches the ship, he still once again warns the men about the herds of Helios and makes them swear they will under no circumstances touch the animals. Of course, they swear.

If you miss the wonderful irony of the oath (this entire course of madness really started, after all, when Odysseus got the suitors of Helen to swear the oath that forced them all to follow Agamemnon to war at Troy), Homer brings in another element from the story's roots: the contrary wind. The storm that blew Odysseus off course and on to the Lotus-eaters, the winds from the bag of Aeolus that blew them away from Ithaca, the wind at Aulis before the fleet sailed for Troy, to change which Agamemnon sacrificed his own daughter—contrary winds densely populate the stories of *The Odyssey, The Iliad,* the entire Epic Cycle. They remind you yet again: Go ahead, mortals, make your plans—the gods will do as they wish. So when the crew says to Odysseus, "Just for one night! Come on, we're not all Superman like you, can't we just stop and eat?" Odysseus tries only once to say,

"Anyplace—*anyplace* else. Just not here." But he sees the will of the gods, does his best, then gives up. They stop, just for one meal and a night's rest.

Cue contrary wind.

It blows for a month, during which the crew runs short on food, trying to get by on such fish and birds they can catch on Thrinacia. Things get worse. Odysseus apparently sees it coming and can't stand to watch; he reminds the men once again to keep their hands off the cattle (it's the third time he's told them) and goes off to pray for the guidance of the gods. The gods, jokesters as ever, put him to sleep.

While Odysseus sleeps, Eurylochus—who else?—starts talking. They can build a nice temple to Helios when they get home, he says; Helios won't mind if they eat a few cattle. And if before then an angry Helios wrecks their ship, better "to gulp at a wave and give up the ghost all at once, than have life leak out drop by drop on a desolate island!" The hungry men buy in; let the barbecue begin. Supplies are so low the men don't even have wine for a proper libation to the gods, so they use water. Proper libations wouldn't have saved them, but the snub has to add insult to injury. The sun god misses nothing; he demands that Zeus punish the crew—if not, Helios threatens to go shine in the underworld. Zeus tells him to relax: "As for the offenders, I'll soon strike their swift ship with a bolt of dazzling fire."

There's a nice reaction scene when Odysseus, like Moses coming down from Sinai and seeing the worship of the golden calf, comes back from communing with the gods to smell the burning meat. Whether it's a spit-take, a whap of palm to forehead, or just a slow shaking of the head, you feel Odysseus thinking: "Oh for pity's sake, what next?" The hides of the cattle begin crawling along the ground, and the meat "both roasted and raw" begins to bellow. You want to know hungry? For an entire week, the men continue to eat meat that's actually mooing at them. That's hungry.

Zeus stops the gale. The men clamber aboard. And as soon as they're out of sight of land here come the clouds, then the hurricane winds, and finally the lightning bolt we've known would come for the crew since the first lines of the poem: "Thus [the Gods] took their returning from them," Homer tells us. In the final analysis, the only person you can really be responsible for is yourself, and after this adventure, that's who Odysseus has left. From twelve full ships, he's down to one guy floating in a storm on a raft he's made from a couple pieces of the shattered ship.

He's washed back to Charybdis, the whirlpool; he leaps up to the bark of a fig tree just above it. He clings there like a bat from dawn, when the whirlpool first sucks down his raft, until the end of the day when she disgorges it and he jumps back on. After that he drifts another ten days, ending up where we first met him: on Calypso's shore. Then come seven long years there, then Hermes visits with the note from Zeus that Odysseus can go home, followed by the long boat trip, the shipwreck, and his washing ashore on the island of the Phaeacians. In addressing those very Phaeacians as he finishes the tale of his travels, Odysseus stops when he washes ashore with Calypso: "But why am I telling you this?" he asks. "Just yesterday I told this part of my story to you, and I strongly dislike repeating what I've already said as well as I know how to say it."

FROM MY JOURNAL: *Taormina: a place where cattle are eaten to deleterious effect. No doubt, but it's not the visitors eating the cattle: the visitors are the cattle. I like the four-euro map better than the town.*

The map really is very nice, but, of course, really so is the town—that's why it's on the itinerary of every single package tour and cruise ship in the Mediterranean. My snide attitude may have had something to do with seeing Taormina—a mountainside town with narrow, cobbled streets; pale yellow and white buildings with red tile roofs; and second-story balconies covered with bougainvillea—after having seen Positano, and Capri, and Amalfi, and Bonifacio, all of which fit that general description. Or Taormina may have just fallen so late in my travels that I was tired and it was time to get my jaded eyes home—surely, when you're in one of the most beautiful cities in the Mediterranean and you're rolling your eyes, it's time to go.

For me, in fact, it was. I had left home with the idea that I was beginning the first leg of several in making my complete Odyssean journey. I planned to go as long as I could until exhaustion, lack of funds, or something at home made me stop, and then reassess. But one place led to another, sometimes surprisingly smoothly, and for a period it even seemed plausible that I would complete my entire journey in one long go. Then work called me home, and from the south of Italy I planned my return flight from Rome. Taormina, I knew, would be my last stop on this portion of my journey. As I wandered Taormina's charming plazas, the side streets that went up steps deeper into the side of the mountain, I realized that its well-touristed streets would be the far point of my journey, and I think I was just haughty with how far I'd gone. I visited the obligatory Greek theater, this one improved by the Romans and very well preserved, with a lovely view of Etna over the stage, and my journal reads, "4 euros fifty for the peace of knowing I didn't miss something."

Fortunately, Taormina is so genuinely beautiful that I got over myself pretty quickly. I walked down the Corso Umberto, the town's lovely, narrow main drag that every now and then opens up into a tiny but breathtaking piazza. Since the town bans cars in its pedestrianized center, walking is pleasant, even among the mob of tourists (the day I was there a cruise ship had anchored offshore). Three cobblestone gates, remnants of ancient city walls, arch over Corso Umberto—loveliest of those is the middle one, Porta di Mezzo (it has a two-story stone clock tower, added in 1679), presiding over the checkerboard-tiled Piazza Novo Aprile, surrounded by cafés and churches; I got a coffee and sat on the steps of the church of San Giuseppe. I climbed a long, steep fall of stone stairs; burbling fountains graced the terraces, faces spurting water. I arrived at the sixteenth-century Santuario Madonna della Rocca, carved directly into the side of the mountain and open, I was told, only once a year—not the day I was there. Still, the view was spectacular: cypresses spilling down the side of the mountain, the city nestled in below, the vast blue sea beyond.

Since my main goal for the day was to not enrage the gods by eating forbidden cattle, I assembled for myself at a little alimentaria a vegetarian lunch of grapes, cheese, olives, bread, and water, which I ate in the city's absolutely dreamy terraced public garden, affording not only shaded benches, fountains, and cypresses among the sandy pathways, but also a vast terrace with a brick balustrade, between whose urns filled with plantings you can again gaze out toward the sea. Finally, I visited the small Duomo, which though not a cathedral (as its name implies) has lovely exposed dark beams, a beautiful wooden ceiling, and a castellated cobblestone Gothic facade that comfortably presides over the plaza before it. "It has thirty-two types of marble," one Brenda Jenner told me. "That's the only thing it's famous for."

I STOOD IN THAT PLAZA WITH BRENDA because even with my map, even in a town so small as Taormina, I had managed to get lost. I followed my nose up and down the staircased side streets, finding peaceful empty plazas with terra-cotta diamonds in the brick streets, empty benches in the shade, and potted geraniums and cacti framing ancient gothic arches with thick wooden doors. All beautiful enough, but then I found myself somehow outside the town, on roads where cars whizzed by, wondering how to find my way back to see the Duomo, and the statue before it of the half bull, half woman that is the city's symbol. Then came Brenda.

She was carrying out some trash, and instead of asking me to vacate the stone wall on which I sat, poring over my map, she invited me inside. Thus I entered the house she told me was named Casa Cuseni, home of her employer, a ninety-three-year-old deaf, bedridden woman named Daphne Phelps, whom Brenda didn't notify that I was in the house. Brenda was English, from Kent, and it was never clear to me how she came to be Daphne's caretaker, though she said several times: "This is where I have to live . . . looking after Daphne." Daphne, Brenda told me, had been a great friend to the international artistic set that has frequented Taormina. The house felt like an English country home, with bookcases bursting with volumes of Yeats, Byron, and Pepys, art everywhere on the walls.

According to Brenda, Daphne had been quite the hostess in her day. Dispatched by her English family in 1947 to sell the house, she instead fell into the Taormina life, fending off marriage proposals from land-hungry Italians and opening up the house to guests, paying and nonpaying, like Tennessee Williams, Bertrand Russell, and the drunken widow of Dylan Thomas. Daphne wrote it all up in a book called *A House in Sicily,* Brenda said, but unfortunately my eyes were kind of glazing over. I was having trouble enough keeping up with Odysseus and his friends. Did Brenda know how to get back to the Duomo? She led me there, using her own camera to take a picture of me standing cheerfully in front of the statue of the half-bull woman wearing a crown and holding the orb and scepter of state. Whether this was the island of Helios or not, clearly in Taormina they still deeply respect their cattle. Brenda sent me that picture. Daphne died, I later read, in 2005.

TWO LESSONS SHIMMER BENEATH Odysseus's experience among the cattle of the sun god—one epic, one commonsensical. Regarding epic, for a guy who'll do whatever he needs to win, we get yet another glimpse here of the fact that Odysseus is surprisingly reverent. Throughout his story he does everything he can to follow the advice the gods send him, constantly making the appropriate sacrifices; and when he's in trouble he goes to the gods for more advice. He complains when the gods plot against him, but he never blames them for his misfortunes. He never forgets who's in charge.

This places Odysseus in contrast with more than just his crew. The events of *The Iliad,* after all, began when Agamemnon offended Apollo by taking one of his priestesses as a concubine. When Apollo's vengeance on the Greeks (a plague) convinced Agamemnon to return the girl, he assuaged his feelings by taking another from Achilles. Later, Achilles' son Neoptolemus kills the Trojan king Priam at the altar of Zeus; Locrian Ajax rapes Cassandra at the altar of Athena. Agamemnon and Menelaus argue about how to appease Athena, though neither of them succeeds particularly well. That is, by sacrilegiously consuming the immortal cattle of Helios, by not even appropriately sacrificing before they do, Odysseus's crewmen merely uphold the Greek epic tradition of asinine insult of the gods. Eating meat for a week after it begins lowing even on the spit has to receive commendation for special effort in idiocy, but it's nothing new. Anyhow, it gets them all killed, which is what they were scheduled for, as we know from the proem, from the very start.

Against this tide of impiety, consider Odysseus. When his crewmen seal their fates, Odysseus is off praying. When Odysseus learns in the underworld that Elpenor needs a decent burial, he goes right back to Circe's island and takes care of business. Early in the poem, you'll remember, when Telemachus visits Nestor, the old man describes the close relationship between Odysseus and Athena as utterly unique. Even Odysseus's persecution by Poseidon is his own fault, and he seems to understand that. So in case Homer hadn't made it clear before now, on the island of the cattle of the sun he underscores it: Odysseus shows respect for the gods; his crew does not. Check the result.

The more quotidian lesson I gleaned from this bad experience with the sun god I had recognized long before I got to Taormina, and it's pretty simple: In the Mediterranean, in the summer, the sun is not your friend. From my terrible walk in Sparta to my constant application of sunscreen, every day of my travels found me strategizing against the sun. I secreted extra water in my knapsack in places I thought it might not get too hot; a bandanna around my neck could be dipped in the ocean, an irrigation canal, my own drinking water, to help cool me. When I swam, more often than not I kept sunglasses and white canvas hat on, like one of those nice neighbor ladies at the community pool, to keep my retinas from burning in reflected glare and the sun from frying the increasingly unprotected top of my dome. The sun felt like an enemy every day, and I never didn't think about it.

So when Odysseus gets into trouble with Helios, the sun god, I had to think: Well, it figures; around here, the sun is just a bad guy, and maybe this episode is code for that.

IN ANY CASE, from Taormina I turned around, heading back home for a caesura to my travels; after a couple of months, enough things at work finally required attention that I had to go there.

I took an overnight train—virtually empty—to Rome, on which I shared a sleeper cabin with an Italian family. Each bed came with a little package: a pillow cover, a wet nap, a little sealed cup of water, and a pair of paper hospital slippers, I suppose for those late-night shuffles down to the restroom at the end of the carriage. I was thrilled to kick off my boots and put them on. Thereafter, the four of us—and a German traveler who joined us from the corridor, plus the conductor in charge of our car—talked so cheerfully about *The Odyssey* and our various travels that I felt like I was at a slumber party; using Italian, German, French, and English, we puzzled out each other's jobs, goals, families. The conductor for some reason made a project of me, ensuring that I didn't miss the spectacular view from the deck as the ferry carried our train car for the twenty-minute trip across the Strait of Messina. I thought about explaining that this was about my millionth ferry journey in the last couple months, but then I remembered: Take assistance, and enjoy it. I had my little cup of water, the wind over the water ruffling my T-shirt, drying it nicely for sleep. When another ship passed nearby, you saw the people moving about on its deck, and they looked unreal, like an electric train layout or terribly clever animation. I stalked the deck in my ridiculous hospital slippers and sipped my water like it was cognac, then rejoined our party. Someone down the corridor was playing the harmonica badly, but before midnight he stopped, or at least closed his compartment door. We all slept well and woke up in Rome, where I caught a plane.

AT HOME I saw June again with a gasp—the woman who was thickening around the middle when I had left now demonstrably contained a prize inside. She had passed stealing-a-basketball and had reached swallowed-an-army-helmet, and she glowed like a lighthouse. I had feared that seeing her midjourney would either reduce my spirit for the rest of the trip or attenuate my longing for home afterward, but I found the opposite: Suddenly seeing that this child the doctors kept telling us about was actually there and getting bigger made me wish only more urgently to get back out—and then home for good. With the remainder of my trip waiting and time getting short, now was not the time for storytelling; this was no real homecoming. So I hustled to take care of business, figuring the sooner I left, the sooner I would return. And before long, there I was back on a plane to Malta.

And I loved Malta, and I had adventures there, but by the time I left Malta for Sicily, to board the *Clelia II*, I was already thinking about the finish line. With a demonstrably pregnant wife at home I was a man on a mission. Another thing—I was used to traveling by then. Thus, arriving in Sicily before dawn at a tiny regional airport didn't concern me a bit. A bus stop sign with a picture of a choo-choo assured me I had found the way to the train station, and despite the airport's lack of ATM or *bureau de change* I had enough stray euros in my pocket to get me aboard. Train station breakfast, train to Messina, a walk down the quay and aboard the *Clelia II*. But as Odysseus says to the Phaeacians, I've already told you this once.

Chapter 15

Among the Phaeacians II:

Corfu and the Journey by Night

When they reached the ship and the sea, right away the noble young men of the crew took all of these things and stowed them away aboard ship. On the deck at the stern they prepared a soft pallet with linen sheet on which Odysseus was to sleep. Then he came aboard and lay down in silence. They cast off from the bored-stone mooring and sat down in their places to row. And with the first flash of brine from their oarblades a sweet sleep fell on the eyes of Odysseus.

—*The Odyssey*, Book XIII

WHEN ODYSSEUS FINISHES telling his story to the Phaeacians at the banquet, they're stunned: "Throughout the shadowy halls his listeners sat in silence as if enchanted," Homer tells us, instantly resuming his own narrative voice, now that Odysseus is no longer doing the talking. And I wish I could say that when I finished telling the five nice women at my table aboard the cruise ship where I'd been and why, I encountered nothing but enraptured gazes. Instead, I had one of those moments where you notice that everyone else has mostly finished their entrée and yours alone stands uneaten because you've been talking the whole time. Once you're there, all you can do is brazen it out; I thank goodness that they were polite, and I just hoped I had got most of it right.

But I confess a certain satisfaction. By relating my tale to my new friends aboard the *Clelia II*, I had participated in the oldest tradition imaginable: I had spoken my tale aloud.

This oral repetition was central not just to *The Odyssey* but to my pursuit of its locations and its meaning. In Taormina, for example, I heard Brenda's stories about the high jinks in the Casa Cuseni, and then when I later ran across book reviews of *A House in Sicily* and ultimately the obituary for Daphne Phelps, I found that Brenda's stories had been around 70 percent on the money—most of what she recounted to me was true. I figure that ranks her pretty high on the source-trustworthiness scale, given three elements affecting repeated stories: the unreliability of human memory, the universal need to organize stories (and improve our own parts in them), and the fact that even things repeated correctly might not have been true when somebody first told them. In thinking about *The Odyssey*, you have to add in a fourth factor that trumps all the others: Does it work?

Because if not, you're allowed to change it.

THE ODYSSEY, everybody agrees, first appears written down sometime in the eighth or seventh century BC. Before that, in some form or another, it was passed along orally, mouth to ears, for unknowable generations, probably in performance-sized fragments sung at competitions, festivals, or feasts by poets who plucked a lyre as accompaniment.

Even the ancient Greeks recognized that the Homeric poems had their origins in oral stories. Bards performing these stories—they do so several times in *The Odyssey*—would entertain gatherings by relating one or another episode from the vast shared mythology of the Epic Cycle. To put it in a more modern sense, return to my friend and guide Narcy Calamatta from Malta: "Heroes and gods were their celebrities," he said of the ancients—they didn't have *American Idol* or sitcoms, televised sports or even a single variety of *Law & Order*. Instead, they had the myths and stories of the gods and the age of heroes. Homer describes the great respect with which the poets are treated, and the rapt attention they receive, when the blind poet Demodocus is gently led in to sing for the Phaeacians: "Throughout the earth, the portion of poets is honor and reverence," Homer notes, presumably with a blush. Nestor concurs earlier in the poem when he tells Telemachus that Agamemnon protected Clytemnestra's honor by leaving "a bard . . . there with her." (Clytemnestra succumbed to the flattery of Aegisthus, her paramour, only after Aegisthus carried off the poet and abandoned him on a desert island.) Poets, that is, had respect.

And poets, being performers, did just like anybody who's ever told a story more than once, anyone who's ever had a funny or interesting anecdote that became a dinner party staple: They worked on it. If the "No-Man" trick got a laugh or a gasp, it stayed. If during another description of landing boats or eating sheep half the people at the table fell asleep, that would probably get trimmed or deleted. The story would assert itself through generations of telling. This explains not only how various versions of the myths emerged, but also how the myths themselves achieved their final form.

Twentieth-century researchers have actually traced this process. Harvard professor Milman Parry, trying to understand the different epithets in Homer, went to Yugoslavia, where he listened to illiterate bards who still had the job of performing traditional poems. Parry noticed that the performers were doing less reciting than improvising—that is, these oral poets were less like classical musicians who have memorized a strict score than like jazz performers improvising on established themes.

Greek-American scholar James Notopoulos, who after World War II studied similar oral storytellers on Crete, found an actual example of how a story developed. He asked a local bard for a tale about a famously daring wartime operation on Crete in which two British officers parachuted in and with help from Cretan guerrillas kidnapped a German general. The bard proceeded to sing a tale in accordance with some of the main facts, but starring Cretan protagonists, with added specious elements like the sacrifice by a beautiful young woman of her honor for the good of Crete. Notopoulos found this massive change in the story a mere nine years after the events, in an age when the facts of the events were everywhere recorded. Imagine the development in story, in presentation, in character, in location, during the hundreds of years between the possibly real events of the plausibly real Trojan War and the commitment to paper of the epics by the possibly real poet possibly named Homer, maybe in the eighth century BC, at the dawn of the age of writing. All of which is to say that the more I learned, the more my goal focused on what had first captured me when I returned to Homer, before I had begun digging into theory and research: the desire to understand the episodes, not their specific geography.

Anyhow, it's no wonder that even by Homer's time different versions of these myths appear; the amazing thing is how strong the core of the story has remained for millennia. Who's to say whether the Cyclops didn't once eat all the crew except Odysseus, or that the story was just a little flat until the "No-Man" trick entered, and then the bards found it a crowd-pleaser? Who knows whether Odysseus didn't once have an adventure with the Wandering Rocks until bards found out that between the Sirens and Scylla and Charybdis that just made one sea adventure too many, and stopped using it, though they still mentioned it? These stories, then, developed as a kind of collaboration between the skilled bards as tellers and the audience: the world's first focus groups. No wonder these stories still seem to reach so deeply into us, the listeners, into our personal understandings of the world: In a sense, they emerged from there in the first place.

The same thing goes on even now, of course. We have our own mythological pantheon—including Spider-Man and Batman, say, or James Bond, or Luke Skywalker—and every now and then somebody crafts a new way of telling their stories, flings it out there, and sees what sticks. We're on at least our seventh Superman cycle, for example, and the Internet is full of new stories, called fan fiction, about the *Star Trek* characters—commonly about them having gay sex, in fact—and who's to say what will last? Telling stories—telling the oldest stories—is something people have been doing since the dawn of time. Homer did it, and for the series of adventures for which he is best known he made Odysseus do it among the Phaeacians. And I did it among Phaeacians of my own there on the *Clelia II*. I wondered whether my stories, too, had received subtle, unconscious editing even as I told them—even, for that matter, as I wrote about them in my journals when they happened. I told the stories as candidly as I could, and I didn't notice any yawns. Maybe I just wasn't looking.

Dinner ended with the ritual exchange of e-mail addresses—that constant modern low-cost guest-gift shared among travelers. At night, with a few of the younger passengers, I stood on deck as we steamed toward Corfu, marveling at the midsea visibility of the stars. Discussion of the Southern Cross and who had seen it began an initially genial dispute about whether if you put a tub of water with a hole in the bottom down ten feet north of the equator the Coriolis force would make water drain in a counterclockwise whirlpool, whereas a similar tub ten feet south of the line would drain clockwise. When the argument gained heat, a woman of about my age traveling with her mother suggested that perhaps dancing beneath them took better advantage of the stars than argument. It was hard to disagree.

The next day we landed in Corfu, where I expected to leave the *Clelia II*. The management had specifically invited me only for the overnight passage to Corfu, and I didn't want to overstay my welcome, particularly after my adventure with the General and the Coriolis Affair. I ended up staying aboard another night, for which to some extent I blame the crew, who told me I was welcome to stay on as long as I pleased—they said they liked the way my forty-four years lowered the average age aboard ship. I might have resisted, figuring the crew for being merely being polite. But something that happened later convinced me that my journey would best be fulfilled by sailing on with the *Clelia II*.

CORFU HAS BEEN CONNECTED with the final hosts of Odysseus since Thucydides, who called it "an island whose nautical renown dated from the days of its old inhabitants, the Phaeacians." This identification works, given that Calypso had told Odysseus to sail with the Great Bear on his left—that is, eastward—and he does so for seventeen days, which will get you to islands off the west coast of Greece from just about anywhere in the western Mediterranean. Moreover, if you're drawing on a map, the hundred miles or so between Corfu and Ithaca, while probably more than a mere night's journey, certainly makes a good brief, magical final hop on Odysseus's path.

I couldn't land in Corfu as Odysseus had done—he washed up, don't forget, after sailing seventeen days from Calypso's isle and spending two more bobbing naked in the sea following his shipwreck. In terms of his human journey, though, this arrival carries a lot of weight—Odysseus emerges from the salt water naked and alone, with not even clothes to protect him: as good a metaphor for rebirth as you're ever likely to find. He even goes to sleep beneath "two olive bushes, one of them wild"—itself a wonderful metaphor for the combination of native vigor and civilizing self-control that Odysseus has honed through his travels. And a large part of what Odysseus does among the Phaeacians is resist his final, most earthly temptation: to give up his return and be treated like a king alongside the coltish Nausicaa, who clearly desires him as her husband.

After escaping the supernatural wiles of Circe and Calypso, after slipping by the Sirens, and after suffering only the minimum damage from Scylla and Charybdis, Odysseus could be forgiven for being tempted by, at last, a real human girl who clearly meant him no harm and could have given him a wonderful and happy human life. Calypso, Circe, the Sirens—these are all supernatural beings and easily resisted by the clever Odysseus. But the good girl Nausicaa, reverent, kind, and beautiful, is like Penelope 2.2—a newer, faster, sexier version of his wife. Think of her as Isabella Rossellini, with Odysseus managing to remember he's married to Ingrid Bergman, and finally—easily—sticking with the original. Maybe he sees that she's the age of his son, and temptation withers; in any case, he proves how far he's come by remaining entirely paternal toward Nausicaa, his eyes fixed on his home. Resisting her small temptation appears perfectly easy for him—it's like a valediction to his journey, a symbolic end to his wandering.

The entire episode with the Phaeacians has proceeded in this vein. The king and the queen have celebratory dances and games in his honor, and when a participant sneers that Odysseus won't compete because he's probably just some merchant, Odysseus leaps up and throws the discus farther than anybody else, lest those Phaeacians—or we listeners or readers—think that in his middle years he's lost any of his vigor. But then, instead of giving in to anger at the insult, Odysseus cheerfully boasts a moment and then takes his seat for the dances and stories—he chooses the role of elder rather than competitor. His day is past; more, he has nothing left to prove, certainly not to idle boasters. King Alcinous, in every way impressed, urges his twelve chieftains to join him in each providing "a fresh cloak and tunic and a talent of precious gold as gifts for our guest"—thus Odysseus, who already knows he's got a ride home, can now expect to arrive with more valuable booty than he would have had even were all his ships from Troy still sailing. (Alcinous also reminds his chiefs that "we in turn will pay ourselves back from the people," giving a nice reminder that ancient taxation policy differed little from our own.) Queen Arete gives Odysseus a chest, which she urges him to fill with his booty—he does, "making it fast with a cunning elaborate knot great Circe had taught him." He knows he'll sleep in the boat home, and he's learned how dangerous that can be.

ODYSSEUS'S TRAVELS ARE NEARLY OVER, but he's not yet on Ithaca, and Poseidon still simmers. So when the time for departing comes, among many fine speeches and appropriate sacrifices to the gods, you know something still has to happen, and it does—but not to Odysseus. Odysseus lies down in the Phaeacian boat, falling into "delicious deep sleep like nothing so much as death," and the magical ship springs forward for Ithaca so fast that "not even the circling hawk, the fastest of fowls, could have kept up with her." The Phaeacians reach Ithaca before dawn and deposit Odysseus there, still asleep, piling his gifts at the base of an olive tree. Odysseus is home at last.

But not yet the Phaeacians. Poseidon, annoyed, asks Zeus how he can expect respect from the other gods when the Phaeacians, whom he says are his kinsmen, have ferried Odysseus safely home despite Poseidon's antipathy. Zeus tells Poseidon to express his rage however he likes, and Poseidon decides to smash the returning ship and surround the Phaeacian city with mountains. Zeus has a better suggestion: Wait until the ship nears shore, and then instantly turn it to stone—that will make a stronger impression. Just so—the ship approaches shore and suddenly turns to rock, leaving the watching Phaeacians "in trembling amazement." Alcinous remembers that his father had predicted just such an event should they continue "safely conducting strangers over the deep"—I imagine him slapping his forehead—and he remembers that the next event in the prophecy was Poseidon surrounding the town with mountains. Alcinous quickly arranges sacrifices to Poseidon and promises to stop transporting strangers, and there we leave the Phaeacians, so poorly repaid for their hospitality. Even *xenia* suffers the whims of the gods. We never find out whether Poseidon follows through with those mountains.

But the story of Odysseus's wanderings is over. As Odysseus began his tale in the real world by fighting the very human Cicones, Homer has him end in the almost real world with the almost entirely human Phaeacians—and their story ends with them renouncing their magical sea prowess. With the Phaeacians, clearly the magical portion of *The Odyssey* has ended. From now on we'll be, with Odysseus, on solid ground.

I DON'T HAVE A MAP FROM CORFU—an indication of the cruise experience. Had I traveled there on my own, I would now have, in a pile somewhere, a map of Kérkyra (or Corfu town); a map of the island; ferry and bus schedules and receipts; pamphlets from this museum and that church. Instead, what I have is a leaflet from the Archaeological Museum of Corfu and a few hours of pleasant memories. For this, along with the ship's crew, I blame Stella, the Greek guide who in Corfu came aboard the *Clelia II*.

Two places on Corfu have Odyssean connections: a highly touristed place on the west coast called Paleokastritsa, associated with the city of the Phaeacians, and a resort town about ten kilometers south of there called Ermones, where the Ropa River emptying into the Ionian reminds some of the river mouth into which Odysseus finally swam when he came ashore after his long journey from Calypso's island. I thought I could see the two in a day, then figure out how to make my way by ferry to Patras, the main western Greek port, and then back out to Ithaca. But after I got into the usual discussion of my quest with Stella, who planned to lead the brief tours both on Corfu and the next day on Ithaca, she almost shook with delight: If I stayed aboard the ship, she thrilled to note, the *Clelia II* would deposit me early the next morning on the shore of Ithaca—exactly as the Phaeacians' ship had deposited Odysseus. Surely I would not deny them the opportunity to make this perfect expression of *xenia* on my final Odyssean journey.

The only downside was that while Stella planned to take us all by bus to Paleokastritsa, we would skip Ermones; we would take a look at the rock that residents of the island claim is the boat fossilized by Poseidon, but we wouldn't stand in the river they claim as Odysseus's landing spot. Staying on the ship meant a second night of luxury; leaving meant five minutes with my feet in a river followed by two days of miserable ferry travel. As choices go, Scylla and Charybdis this was not. When we loaded onto the buses the next afternoon to go to the Archaeological Museum of Corfu, my bag remained in my palatial suite. When your trip nears its end, you're allowed to be smart.

THE ARCHAEOLOGICAL MUSEUM was filled with what I could only describe at this point in my travels as more ancient Greek stuff: a seventh-century BC stone lion, a sixth-century BC pediment, statues of Aphrodite, and plenty more like it. Kérkyra began as a colony of Corinth, and when it came into conflict with its mother city in 435 BC it helped cause the Peloponnesian War. Interesting, of course, if post-Homeric. Anyhow, used to traveling at my own pace, I felt almost stifled traveling with a group and a guide. Fortunately, the museum visit lasted less than an hour, after which the bus drove us across the island to Paleokastritsa, tracing tortuous mountain roads giving glimpses on one hand of the sea and its rocky shore, on the other endless stands of cypress climbing Corfu's steep slopes.

With two main harbors, Paleokastritsa also features a breathtaking monastery atop the central headland, reached only by causeway, perfectly fitting the Homeric description: "the way leading in is narrow, . . . since a fine harbor lies on either side." An almost Spanish-mission-looking place of stucco walls and a cooling arched loggia, the monastery houses a museum, though you'll likely be drawn instead to the lush courtyard gardens and passages, from which through the arches of the monastery walls you can see, directly below the headland and just outside the harbor, a long, narrow, gray-brown rocky shoal—just about ship size. The locals naturally point it out as the ship fossilized while returning from dropping Odysseus in Ithaca. Of course, the locals also like to identify the monastery as the palace of Alcinous, though it wasn't founded until the thirteenth century and the current structure was built in the eighteenth.

Impatient with tours and aware that with no stop scheduled for Ermones Bay this was our only Odyssean moment in Corfu, I refused to leave without wetting my feet in the Ionian. With another member of the cruise's small under-fifty contingent and her mother, I descended the steep street from the monastery to the causeway, shedding shoes and socks to wade into both the sandy harbor and the stony harbor, snapping pictures for proof of our daring. In the snapshot, I'm grinning like a fool.

That evening the three of us, all looking for cheap eats, wandered for dinner among the winding streets of Kérkyra's quaint and busy tourist district, off the vast green esplanade by the dock. We found a window selling 3-euro souvlaki in a paper wrapper that dripped sauce down your arm, then sipped espresso and ate baklava for an hour for another 10 euros total. When we later compared experiences with shipmates, we didn't find a single person who had eaten a single meal for less than the three of us together had spent on our entire evening. I allowed myself a Lonely Planetoid superior sneer.

BUT ONLY FOR A WHILE, for we later learned from fellow passengers that as delightful as the wade in the Ionian had been, by taking it I missed something I'd have liked to see: a face-off between our guide and one of our resident professors about whether Odysseus was a real person. Stella, a Greek, asserted that Odysseus was as real as Davy Crockett or Daniel Boone—sure, his exploits have been exaggerated, but he was a man of history. He shows up on coins and in artwork and has a heritage unparalleled in Greece; telling her that Odysseus wasn't real was like telling an American that Abraham Lincoln was interesting and all, but obviously made up. Saying she "claimed" Odysseus was real would be like saying you "claimed" the earth revolves around the sun. She took the existence of a real Odysseus as a matter of obvious historical fact.

The professor—he subsequently demanded to be known only as "an unnamed learned gentleman of forceful persuasion," which lacks the vigor of "sacker of cities," but I'm just telling you what happened—found the whole thing preposterous; this also described his attitude toward the undertaking of following the route in the first place. He allowed that the *Odyssey* story was powerful and marvelous and had entertained an entire culture for millennia, but trying to pin historical fact to the personage of Odysseus was as ridiculous as looking for the historical Batman or the real Paul Bunyan. He didn't deny that there was plenty of evidence that Bronze Age Greeks traveled in the western Mediterranean, nor did he deny that travel lore—the nine-day blow to the Lotus-eaters; the perfect harbor of the Laestrygonians; the narrow strait of Scylla and Charybdis—showed up in *The Odyssey*. He just stood very strongly among the hair-tearers who regard the literal truth of any part of the story as poppycock.

The story of the confrontation was repeated all evening, as the *Clelia II* slipped southward from Corfu. Passengers gathered around tables on deck to enjoy the lightly moving air, and I heard them describe Stella showing genuine fury when he refused to credit her beliefs, having to be almost physically restrained; the Learned Gentleman subscribed more to the roll-your-eyes-and-shrug species of argumentation. Stella, perhaps offended, didn't wish to discuss it later. The Learned Gentleman said only, forcefully: Odysseus took an imaginary journey.

But the best thing about that discussion was the next issue it raised. If after all the discussion about varying myths, oral storytelling, and ancient history, a historical Odysseus still provokes argument, remember that people argue with the same ferocity over the existence of not only the poem's characters, but also of the poet himself. What's called "the Homeric Question" in classics circles remains unresolved to this day.

REGARDING HOMER, the experts agree on these facts: Homer either did or did not exist; he lived in the ninth century BC, unless it was the eighth, or tenth, or not at all; he wrote *The Iliad* and *The Odyssey*, or one of them, or neither, or perhaps other, lost poems; either he actually wrote or he dictated, since he was either literate or illiterate;

either he was blind or he was not; and he was born, if he ever was, in Smyrna—or in Argos, or Chios, or Colophon, or Salamis, or Rhodes, or Athens. That's the general agreement. If you go beyond that, people begin arguing.

About, say, whether he was a woman, like Butler claimed, or a genuinely blind poet, though most modern scholars seem to think that tradition merely reflects the blind poet Demodocus of the Phaeacians. (Though an alternative tradition makes "Homer" the commonly used term, way back then, for a blind poet.) There's an ancient, very detailed—though entirely fake—biography of Homer that claims to be the work of Herodotus, though it's not; the real Herodotus thought Homer had lived four hundred years before his own time. On the Greek island of Chios, not far from Smyrna, a clan of rhapsodes (or bards) who made their living reciting Homer by the sixth century BC called themselves the Homeridae, claiming to be Homer's descendants, but their story has no greater claim to our credence, as Strabo would have said, than any other.

Just the same, final written versions of the poems themselves had been settled on by around the fifth century BC, and *The Iliad* and *The Odyssey*, recited regularly in public as well as used for instruction, constituted the central literature of classical Greece (historian Daniel Boorstin has said that "of the Egyptian papyri that have lasted into our century, about half are copies of the *Iliad* or the *Odyssey*, or commentaries on them").

By the second century BC, though, people already wondered whether the same person had written both Homeric poems, and whether the real Homer, if there was one, had done anything more than merely stitch together separate pieces into the two long poems we know. The poems remained central, though in the Roman Empire read less in Greek than in Latin translations.

After the classical period, in barbarian Europe, Homer was known mostly among Latin speakers, and mostly through hearsay—proving that some things never change. Especially important were two spurious "eyewitness" accounts of the Trojan War that appeared to fill this vacuum in the early centuries AD. One, by someone called Dictys Cretensis (supposedly traveling with the Cretans), takes the Greek side; the other, by Dares Phrygius, an actual character mentioned in *The Iliad,* tells the story from the Trojan point of view. Through these garbled transmutations most of the Homeric stories made their first forays into western Europe, translated into vernacular languages as they emerged and spreading non-Homeric tales like the story of Troilus and Cressida, eventually retold by Chaucer and Shakespeare. These bastardized versions powerfully influenced medieval Europe— in fact, the first book ever printed in English was not the Bible, not *The Canterbury Tales,* but *The Recuyell of the Historyes of Troye,* printed by William Caxton in 1474. The first full English translation of Homer's actual work was the version by Chapman (completed in 1616) into which John Keats famously looked. Less than two hundred years later, people were already again discussing whether Homer could have written both his epics; whether he might have been a woman; and whether he was real.

So when I returned to the stories of *The Odyssey* after reading my Joyce only to discover that I had been functioning on incomplete or erroneous information for a long time, I wasn't alone: Our entire culture had done that, and the arguments raised by this backdoor introduction never look likely to stop. A book that came out after my trip addresses the question and raises the supposedly shocking prospect: Perhaps Homer was . . . a woman! As a friend sighed when I first started reporting to him the disputes and arcanery I found as I began looking into the myriad discussions and disputes beyond my little blue copy of *The Odyssey,* "It's like the Talmud. Once you start, how do you stop?"

Easy. You do what Odysseus did: You stop when you get to Ithaca. And that's where the Phaeacian sailors of the *Clelia II* bore me overnight, while on my eyes in my magnificent cabin the gods shed a sleep of great peace.

Chapter 16

What These Ithacas Mean

If you don't know what land this is, then you're either a fool or a stranger indeed, for here we have a name and everybody knows it. All those who live between the sunny East and gloomy West have heard the name of this rugged island. For though it's narrow and a very poor place for driving horses, it's not altogether poor. The land is golden with grain and flowing with wine, since there's always plenty of rain and enriching dew. . . . And so it is, strange sir, that even in Troy they have heard the name of Ithaca, and Troy, they say, is very far from this Achaean country.

—*The Odyssey*, Book XIII

MORNING. Silence. The sky a perfect clear blue, the water a perfect mirror, barely a ripple beyond the wake of the *Clelia II*, which itself barely stirs the surface, moving slowly toward the harbor as if in a dream. I stand on deck, holding a cup of coffee, leaning on the rail. Before me slide hills, rocky bluffs, the occasional tiny cluster of houses perched on the edge. The boat turns and we head southeast, directly into the sun. A tiny island in the middle of a long, narrow fastness, the whole surrounded by square white stucco houses, red terra-cotta tile roofs running halfway up the surrounding mountains; thereafter just green scrub brush, brown dirt, gray rock. Vathy Harbor, the main port of Ithaca.

Last stop.

The crew invites me to join them as they pile aboard buses for their two-hour tour, but I decline. I plan to stay several days and figure I am better off on my own, so as I stand on the quay with my backpack the passengers of the *Clelia II* bid me a friendly farewell. The buses roll off. My guidebook lists two cheap hotels; the Odysseus, near the quay, is abandoned, behind a chain-link fence, so I stay in the Mentor, at the opposite corner of the squarish harbor of Vathy, largest town of Ithaca: a main row of shops, open-air cafés, and restaurants along the harbor, a less-busy street behind it, and beyond that mostly cross streets quickly straggling out as they climb up Mount Neion, the central peak of southern Ithaca. My upstairs room has a view of the harbor and the town from its little balcony. When later I leave the door open to let in the cool evening breezes, the room fills up with mosquitoes. They don't move too fast, so the walls are soon smeared with their blood. You can kill the ones on the ceiling by throwing a phone book straight up.

ITHACA IS HOME TO ODYSSEUS, but, of course, it's not quite home, too—he's been gone twenty years. He returns at almost exactly the halfway point of the poem—early in Book XIII—and spends the remainder of the book, in a way, earning his safe arrival and fulfilling the prophecy that he return to a house full of trouble. He faces challenges that if not as fantastic as the witches and monsters he met on his travels at least give him the opportunity to show what he's learned—more important, to prove himself to his wife and son. He has to make Ithaca his home again.

He wakes up literally in a fog, alone on the beach beneath an olive tree, naturally enough presuming he's been hoodwinked once again, abandoned by the Phaeacians on some strange shore: "O not again!" he cries. "Among what manner of mortals can I be now?" He wonders whether he would have been better off going to yet another king; he wonders what to do with his stuff, piled around him; he wonders where he is. He's like a traveler showing up in a new town, and what he needs is the tourist office.

The tourist office arrives, in the form of Athena, disguised as a shepherd. The shepherd describes the land "golden with grain, and flowing with wind." Everyone knows this place: "even in Troy they have heard the name of Ithaca, and Troy, they say, is very far from this Achaean country." Ha-ha, get it? A long way from Troy, indeed.

Odysseus has earned his reputation for craftiness, and he doubles and quadruples it now that he's home. He instantly begins telling lies, telling so many it's a wonder anybody can keep them straight. To the shepherd Odysseus lets loose a string of falsehoods about starting off in Crete and so forth. Athena, thrilled, shows her true form and revels in the cleverness of her favorite; they're two of a kind, she says: "Just as you surpass all men in planning and speaking, so I am famous among all the gods for wisdom and cunning." She applauds him for not running directly to Penelope but instead waiting to check the situation first. She helps him hide his treasure in a nearby cave dedicated to the nymphs called Naiads. To help him as he scopes out his homeland under cover, she changes his form so that not only is he clothed in rags but he even looks old and wizened. She explains to Odysseus that she hadn't simply reassured Telemachus but had instead helped him on his journey so "that men might think well of him for going." As if Odysseus, of all people, needs reminding that a journey offers opportunity for growth. With a promise to help Telemachus get home and to be with Odysseus when he finally challenges the suitors, off she goes.

Disguised, Odysseus spends the next several books telling more lies. He makes up a new version of his life story to tell Eumaeus, the swineherd who has remained faithful in his long absence; Eumaeus shows him great hospitality, promising even greater hospitality should Telemachus return and greater still should his long-lamented master, Odysseus, ever get back. Telemachus does, of course, return from his travels, avoiding the suitors' ambush and, with Athena's guidance, coming home by way of the swineherd's hut, where he is welcomed like Eumaeus's own son.

When Telemachus sends Eumaeus to inform Penelope of his arrival, Odysseus reveals himself to his son—again changed by Athena into his most impressive physical form. When Telemachus is convinced that the father he's never known has truly returned, the two embrace, weeping. But like father, like son—they instantly fall to scheming, setting up a plan by which they can eventually rout the suitors. By the time Eumaeus gets back, Athena has returned Odysseus to his disguise.

The suitors, meanwhile, have returned to Odysseus's palace, and even though they failed to kill Telemachus and have shelved, for the moment, further plans against him, they're living large in Odysseus's house. Odysseus in disguise walks to town the next morning, receiving harsh treatment from some of his servants. Telemachus has preceded him with a seer, who tells Penelope that Odysseus has reached Ithaca and even now plans revenge on the suitors, but Penelope, who after twenty years has heard her fill of false prophecies, dares not believe. At the gates of the palace, Odysseus sees his old dog, Argus, mistreated by the suitors, lying on a pile of dung. The dog's ears prick up as he recognizes his master, but he lacks the energy even to move, and there, aware at last that his master has returned, he dies. Odysseus brushes away a tear. The suitors not only jeer at Odysseus but also throw a stool at him: an echo of the Cyclops tossing that mountaintop. This time Odysseus doesn't lose his cool, so it's a foreshadowing, too—things didn't go too well for the Cyclops, so inhospitable to Odysseus, and that was when Odysseus lacked self-control. Now he's at the peak of his abilities.

Matters simmer. The suitors continue to mistreat Odysseus, who is jeered even by the palace's regular beggar, who challenges Odysseus to a fight. He soon regrets it, of course; in another small foreshadowing of what's to come, Odysseus thrashes him, causing some of the suitors to raise an eyebrow: Who is this guy? Odysseus approaches one of the less-culpable suitors, advising him to leave the palace before trouble begins, but the die has been cast, and he resists the advice. Leaving Odysseus as a beggar in his own palace, the suitors go home for the night.

SO: A HARBOR, "protected on either side by cliffs that extend far out into the deep"; a cave, full of treasure or suitable to be so; Eumaeus's hut; Odysseus's palace. No shortage of places for the *Odyssey* pilgrim to visit, and once you're on Ithaca, you can find them all. In fact, you can find each of them several different places and on several different islands. What, you thought that just because Odysseus lived on a Greek island called Ithaca and there's still a Greek island called Ithaca that the search was over? Have you been paying no attention at all?

The Greek island of Ithaca has been known by its current name for as long as people have known about Greeks and islands, and its name shows up without change in *The Odyssey*. Just the same, Odysseus calls it "well out in the sea toward the gloom of twilight, while the neighboring islands of Dulichium, Samos, and wooded Zacynthus lie nearer the rising sun." He also mentions "leafy Mount Neriton," visible for miles, and Mount Neriton still stands in northern Ithaca. Still, this description seems to make Ithaca the westernmost island of a group of four, whereas Ithaca is actually part of a group of three islands, of which it's the farthest north, due east of Kefalloniá, one of the others. Zacynthus to the south still bears a Homeric name. Lefkáda, to the north, is actually connected to the mainland by a causeway, so you might or might not want to call it an island (it's separated by a dredged canal these days). When people count the main Ionian Islands they usually count six, starting with Corfu and including Lefkáda; common practice regarding Homer is to leave Corfu and the tiny Paxol off to the north, equate Lefkáda and Kefalloniá in some way with Dulichium and Samos, and forgive Homer—a blind, possibly illiterate guy who lived before the age of compasses or accurate mapmaking—for getting the geography a bit wonky.

In any case, you've already got space for debate, and you can bet there's been plenty. In fact, after I got back from my trip a new book, *Odysseus Unbound,* appeared, summarizing millennia of argument and supporting the claim, itself at least a century old, that we've had the wrong Ithaca all along, and the real one is actually a peninsula on the west coast of Kefalloniá, which was a separate island until a long-forgotten earthquake smashed the two together. It pleads its case for nearly six hundred pages, using satellite images, detailed maps, and a lot of expensive photographs.

The authors could certainly be right, though the level of detail they find in Homer's geography on Ithaca would be far greater than Homer demonstrated anywhere else in *The Odyssey,* real or imagined. More important, once you've been among the floating islands and witches and sea monsters and man-eating giants, you've pretty much given up on specific correlations between Odyssean maps and your own. I was glad the book came out after I got back. That way I was left—like Strabo, among others—to treat Ithaca as though it were Ithaca. I don't regret it.

MY FIRST AFTERNOON, I gathered such little information as I could. The lack of a tourist office sent me to car and scooter rental places, which offered only a smudgy, photocopied map, so I bought a nicer map in a

quiet souvenir shop; most of the other souvenirs were tiles and
T-shirts showing Greek figures seemingly from vases engaging in
shocking sexual activity. I didn't buy any. After that I grabbed a towel
and my bathing suit and trooped over the hill from Vathy to a tiny
little harbor off the main harbor, identified by an actual sign poked
into the ground as Dhéxa beach, or "Phorkys Bay"—directly quoting
the line from *The Odyssey* that notes that the Ithaca harbor is "dear to
Phorcys, that briny old man of the sea." The long, deep harbor of
Vathy is called one of the largest in the world, thus perfectly fulfilling
the Homeric description of those long cliffs, protecting so well from
waves that "ships within lie completely unmoored, and safe where the
sailors leave them." So in Phorkys Bay, along the pebbly beach,
beneath a couple terraced rows of olive trees, I swam, sketched, and for
the first time tried to call my journey over. Here I was—on Ithaca—and
swimming, just as I had in the Bosporus, the Aegean, the Ionian, the
Mediterranean. Tiny waves lapped the stony beach; I heard the rattle
and tonk of goat bells. I skipped stones, ate bread and goat cheese,
reread parts of Odysseus's return. I even, feeling rather foolish, bent
down and kissed the beach, as Odysseus does when Athena dispels the
mist and he finally sees his homeland. The beach was lovely, the swimming refreshing, the olive trees genuinely breathtaking, the little bay off
the greater harbor lovely almost to distraction. Still—I didn't feel done.

Okay; no problem. A nice dinner of lamb, potatoes, and rice at one
of the many nearly empty cafés along the Vathy strand left me plenty
of time to sketch the fishing boats gently bobbing in the Vathy port
and watch the locals and the few straggling tourists gather among the
kiosks and little cafés. I read my guidebook and found four more
specifically Odyssean sites I could visit.

Up the hill from the Dhéxa beach was Marmarospilia, the "cave
of the Nymphs," where Odysseus and Athena hid his treasure; a little
farther from Vathy was Alalkomenae, ruins of an ancient settlement
that no less a personage than our old pal Schliemann had once identified as the palace of Odysseus. Way north, near Stavros, the island's
other largish town, was Pilikata Hill, identified with Odysseus by
more recent archaeologists. And together, far south on the island,
were Arethousa Spring and Raven Rock, where Athena sent Odysseus

to meet Eumaeus. The cave, the spring, and the rock looked walkable; the other places required transportation. When my first foray toward the cave met with resistance in the form of scary untethered dogs, and since my queries about buses received only raised eyebrows, I admitted defeat: After having avoided one for my entire trip, at my last destination I finally rented a car, an awesome little two-seater called a Smart Car, with a three-gear semiautomatic transmission, purple upholstery, and no backseat. The radio played pop music I recognized from Italy.

MY FIRST DESTINATION was also Odysseus's: the cave of the nymphs, where he and Athena stashed his treasure. Near the top of the mountain directly above the Dhéxa beach, the cave is perfectly suited to match Homer's description—it even turns out to have two entrances, as Homer says, one for mortals, and another, "a sacred way though which pass none but immortal feet." Everyone told me the cave was closed, but I powered up the road after it turned to dirt. You have to drive slowly because sometimes goats get in the path. But in the car I didn't mind those frantic untethered dogs, and not long after I left them behind I came to an iron gate, made fast only by a loose, long-shackled lock, as if to say, "Well, okay, but we warned you." A rotting little green shack probably once housed a ticket booth, a broken fence required little more strenuous than a squeeze, and then . . . a triangular opening in the rock that led to total darkness.

I sat inside for as long as I could to let my eyes adjust. First, I made out a gentle glow from above—diffuse sunlight from that other opening, the one for the gods. My tiny flashlights offered almost no help, so slowly I crept forward, feet, hands, and butt sliding on damp, sandy rock. Finally, something about the chill in the air or the quality of echo made me feel I was in a larger space, so I stopped. Still unable to see, I took out my camera and hit the flash, hoping to get a better—if brief—sense of my surroundings. I did, seeing suddenly a precipitous drop, a yard beyond my boots. Also stalactites, stairs, and, though no treasure, a chaos of beams and cables, electrical wires, and broken struts. No wonder the cave was closed. I decided I'd gone as far as I needed to go and cautiously made my way back out into the hot sun, among the cypress and the olives, the silence up on the mountain broken only by buzzing insects and those omnipresent goat bells.

On my way back down, I made perhaps the final silly mistake of my trip.

YOU CAN'T GET AWAY FROM THE OLIVE in the Mediterranean—nor should you want to. Everywhere you go you find olive orchards, the long silvery leaves and twisted trunks of olives becoming part of your background perception, like the smell of wild sage and pine resin, the sound of goat bells, the rocky limestone outcroppings. Olives have been cultivated in the Mediterranean for at least five thousand years; some say that clear-cutting for olive groves, in fact, turned the once-deciduous Mediterranean into the rocky, scrubby landscape it is now. Legend says that when Athena and Poseidon competed for the patronage of Athens, Poseidon struck the rock of the Acropolis and caused a spring to rise, which is pretty good; but Athena caused an olive to grow there, providing food, oil, wealth—and the Athenians had their patron.

In the fall you start seeing people harvest their olives. Nets are spread on the ground and someone climbs among the branches, whacking them with sticks to shake off the ripe fruit. You see the nets stored in crooks in the trees themselves, and the harvest, too, becomes something you almost don't notice. But on my way down from the cave of the nymphs, I had to laugh when I saw a man of around my own age sitting on a rock wall smoking as a woman of sixty or more—his mother, he later said—climbed in the tree, harvesting and pruning. The man had stopped me on my way up the hill, assuring me that the cave was closed. On my way down, anxious to boast, I rolled to a stop, lowered the window, and told him I'd been inside the cave. He admired my enterprise, asked what I was up to—and then, of course, assured me that as a lifelong resident of Ithaca he could show me things about Odysseus that I'd never otherwise see. Before I knew it, we had an arrangement to meet on the Vathy central square at 1 p.m.

Oy. I had a full day of places to see, the happy company of that cheerful Greek pop music in my Smart Car, and nothing between me and the end of my journey but a delightful day of driving the twisting roads of this tiny Greek island. I can't explain my decision to invite into my journey a sweating, chain-smoking man who let his own mother harvest his olives. Perhaps I wanted to make sure I left no stone unturned; or maybe the gods weren't through with me yet.

In any case, once I had agreed to meet him I felt obligated to honor that, so I made the best of what remained of my morning alone by heading north of Vathy to Alalkomenae, the site Schliemann had identified as Odysseus's castle. I parked by the side of the road—in the shade of an olive, of course—and found the beginning of a red-and-white-blazed trail leading up, up, up the steep side of a hill. Ithaca looks like two mountains connected by a hilly isthmus, and Alalkomenae perches atop the central hill of the isthmus. I climbed for a good hour, passing stone walls ancient and modern, climbing stiles between pastures, stepping over goat pellets and goats, always going higher. The views grew more spectacular until finally, at the very top, I reached a stately set of terraced stone stairs, alongside which stood a blue sign with lettering in yellow: Alalkomenae Castle. Cyclopean walls nearby, giant rocky things, ran near the top of the hill, and I climbed on those. To the west I could see the Ionian and Kefalloniá; to the east, the harbor and off a ways toward the mainland. To the north towered Mount Neriton.

Archaeologists argue that these stairs and walls are too recent to be those of Odysseus's castle, though others claim this still might be the site of the Homeric city of Ithaca. Schliemann, ever imaginative if nothing else, had claimed he could tell which corner of the ruins would have been the bedroom in which Odysseus had built his famous bed, one post of which was a living olive tree. No such imagery came to me: I saw a field of dewy grass and clover, simple if lovely ancient rocks among violets and tiny tulip-looking flowers. I lay in the breeze and merely thanked the gods I had made it to the top.

I still didn't feel done.

BACK DOWN TO THE SMART CAR, and then back to Vathy Harbor to pick up my guide—and then a bracing drive along the cliffside road carved into the side of Mount Neriton of the northern part of Ithaca. My guide told me his name was Nikolas, and he promised me he was the brother of the president of Ithaca, if there even is one. He smoked in the car, cringing in fear at our speed. He might have made a better impression had he not exhaled such alcohol fumes that I feared his cigarettes might ignite the air in the car. Just the same, there he was, so when he told me we had to go see the capriciously described "School of Homer," that's where we headed. First we stopped in Stavros, the tiny town that is nonetheless the largest in the north of Ithaca. There I ran instantly to the little town green, where a rather intense bust of Odysseus stands on a pillar, next to a relief diagram of the Mediterranean, showing the supposed route of Odysseus. It agreed with mine about half the time. I took my picture next to the bust while Nikolas chatted with a café owner.

Nikolas thought the next thing I ought to do was buy him a drink at the tiny café overlooking the square, but I was a man on a mission and wanted to see the archaeological sites, so looking rather put-upon he climbed back into the Smart Car, and we bounced down a dirt road to the School of Homer, part of the Pilikata Hill area, the other main claimant to the title of Homeric Ithaca. These ruins, mostly overgrown, are definitely Bronze Age, though nobody has found anything they can genuinely link to Odysseus. Aware that I had the car for only a day, I skittered among the ruins, peering off toward the sea and sitting on ancient walls, walking along the boardwalks protecting the ground beneath our feet. Among the olive trees and the lichen-covered stones, I can't say I ever felt like I had found the power center of Odysseus, but I may just have been too aware of Nikolas, skulking nearby, smoking cigarettes and occasionally giving me specious advice like "The Christians, they destroyed our old culture. Remember what I tell you!" and then picking up some random shard of terra-cotta and handing it to me, telling me he was sure it was valuable, and that it would be okay if I slipped it into my bag and took it home. No? "Okay, maybe I give it to Fotini."

Fotini was Fotini Couvaras, the curator of the Stavros museum, two tiny rooms on a backstreet filled with ancient pottery shards and, especially, a series of eighth- or ninth-century BC bronze tripods found in a cave below Stavros, at the end of Polis Bay. One was found by the landowner in the nineteenth century, and twelve more were found when British archaeologist Sylvia Benton made a careful study of the cave in the 1930s. The thirteen tripods—exactly as many as Odysseus describes bringing with him from the Phaeacians—prompt the expected debate. Some claim them as the genuine article; others that they indicate cultic worship of Odysseus and were placed in the cave to re-create Odyssean details; still others suggest the cave and the tripods were absorbed into the Homeric tale. As ever, more debate than anything else. Fotini was delightful, pointing out a triangular piece of terra-cotta with an inscription meaning "glory to Odysseus"— clearly a cult offering—as evidence: "This proves he did exist, he was here on Ithaca." The piece was dated 200 BC, a thousand years after the supposed events of *The Odyssey*. "If they remembered Odysseus a thousand years after he existed, and worshipped him," she concluded, "then he was very important."

Granted without argument. With relief I dropped Nikolas off back at Vathy and spent the last couple hours of light scrambling in the south of the island, looking for a hut or cave supposed to have belonged to Eumaeus. Several nice Greek-speaking old ladies in babushkas tried to help me, but all I found were a few scarcely marked trails, and I ended up muddy and running away from dogs. Knowing I'd be back the next day to look for Arethousa Spring and Raven Rock, I drove back and turned in the car. In the evening I sat on a bench by the harbor, drinking orange pop, watching the reflections of the white houses waver in the ripples in the green water caused by the bobbing of the fishing boats. Then I went up to my room, killed the day's squadron of mosquitoes, and went to sleep.

THOSE TWO FINAL ODYSSEAN SITES REMAINED, and I set out on foot the next morning. Almost directly from my hotel led a road southward, toward Raven Rock and Arethousa Spring, both described by Athena when she sends Odysseus off for Eumaeus, his faithful swineherd, after their meeting on the beach: "You will find him tending your swine by Raven's Rock at the spring Arethousa." Above the town the road climbs into the rough rocky brown soil of Mount Neion, running between olive plantations until it reaches a windy plateau of little more than gorse and wild thyme. The road ends and turns into dirt where the trail to the fountain—directly below the rock—was supposed to turn off. When I couldn't find it, a helpful guy and girl on a scooter stopped to point me in the right direction, and from there I hoofed along a silent pebbly trail among the brush. As it curled around the mountain, it entered a long gorge and descended some stairs. Suddenly, I found myself on an ancient grassy track, terraced with stone walls into the side of the mountain. And there, where the gorge came to a cleft in the mountain, was a little rocky cave, in which a tiny trickle of water—a dampness, really—spread among mossy rocks: Arethousa Spring. Directly above, where the steep gorge met the plateau above, was a stark white cliff: Raven Rock.

I walked around the lovely stony walls, the grassy track, feeling the breeze hitting the side of the mountain direct from the sea. A tiny island floated just offshore, below the cypress trees, the low scrub, the crumbling mountainside. Directly below was a little secluded shore—on another day I'm sure I would have scrambled down to its rocky beach and read, wrote in my journals, planned my next steps. But not this time. I realized, finally, that I had no more steps. This was as far as I was going. I held my camera out at arm's length and took my own picture, with the spring behind me. In the picture, I look tired.

When I trudged back into Vathy, I ran into the two English speakers who had set me on the path for the spring. We sat down for dinner a block from the harbor at a little corner restaurant called Kalkanis, where the owner kept the beer and souvlaki coming. Tourist season was about over, and we constituted the only occupied table. Neil, it turned out, was about my age, and he lived in an old stone shepherd's cottage near the tiny town of Frikes, in the north of the island; Jude was visiting.

"I came here totally by accident," he said. An Anglophone from Kenya, he said he was a displaced person wherever he went, so why not set up shop here? After the upheavals of World War II, followed by the terrible Greek civil war, the Ionian Islands were devastated by a 1953 earthquake, and the vast majority of the population up and left—Neil described finding trunks and furniture in his cottage when he moved in, left behind by occupants who simply walked away. So what made him want to stay?

"That's really the million-dollar question about this place," he said, laughing. "And nobody has an answer. This is a place you curse. I've seen far more beautiful places in the world than this bloody rock sticking out of the ocean. People look forward to getting away from here—and then look forward to getting back. I look at that as the Odyssey-type syndrome."

Since he brought it up, I told him my story—very briefly. And I mentioned that as much as I had hoped for some powerful moment of completion to my travels, I had never quite had it, even there on Ithaca, where I'd reached my goal. "I think to have that feeling on this island," Jude piped up, "you need to have made your journey."

I wasn't sure I liked the implications of that. Still, whether I felt the full-bore emotional hoedown I hoped for or not, Ithaca was the final stop on my pilgrimage. That checklist of places was complete. In fact, inside the front cover of my totem copy of *The Odyssey* I had, early into my thinking about the trip, listed the page numbers on which each episode appears. I took pleasure in running through them, and I showed them to Neil and Jude. They looked politely before they hopped on their scooter and headed away.

I THOUGHT A LOT, TOO, there on Ithaca, about "Ithaca," the marvelous poem by Constantine Cavafy that I had read at my friend's wedding—its appearance in my e-mail in-box had been part of the midsummer *Odyssey* attack that got me started publicly griping about Joyce in the first place, which had led me, inexorably, to Ithaca. And like its predecessor, Cavafy's poem, too, had renewed wisdom for me.

"Hope your road is a long one," Cavafy advises each of us setting off for Ithacas of our own. He's a modern, and like most of us he wants the journey itself to be more important than the destination. He hopes we visit "Phoenician trading stations" to purchase jewels and perfumes and "many Egyptian cities" to learn from scholars. "Keep Ithaka always in your mind," of course, but take all the time you can. We can expect to meet only such Laestrygonians and Cyclopes as we carry in our hearts—ours is to be an inward as well as an outward journey. And when we finally arrive, Cavafy knows Ithaca is almost sure to disappoint us, as any traveler knows; as I was in the process of discovering, the final destination always does. But if we've learned from our travels, "Ithaca won't have fooled you. / Wise as you will have become, so full of experience, / you'll have understood by then what these Ithakas mean."

It's a lovely sentiment, and certainly one with which I agreed: The journey makes us wiser and better, and for most of us the journey is the point. Just the same, as I came to its end, I couldn't help thinking how far off the mark Cavafy was regarding Odysseus himself—or anyhow, how much Odysseus wouldn't have agreed. Odysseus wouldn't have seen the Laestrygonians as manifestations of his own internal conflicts: Odysseus saw them as monsters who ate up eleven-twelfths of his crew. And especially after he left Circe, Odysseus in no way saw his travels as opportunities to learn and buy gifts. Odysseus just wanted to get home. And there on Ithaca he was home.

BUT, OF COURSE, I wasn't, and could any realization come more powerfully at the end of such travels? I had made it to Odysseus's home—but not to my own. No wonder epiphany evaded me. And so after my journey with Odysseus I had to start for home for real. My return airline ticket, organized with uncertainty in mind, left a week later from Athens, and loitering around Athens for the better part of a week actually sounded awful. Anxious to return to my wife, a baby no more than a month away, I could anticipate no pleasure in additional travel. Between beers and staring at the harbor from my chair in the Vathy Internet café, I started working the phone and the computer. Only a day or so passed before I found myself in possession of a ticket from Rome to London to Philadelphia and, finally, to Raleigh. The next morning I got up very early, dropped my key at the desk of the Mentor, and boarded the morning ferry for Patras. There I easily booked passage on the Superfast ferry line for that night's crossing to Bari, on the east coast of Italy, from where I could catch trains to Rome and, then, a plane home.

Perhaps feeling premature nostalgia for my days of rough travel, I booked only deck passage, which meant that as the heat of the day evaporated into a fall evening that grew rather chilly, I sat at a deck-side table with two new friends, Jawad Ali and Anayat, playing a Pakistani version of gin rummy (twelve cards each; two wild cards) while two tables away a couple dozen Albanians in leather jackets crowded around one of those games whose chief action consists of face slapping. Jawad Ali, Anayat, and I had decided that our table was defensible for the night, and in truth they rolled up in blankets and appeared to sleep soundly in the chilly air. I tried a bench, a deck chair, and even the rubber mats of the caged children's play area, sleeping in each for a couple hours before awaking from cold or cramp, finally passing my last hour or so in relative comfort on a bench in a little bar on deck seven. After about 2 a.m. they let you sleep anywhere. Around seven they start poking you awake.

In Greece, they read the newspapers to you on TV in the morning, and that's what everyone on the *Superfast XII* watched while consuming their coffee. In Bari I found the train to Rome with little trouble, and I killed my day in Rome failing once again to get into the Capuchin crypts and paying my respects at the grave of John Keats, thereafter engaging in a brief dispute with a museum docent over whether his epitaph, "Here Lies One Whose Name Was Writ in Water," constitutes iambic pentameter, which it does not, no matter what they say at the Keats House near the Spanish Steps.

But that's all really the beginning of another story.

Chapter 17

Home at Last:

Penelope and Odysseus

Nothing is better or greater than a home where man and wife are living harmoniously together, the envy of evil minds, but a very great joy to men of good will, and greatest of all to themselves.

—*The Odyssey*, Book VI

ODYSSEUS COMES HOME TO A PALACE FULL OF SUITORS and has to murder every last one of them; I came home to a house full of contractors, and my only weapon was a checkbook. You decide which is worse.

Okay, that's not completely accurate. Actually, the contractors worked all summer, while I traveled, adding a second bathroom, and when I came home there was plenty to take care of but no crisis; beyond painting, they were virtually done. But there's truth in the metaphor, too—you spend your time gallivanting the globe and by the time you get home there's bound to be trouble: Accounts get over-drawn, pets get fleas, maintenance isn't performed. Your wife—or partner or roommate—can cover for you, but it won't be the same. Actions have consequences; you can't be everywhere. June had done much more than her share while I was away, and just seeing her was tonic—but still I had plenty to do when I got home.

Just like Odysseus.

Homer has Penelope and the disguised Odysseus finally meet in Book XIX, where the beggar tells Penelope that he's sure Odysseus will be home any minute. Penelope seems to at least suspect the beggar's true identity, telling her own story of resisting the suitors, then having Eurycleia, the faithful maid who nursed Odysseus as a baby, wash the beggar's feet. When Eurycleia does so, she discovers on Odysseus's leg a scar he got as a boy when, visiting his grandfather, he was injured by a boar. Startled by recognition, she drops his foot, splashing water out of the basin; Odysseus warns that she had better not let on that she knows. Of course, she complies, pointing out that when the moment is right, she'll be able to identify which servants have remained faithful.

Odysseus has already counseled Telemachus to remove all the armor and weapons from the hall where the suitors gather, so when Penelope tells the beggar that the next day she plans to take out Odysseus's famous bow and marry whoever among the suitors can string it and shoot an arrow through a row of twelve axes, the beggar strongly approves.

The next morning, continued mockery by the suitors. Penelope announces the archery contest, then returns to her room. The first to try to string the bow is Telemachus, who fails three times; when on his fourth try he's about to succeed, a glance from Odysseus tells him not to. As one by one the suitors fail, Odysseus slips off with Eumaeus and Philoetius, a similarly faithful goatherd, to announce his identity and his plans for the suitors, which include not only hiding the armor but bolting the doors so they cannot escape.

Back among the suitors, Odysseus asks for the opportunity to string the bow. Amid jeering, the beggar easily does so, then succeeds at the impossible arrow shot. He stands to face the suitors, Telemachus joining him. Odysseus shoots the leader of the suitors, then announces his identity and his plans. Joined by his son and his two faithful servants—and, of course, Athena—in a bloody battle Odysseus finishes off the 108 suitors; he spares only the herald and, of course, the bard, both of whom served the suitors unwillingly. He forces disloyal maids to clean up, after which they are hanged. Everyone washes and pretends a wedding is going on in the palace so outsiders will not suspect the slaughter.

When a delighted Eurycleia brings Penelope down to see the conquering Odysseus, cautious Penelope resists belief that her husband has finally returned. Odysseus sends Telemachus away so the two may talk freely. Penelope finally claims she will allow this person, whoever he is, to sleep in her own bed, which she orders moved out of her bedroom for his comfort. Odysseus had built this bed himself, so he knows that one leg is made of a living olive tree still rooted to the ground. He cries in rage that his fine bed has been destroyed—proving, finally, to Penelope that he is who he claims to be. The couple embraces, weeping, and repairs to bed, each telling the other their entire story (including, from Odysseus, the prediction of that final voyage with the oar). To give them plenty of time for storytelling as well as lovemaking and refreshing sleep, thoughtful Athena holds back the dawn.

The next morning, Odysseus reunites with his father—again in disguise, this time somewhat inexplicably. After he has revealed himself, Odysseus, his father and son, and the two herdsmen face a group of enraged family members of the suitors. Athena cools tempers, though, and there the story ends.

SO YOU SEE HOW IT IS. After the long journey encountering bullies and temptations, gods and monsters, Odysseus arrives home to face bullies and resist temptation, address gods and the monstrousness of the suitors. He passes every test, resisting even, for example, the temptation toward cruelty—when Eurycleia exults over the piles of dead suitors, Odysseus scolds her: There's nothing to exult over in death, even that decreed by the gods and made certain by the men's own iniquity. Odysseus hasn't forgotten the solemnity of death—and among other things he's become that rarest of all men, a good winner.

Odysseus shows that on his journey everything has changed—and nothing has. He's still the same clever guy, still willing to hack to death a hundred or so people if it suits his needs. On the other hand, with the experience he's gained on his travels, Odysseus makes all the right moves in this, his last battle; Telemachus and Eumaeus each get a scratch, but for 4 against 108, he's managed things pretty well, though having Athena on their side certainly didn't hurt. The second half of the poem brings home the wild elements of the first half, and Odysseus becomes a great man around the house as well as a great man out in the wide world and beyond.

Contractors or no, I had nobody to kill when I got home. But I knew long before I left that applying what I'd learned from *The Odyssey*— both Homer's poem and my own travels—was a lifelong project, and nothing I planned to ritually re-create at home. Just the same, I almost did something quite stupid. At one point, for several weeks, I had it in mind to reenact Odysseus's return in disguise.

It's odd, because I had never thought of my trip as reenactment. In fact, I hate reenactment. Not for me the grimy men in thick wool Civil War garb sweating through a "battle" playing dead for hours in the hot August sun. If I go to Williamsburg, I'll be happy to watch them shoot the cannon, but if they're wearing felt hats and talking in fake-sounding accents, I'm going to give them directions to the Renaissance Faire.

To me reenactments smack of the inauthentic, the falsified, the kind of fakery that degrades what it aims to demystify. I'll gladly go to Gettysburg or Independence Hall, but I think silence best venerates their famous events. In fact, while I was in Malta, I actually stumbled upon a reenactment of the plague—people in ghastly makeup writhed around in straw, with medieval doctors occasionally hauling them off in carts. In my journal I called it Plague Fantasy Camp; it reminded me of everything I meant my trip not to be. I traveled in modern vessels, wore modern clothes, tried to reach the touch points of my journey in a modern way: following, not playacting. Which renders it especially odd that before I left for the final portion of my journey I had decided that the thing to do was, like Odysseus, return before my wife knew it. I could, like Odysseus, cast a wayfarer's eye on my home situation, see what was up before revealing my true identity. I had retraced Odysseus's path, after a fashion; why not reenact his homecoming?

This terrible idea had begun percolating weeks before my final trip, when I considered my eventual return home. I'd be arriving right around Halloween—a significant coincidence, considering Odysseus spends such a large part of the second half of *The Odyssey* in disguise. I couldn't help thinking: Surely, among all our friends, there would be some costume party somewhere. I could arrive home early, not informing June . . . I could attend such a party concealed: a gorilla suit, I figured. I could sneak up to my wife at the party . . . and thereafter I envisioned the most lovely and hilarious recognition sequence: a shocked cry, perhaps a spilled drink, and then squeals of delight, tears, hugs, and photographs of the two of us, me with my gorilla head jauntily under my arm.

I discussed the plan with friends, who either thought it was a hilarious idea or took me by the shoulders and begged me not to do the stupidest thing I had ever considered in my entire life. Those in the former camp pledged to make sure that the by-then-immensely-pregnant June was invited to a Halloween party. So when I finished my journey in Ithaca, Odysseus's homeland, with nothing like the crash of cymbals I'd hoped for, I almost caused terrible mischief.

It must have been the work of Athena that finally, hunched in Ithaca over a public telephone for yet another complicated long-distance call to an airline trying to arrange my surprise return, I suddenly realized that my plan was just stupid. By the grace of some god I finally considered the wisdom of not only keeping a secret from June, but also delivering a huge shock to a pregnant woman. I quickly changed my request to the airline: How fast can you get me home? And then I did the smartest thing I did on my whole trip: I ran back to the Internet café along Vathy's main drag and I e-mailed June, telling her exactly when I planned to be home.

She said she couldn't wait.

If any part of my journey truly ended in Ithaca, that's when it did.

THE IDIOTIC REENACTMENT SEQUENCE attracted me because, I think, even that late in my travels I still wasn't quite comfortable with what I was doing. I had snorted at the geographers, yet gone on my geographical journey; sneered at reenactors, yet engaged in something that if not reenactment was a lot like it. I was finally, at that late hour, discovering the nature of pilgrimage.

That discovery had begun many months before, in Dublin, on Bloomsday. As my plans began, June and I couldn't fail to notice that Bloomsday, June 16, loomed near in the calendar. More, it was the hundredth anniversary of June 16, 1904, the day *Ulysses* is set. With a wedding present of round-trip transatlantic ticket for two still unused, we determined to go, together, to Dublin before my trip began—and before June's pregnancy grew profound enough to limit her travel. We cut that last a little close, it turned out.

Bloomsday in Dublin is like a science fiction convention spread out over an entire city. Wherever you go all day long you run into people, noses in *Ulysses,* pointing to buildings and checking watches, trying to be where Bloom and Stephen Dedalus were at different times. Joyce wrote his book expressly so—he interlocked characters' passages, left clues of time of day, used actual landmarks for his characters. He claimed he was "more interested in the street names of Dublin than in the riddle of the universe," and *Ulysses,* presumably about the latter, has for a century kept people occupied about the former.

Once I had read *Ulysses,* though, Bloomsday became less preposterous than merely fascinating. I still couldn't see making the book central to my life, but seeing firsthand how deeply it affected so many others—especially when I was planning my own journey based on a book—sounded like fun. We checked in to a relatively cheap bed-and-breakfast, meeting cheerful festivalgoers who immediately identified us as outsiders; "civilians," they actually called us. I believe the word *Trekkie* first crossed my mind less than five minutes after we arrived at our hotel. The veterans remembered each other from previous Bloomsdays and other symposia: "Didn't I see you in Trieste?" or "Oh, I know him—we got drunk at the Ormond in 1999."

We walked to O'Connell Street for a free fried kidney—when readers first meet Leopold Bloom, Joyce's Odysseus character, he's frying a kidney—with ten thousand or so others in a vast public breakfast. We watched a bizarre evening street performance, including giant puppets and African drumming, of the episode Joyce based on Odysseus's visit to the island of Aeolus. One day we took a bus tour to the Martello tower where the book begins (the bus tour also included a stop before the house mentioned as the birthplace of Bloom's long-dead father, which actually had a blue historical marker; people took each other's pictures in front of it). We walked along O'Connell Street, following brass markers sunk into the sidewalk, detailing spots mentioned in the book. And each day, around an hour after lunch, we discovered that June, while not too pregnant to travel, was too pregnant to travel all day long, so in the afternoon while she napped I took a long walk on my own. Thus it was that on Bloomsday I was alone for two affecting encounters.

The first took place at F. W. Sweny, Chemist, where Bloom stops to buy some lemon soap. So did I, from a huge column of cases of lemon soap set up to satisfy the Joyceans who assaulted the shop that day. "You can get it yourself, dear, can't you?" said the woman behind the counter. "My feet, you know. It's been quite a day." I did. And then afterward, while I idly gazed into the pharmacy's window, which displayed pictures of Joyce and copies of *Ulysses,* four suited young businessmen walked by, instantly sizing me up: "Oh, we're on a pilgrimage," mocked one, "we're on a sacred pilgrimage." The others laughed and were gone, but I blushed. That didn't seem fair: I didn't yet consider myself a pilgrim, certainly not after anything Joyce had to offer. I dismissed the idea.

But it didn't stay dismissed. Later that afternoon I crossed a bridge over the Liffey to the Ormond Hotel, where the episode based on the Sirens took place. The bar was filled with sweating people wearing boater hats and other Victorian affectation—"the thinking man's Deadheads," one observer offered—and with plainly dressed onlookers like me. At the center of the room, several costumed singers performed songs related to *Ulysses,* which is famously filled with melody. In some ways it felt like any other group singing in a bar, though the size and dress of the crowd reminded you constantly of the special day. Then a tenor began the instantly recognizable tune of "Love's Old Sweet Song," the unofficial theme song of *Ulysses* for Joyceans. Joyce treats Penelope's faithfulness ironically (Molly, Bloom's wife, spends the entire book in bed, some of it having adulterous sex); Molly's a singer, and on an upcoming tour she plans, with her lover, to sing "Love's Old Sweet Song," which both underscores her adultery and also hints at a possible reconciliation with Bloom.

In any case, the tenor sang the first verse, and then, after a long pause, launched into the chorus:

> *Just a song at twilight, when the lights are low*
> *And the flick'ring shadows softly come and go.*

HOME AT LAST

Though the heart be weary, sad the day and long,
Still to us at twilight comes love's old song, comes love's old
  sweet song.

The entire room, softly at first, joined in, and then louder, sang along. The hair stood up at the back of my neck. As the voices swelled, as tears coursed down cheeks in the overheated barroom, for the first time I abandoned my sneering stance. This was significant—these pilgrims were getting something real from being together, from celebrating their love of something they all agreed was important, even central. I hoped I might find something like that community of interest on my own trip.

I DIDN'T, OF COURSE. On my trip, I was almost entirely on my own, stopping at places where many times even the locals didn't know of their supposed Odyssean connections. And only as the journey progressed did I slowly come to understand how completely I was doing the same thing as those Joyceans. And that if those disdainful businessmen were right—that I was on a sacred pilgrimage—that was nothing to feel embarrassed about. I had resisted the idea of pilgrimage because Odysseus wasn't a pilgrim, and I was trying to be like Odysseus. But a pilgrim, I finally recognized, approaches his journey not with understanding but with hope, not to discover something new but to rediscover something ancient. A pilgrim wishes not to understand Lourdes or Mecca or Jerusalem but to be near it, to be nourished by its power. This, I realized as my journey went on, was what I was doing.

Long before, on that Asian journey with my wife, we had learned to resist the haughtiness of Lonely Planetoids, scornful of seeing anything once the tourists had found it. We were right to resist; that's the opposite of the pilgrim spirit. A pilgrim is not a pioneer—the pilgrim wishes to be not the first or only one to see but to join the community of those who have seen. Sure, millions have seen the Mediterranean and walked every foot of my trip—and millions have read *The Odyssey*. But *I* had never traveled those paths before, so those ruins, caves, and islands had something brand new to offer to me, as did *The Odyssey* when I found it. No, I couldn't see those lands the way No-Man had seen them. I couldn't learn what he had learned—he'd already done that, and his story was now familiar. But by emulating Odysseus I could learn, instead of *with* him, *from* him—and thus learn my own lessons. Plus, by walking those paths I helped bring his world to mine, and anything that helped spike the plan of myth onto our own quotidian plane is worth it.

In fact, that was entirely the point. Just as the Joyceans put *Ulysses* at the center of their lives, had I not done the same with *The Odyssey*? Initially, I scoffed at their persnickety geographical devotion: Who could possibly want, as we did on that Dublin tour, to visit the house in which a character who doesn't even appear in the book was supposed to have been born? But by making my own choices on my *Odyssey* trip, I was doing the same: hoping that by going to the places associated with the story I could better internalize and better appreciate the story, better absorb it as my own. I wasn't reenacting any more, or any less, than they were—like them, I was celebrating.

And *The Odyssey* has lasted through the millennia because it's worth that celebration. Because it addresses the essential, probably unanswerable, questions we all face all the time—the questions we always will face. What to do against unreasonable power that can destroy you? How to make choice? Temptation will come; what then? If I spend the energy to distinguish myself, what of my family? If my lot is to be home with my family, what of my own gifts? This isn't something you retrace; this is just your life. A man, past his prime, proving himself yet again; a woman, long-suffering, patiently pretending to allow herself, once again, to be rescued by her partner. A dance as lovely as any that we do.

"The whole sense of the ubiquitous myth of the hero's passage is that it shall serve as a general pattern for men and women, wherever they may stand along the scale. . . . The individual has only to discover his own position with reference to this general human formula, and let it then assist him past his restricting walls. Who and where are his ogres? . . . What are his ideals? Those are the symptoms of his grasp of life." That's Joseph Campbell, and it's strong stuff. Yeah, the "general human formula"—that's just right. Whether your model is Bloom or Odysseus—or Jesus, for that matter, or Spider-Man—you've got a model somewhere. Chances are it's not new. And the thing is not to redo what your model did—the thing is to see what your model did, and then do what you need to do.

And just so, suddenly freed of my idiot desire to reenact the specifics of Odysseus's return to his wife, I was able to truly appreciate my return to my own wife.

I made my ferries and I took my plane, and I got home—almost.

After a hop from Rome to London, my plane flew to Philadelphia. By e-mail June and I had discussed whether I might not be wise, instead of catching my last connection home, to rent a car and drive to New York to visit my sister for a day. She had a raft of baby items for us, and I was going to have to drive up and get them sometime. On the one hand, I was exhausted and wanted to get home as soon as possible; on the other, the thought of soon leaving home yet again for another trip, even a mundane four-day road trip to visit family, sounded awful. I landed in Philadelphia, stood in miserable line after line for passport, customs, connecting flights. I was jet-lagged, dirty, and utterly unsure of what to do next, but the moment for decision had arrived.

I called June.

"I can't tell you what to do," she said. "Either way is fine—I love you and want you home, but I won't want you to leave again, either. I think you have to decide which you'd rather do."

And then, so close to my journey's end, I did a very un-Odyssean thing: I whined. I complained. I whimpered. Did she not get it? I had been traveling on and off for months now. I was tired. I was exhausted. I was at a loss and I didn't know what to do. Could she not please just help me decide?

For a moment silence, and then June's even, loving voice came to me through the pay phone: "Okay," she said. "You're tired. It's time to be done.

"You come home to me now."

You come home to me now. Odysseus, sneaking around in disguise for days on end, never got the chance to hear that. I said to myself, out loud there in that crappy airport, "That's *my* Penelope," and then I took off my backpack and sat down on it. I even cried a little bit. *You come home to me now.*

Journey's end.

*   *   *

LOOKING BACK NOW, I like that. Climb into a cave and wait around to
see if a Cyclops comes? I can do that. Seek temptation only to resist it?
Hell, that's second nature. Search for the lotus, the harbor of man-
eating giants, the dreadful sea monster? Sign me up.

But lie to my wife? I'm out. Odysseus, of course, takes Agamemnon's—and Athena's—advice to keep Penelope in the dark, so he
doesn't get to ask for her help. As a result, after outclevering everybody in the known world and beyond, he comes home and with her
little "move the bed" gambit, Penelope tricks him. The man of many
devices, the man of twists and turns, the trickiest man in the world,
talks to his wife for half an hour and *she* tricks *him*—though, of
course, the degree to which either is actually tricked by the other will
be discussed for millennia. You want to talk about universal truths.

My return home to June was less emotional than we might have
expected. For one thing, I had been home that once, midjourney, so
our final separation was only a matter of weeks; for another, in our
years together we had more than once spent months apart, so finding
each other after something of an absence merely exercised muscles
we had already developed. Most important, though, June's new shape
emphasized the homecoming we both much more strongly antic-
ipated. When I saw June's round belly, we both just laughed. That
night when we went to sleep, she said, "He's trying to bust out!"—
and I felt our baby doing backflips, preparing for a journey yet to
come.

On the other hand, as good a job as June did managing the contractors and choosing the colors for all the rooms in our house and in general keeping things together, when I got back, there was still one task
I had to perform: to paint the room we had set aside for our baby. So
instead of merely boring June to death with travel stories, I got to roll
up my sleeves and put my strength into something for our child yet to
be born. Choosing not to be informed beforehand of our baby's gender, we had no pink-versus-blue color code. June had filed through
decks of paint cards, and from among the "Parakeets" and "Solarias"
and "Rock Gardens" on the palette she chose a lovely misty green for

me to put on the walls in the room where our baby would live. The name of the color chosen by my clever, resourceful wife? "Greek Sea."

That's *my* Penelope.

I'M A JOURNALIST, a writer by trade, so it's no surprise that I had managed to convince myself that going places, following paths, finding things out, is as valuable a thing as a person can do in this world— that a journey like mine had the meaning with which I invested it. I came home from my big trip, my head full of ideas about middle age and life and home and travel, and I found myself recording in my journal that dreams just before waking left behind the phrase "transformational life experience." I was convinced that riding a scooter along a dusty street on a Tunisian island had mysterious deeper meanings. I felt like I had done something.

And then my wife had a baby. And transformational life experiences started flinging themselves at me out of the ether, sometimes a dozen or more per day.

Funny thing. When Penelope and Odysseus spend their magically long night sharing their stories, Penelope tells Odysseus all about her plotting against the suitors and about how they abused the household in his absence. What she doesn't mention is that in Odysseus's absence she has raised their son. She doesn't bring out finger-painted pictures that grew tattered on the refrigerator, doesn't talk about Halloween costumes or his music lessons. Telemachus is grown; that's a done deal, and if there's anything Odysseus truly missed, this is it.

That was exactly what I had raced home for.

I woke from deep sleep early one morning, June standing in front of me, wrapped in towels, still steaming from the shower. "I've started," she said. The way the electricity crackled around her, her face a smiling moon glowing in the light from down the hall, the Greeks would have said a goddess was in the room.

One was. Thirty-four hours of a bone-cracking, mind-piercing, soul-shattering process called *labor* later, any pride I felt in being able to find a hotel room on short notice had shriveled in the awe of what June had done. Then a little boy drew breath, and the word *home* for me suddenly had meaning utterly separate from some Greek island. This life, this breathing, this family, became the center, and far from ever leaving on another journey I wanted to station myself in front of our house, facing outward, holding a pointed stick. I had chosen wisely—two months of travel will not be available to me again for the foreseeable future, nor would I take them if they were. Now, three days away is too long.

I've thought about this a lot. All of the wars, all of the journeys, all of the roaring and the bellowing and the blood—all of this is what men do because we can't have babies. At birth, you are in the presence, literally, of life and death, of the thin line between them. Your accomplishments vanish in comparison to what you see your wife endure as she labors, risks all for the prize against which none compare. I think all the massive enterprises men undertake, we do simply to try to make ourselves feel like a part of something. Not for nothing is Odysseus described after his final battle as exhausted and covered in blood. He washes up on Calypso's shore with nothing but the clothes on his back; he washes up on the shore of the Phaeacians without even that. And he's deposited, sleeping, on his native Ithaca, to say nothing of having gone to the land of the dead and come back. If anybody's ever been reborn, it's Odysseus. And he knows what he wants: He wants to go home.

When Odysseus and Penelope finally embrace, Homer describes the two weeping together: "To her he was as welcome as sight of land to swimmers whose sturdy ship Poseidon has battered and shattered at sea where wind and big wave beat hard upon it, and sweet indeed is the moment when the few survivors, having swum inshore and struggled their way through the surf, set foot at last on dry land." That's pretty welcome, but the image of the two of them weeping came back to me, there in that delivery room with June, and her mom, and doctors and nurses and this unimaginable new creature, this little boy of ours. Weep was what we all did.

There's a ton of weeping in *The Odyssey,* and almost no laughter. At every greeting, every parting, every safe landing, every escape: weeping, weeping, weeping. And I realized: Weeping is the emotion of middle age. Once you get to your forties, no joy fails to remind you of its opposite, or its cost, or those not present to share it; no sorrow fails to get its due. To weep is to be human, to be alive, to have grown up. I keep asking friends how old they were when they could look at their kids without weeping, and the answer is always the same: They'll tell me if they ever get there.

FINALLY, PENELOPE DEMANDS that Odysseus tell her about this journey that Tiresias has prophesied. "I'm likely to learn of it later, I think, so I might as well hear what it is right now." The sensible wife as ever, Penelope just wants the lay of the land. Odysseus tells the story about journeying until his oar is mistaken for a winnowing fan, and she's matter-of-fact: "Well, if the gods are really to give you a better old age, then we can hope that someday your troubles will be over and done with." It's a nice mixed bag—they know that Odysseus has more work to do, more adventures, but they at least have the hope of rest at the end.

June and I felt the same, of course, though we didn't need a dead Theban prophet to explain it. We may have a nice old age, with our troubles over and done with; that we can't predict. But we do have something Odysseus and Penelope didn't: Our next journey goes together. Our next adventure, God and all the gods willing, is raising a little boy.

And that's an adventure even Odysseus never had.

Epilogue

Souvenirs

As for us, we'll sit here eating and drinking and recalling delightful old stories of our grievous misfortunes. It can be very sweet for a man whose wanderings and woes have been many to remember the hardships he had in earlier days.

—*The Odyssey,* Book XV

ANDRA MOI ENNEPE, MOUSA, polutropon, hos mala polla, plankte. . . . I turn on my little recorder and hear, in soft, measured tones, the first words of *The Odyssey,* in ancient Greek, the very words Homer made. "The man—speak to me, Muse, about the man of many turnings, who had to wander very much. . . ." Long after my return, Peter Smith, classics professor at the University of North Carolina, listened to my tale and took pity on me, gladly sitting down in his office and both translating the first ten lines of the poem—that famous proem—on the fly, and then reading them, slowly, aloud. I enjoyed the translation, hearing Smith explain how *polutropon,* which literally means "many turnings," has been the most variably translated word in *The Odyssey.* Wily? Much-traveled? Of many resources, many ways? Ingenious? Versatile? Five words into the poem, and you already have to layer onto it your own interpretation.

Talk about a lesson.

But I especially loved just hearing Smith speak the words, even if I couldn't understand—hearing the beginning of this poem spoken the way a bard might have spoken it, the poem traveling from mouth to ear, as it has since we've had poems. The measured, gently pulsing rhythm of the words, even for the just under a minute it took to read those ten lines, hypnotized like mysterious, soothing music. Smith smiled when he finished, translating the final words. "Tell us, too," the proem ends—a reminder that for every generation this poem will always have something new to share. Or something old but unnoticed, which amounts to the same thing. After all my reading, my travels, my experiences, hearing the words gave me yet another new way to connect to a story that will long continue giving me new ways to read it.

IN ONE WAY my trip failed. One thing I had hoped to do was to feel done—to feel finished, sated, home for good, the way Odysseus felt, or anyhow the way I had believed Odysseus felt. When Odysseus gets home, he knows from Tiresias that he's got one major journey left—the one inland to plant that oar—but after that things look peaceful, and he's happy. As for me, I know another long journey like this one is highly unlikely, and I'm certainly glad to have had a last trip while my shoulders and sacroiliac were up to it, but when I look at a world map now I don't think, Done! I think, Australia. Maybe I just need an oar to plant.

We never really hear about that, or what happens to Odysseus at home. The unknown author of the vanished *Telegony*—the very final chapter of the Epic Cycle, the only one that comes after *The Odyssey*—supposedly tells of the voyage of Telegonus, a son Odysseus has fathered with Circe, to Ithaca in search of his father. Unaware he's on Ithaca, he makes a pirate raid; Odysseus protects his island, and before you can say "Oedipus," Telegonus kills his father with a spear tipped with the stinger from a stingray, neatly fulfilling Tiresias's prophecy regarding death from the sea. According to some traditions, afterward Telemachus marries Circe and Telegonus marries Penelope; according to others, Telemachus eventually marries that lovely young Nausicaa of the Phaeacians. Which is all clever, but probably a bit too clever.

I like to think Odysseus stayed home a good long while, helping Telemachus get started, then soon enough letting Telemachus run the kingdom. I think he made his home with Penelope, tended his flocks, talked things over with Eumaeus and Laertes, kept busy. I think he spent long hours in the palace watching Telemachus—just watching him, his eyes ever thirsty for a glimpse of the son whose youth he missed. I also suspect he got on Penelope's nerves some—used to getting along without him, after all, she probably came to appreciate her time alone, so I figure Odysseus got out plenty, for mischief if not full-blown adventure. Just the same, I think the two had a good time there toward the end, sitting quietly together. I imagine a sigh from one of them making them exchange a glance and maybe a smile, then return to their thoughts, both rich beyond imagining. Maybe *The Odyssey* functions as nothing more than a metaphor for that: All people wish they were at home more with their kids, but have to be away, working more than they'd like; on the other hand, they're secretly pleased when they have to go out on adventure. All people would like more help from their spouses and need to be clever enough to get things done themselves. All children grow up thinking their parents have made a terrible mess of things and that they'd better grow up quickly so they can take charge before things utterly collapse.

I don't suppose I believed I'd come home from the Mediterranean with a list of practicable virtues—any more than I believed I'd really find a Cyclops in that cave. Still, after my season with Odysseus, it was nice to feel like I had at least burrowed closer to the soul of this old sea song. All people face hardships on their journeys: bullies, storms, temptations, starvation, the failure of companions, good advice not taken, bad luck even when you've done everything right. All people face hardship at home: poor treatment by the community; subtle threats forcing you to accommodate outrageous behavior; difficulty raising children when the resources never seem to be enough; trouble with the help. All people face the obstacle of achieving adulthood: parents either absent or overprotective; a paucity of good examples and an awful wealth of bad ones; the terror of knowing that, finally, you have to take those first steps on your own. And always, that awareness that the gods play an unknowable role: Just because things go badly, it doesn't mean you've sinned, and if they go well, that doesn't proclaim your virtue—maybe Zeus just hasn't gone through his mail, and there's plenty of trouble in store for you yet.

Anyhow, Odysseus went on his journey and I went on mine, and when I got back I found the same thing he did, according to Joseph Campbell: Though we undertake "what had promised to be our own unique, unpredictable, and dangerous adventure, all we find in the end is such a series of standard metamorphoses as men and women have undergone in every quarter of the world, in all recorded centuries, and under every odd disguise of civilization." Like all myth, *The Odyssey* is part of our great human story: "a vast and amazingly constant statement of the basic truths by which man has lived throughout the millenniums of his residence on the planet."

MY CURRENT RESIDENCE ON THE PLANET doesn't show too many signs of my recent travels—one good thing about backpack traveling is it limits the purchase of the kind of junk that seems like just what you need when you buy it but doesn't serve any purpose when you get it home. Sure, I have a pocket-size alabaster bust of Odysseus (from Ithaca) on my desk now, a little wooden Trojan Horse on a key chain, even that lemon soap from Dublin. But as souvenirs they function all too well: They bring back memories of themselves, not of my travels. As genuine spurs to memory, I prefer the effluvia of the journey itself, the hoard of ticket stubs and receipts from which I could probably recreate my trip. Boarding passes. Train tickets. Landing cards. A Turkish bus ticket, *"Yolcu Tasima Bileti,"* from Istanbul to Çanakkale, in a little four-color envelope—and suddenly there's bus travel in Turkey: cakes and cologne.

Even those miss the point. The real souvenirs, of course, are memories, and they come when they come. A couscous dinner June makes can have me standing at the sink rinsing the dishes afterward and dreamily remembering Tunisia. When that happens, though I may yearn for Tunisia, I also take pleasure that I'm home, standing at the sink, rinsing the dishes—that I've had dinner with my wife, that my son plays with her in the other room. That I don't have to figure out where I'm going to sleep the next night; I just have to give my son a bath. And as I do that I try to remember the feeling ·of that *tellak's* hands in the Turkish bath—I want my son to feel that confidence, want him to let me bathe him, let my hands clean, caress, comfort him. When the time comes, I'll try to make sure this remains my journey and not his—that like Odysseus did for Telemachus, I'll get out of the way so he can start his own. Just not so soon, I hope. And finally, hanging on our medicine cabinet are three necklaces—first one with a piece of jade from the Hong Kong market, worn on my Asian travels; next, my recent string, with Athena's owl and June's ring; and atop the others a thong strung by June's birthing coach, who put on it not only a special charm for Louie but a bead for each hour of June's labor. Thirty-four beads. As if I needed further reminding that my travels are completely trumped by our home, our little boy.

Sometimes it is my job to help him get to sleep. A streetlight shines almost directly into his window, so we have to draw the pale-green curtains, which makes the room a little too dark for the countless reconnaissance missions we run, checking on him. Early on in the sleepless hallucination of his first weeks, we tried several different night-light solutions, but nothing quite worked. Too strong a light kept him awake, but the deep-green walls of his room absorbed the dim illumination of most nightlights.

Finally, I remembered—out in the office. Internally lit by a fifteen-watt bulb, its soft blue glow would perfectly fill his room at night without keeping him awake. I fetched it, plugged it in, and turned it on: a globe, a spinning blue world all for him. He points to it now, and before sleep he likes to touch it, to see it spin. If he touches someplace I went, I talk: "That's where daddy went," I tell him. "There are caves there, and you can go inside, but you have to be careful." If he touches where I have not been, I hold him closer. "Maybe you will go there," I say. "And you can tell me what it's like." The parallel is unimaginably sweet. I'm home, where I now need to be. The globe is no longer the vast scene of heroic wanderings—it's small, the size of a basketball, nothing more than a serene blue glow to comfort my boy if he wakes in the night. It's the perfect gift from parent to child. Here: The world—it was mine for a time, but now it's yours. Where would you like to go? In any case, it helps him to sleep. Maybe that's my new Homeric epithet: "soother of infants," or "father of sleeping child." I hope when he's older he asks one day about the journey on which I tried to follow Odysseus. "Well," I can say, "let me tell you a story."

* * *

SO IT'S OVER, but is it ever over really? The other way my trip remains uncompleted is that not only am I not done adventuring, I'm not even done with *The Odyssey*. I find countless new *Odysseys* and paeans to *The Odyssey*, retellings of *The Odyssey* and touchstones to *The Odyssey* everywhere I look. The Steely Dan song "Home at Last" delightfully addresses the Sirens; Suzanne Vega gives a thoughtful glimpse inside the head of that protofeminist goddess in "Calypso"; Eudora Welty writes a moody short story, "Circe"; and that's all within reach among the books and records on our first floor.

Go to the library and you'll never get home. The ancient Greeks—Euripides, Sophocles, those guys—mostly hated Odysseus, seeing in him a silver-tongued politician, willing to say anything for victory. The Romans, considering themselves descendants of Trojan Aeneas, mostly agreed: Virgil calls him "ruthless" and "heartless," though the good-hearted Horace, writing at almost exactly the same time, considered Odysseus "a useful example of virtue and wisdom at work."

Modern writers have seen Odysseus more as a questing spirit—Tennyson's famous poem "Ulysses" casts him as feeling a little crazy and cooped up at home and setting out late in life "to follow knowledge like a sinking star / beyond the utmost bound of human thought"; Dante's *Inferno* describes him much the same. At this point Odysseus, that guy who wanted more than anything else to get and stay home, has become his opposite. At which point you've come, perhaps by the back door, to an explanation of why the story remains so popular.

The story has good bones. Whatever point you need to make, this framework might fit. You can cast Odysseus as good guy or bad guy, absent father or courageous traveler; Penelope can be patient and clever or sneaky and manipulative, Telemachus a spirited youth champing at the bit or a troubled lad needing a kick in the butt. Whatever you're trying to say, you can probably get it said with this cast of characters. On my way home from Europe, one of the airline movie channels showed *Pinocchio*, and I laughed: You mean that movie about the journey to full personhood, with temptations and monsters, a boy's journey in search of his father, and a father's anxious return to his son? Is this not just *The Odyssey* again? Isn't it everywhere?

My favorite non-Homeric portrait of Odysseus comes in Plato's

Republic, in a section at the end called the Myth of Er, in which a fellow named Er dies but is sent back to the earth to tell people what the afterlife is like. He describes souls getting the opportunity to choose their next lives. Haughty Agamemnon chooses to be an eagle, a buffoon named Thersites chooses to be an ape, and so forth. Odysseus, as it happens, has to choose last of all. Plato describes him wandering around the corners among the ignored lives, finally picking one of complete obscurity. Odysseus isn't sorry, mind you—he makes his choice gladly, "saying that he would have done the same if his lot had come first."

Which, I'm somewhat embarrassed to say, brings me back, finally, to where all this started: to James Joyce, and *Ulysses.* Joyce's portrait of Leopold Bloom as a guy who just wants to get through his day, who encounters adventures that he'd really rather avoid, who desperately wants a son, and who really wants little more than a peaceful life at home, may be as close to the heart of Homer's Odysseus as anyone's ever come since. Don't get me wrong, I'm not about to go back and reread Joyce; I mean, a joke is a joke. Just the same, I'll admit it out loud: I'm not sorry I read it. Joyce was on to something.

IN MY ENDLESS LIBRARY WANDERING, I finally ran across this, by the first century AD Roman philosopher Seneca, in the *Epistles,* number LXXXVIII:

> You ask where Ulysses will have wandered instead of acting so as to keep us from always wandering? There is no time to listen for whether he was tossed between Italy and Sicily or outside the world known to us—nor could he have wandered so long in a space so narrow. The storms of the soul toss us daily, and iniquity drives us into all the ills of Ulysses. The beauty is not lacking to assail our eyes, nor is an enemy lacking. Here wild monsters delighting in human gore; there the subtle blandishments of gold, shipwreck, and every kind of evil. Teach me how to love my fatherland, my wife, my father; how, even shipwrecked, I may steer towards honor. Why do you ask if Penelope was immodest or caused scandal to her age? If she sus-

pected before she knew for sure that the man she saw was Ulysses? Teach me what modesty is, and the amount of good there is in it, and whether it be located in the body or the soul.

I'm glad I didn't run across this before I decided to take my trip, but it barely differed from something Peter Smith said to me during our afternoon of translation. He cautioned me against straying into euhemerism—after Euhemerus of Messene, a third-century-BC Greek author who wrote a work claiming to trace the Greek gods back to actual historical personages, who over time were deified into Olympian gods with fantastical powers. By trying to turn everything fantastic into something merely historical, something ultimately pedestrian, Smith said, you risk losing what makes it wonderful in the first place. The choice between the whirlpool and the terrible dragon, for example, loses its visceral power if you reduce it to nothing more than an old sea story about a treacherous strait that's been repeated too many times. If it's a folktale, a work of the imagination, it carries transcendent undertones about the human condition; if it's nothing but traveling directions, then it's little better than the MapQuest searches to which I laughingly compared it. Euhemerism misses the point, Smith adjured: "Not the geography," he said, "but the story itself guides you." I ended up writing that down on my wall. With the exception of a few words to Odysseus from a clear-thinking witch, it's the best travel advice I've ever heard.

SO I SPEND MY TIME AT HOME NOW, but I'll never be done with *The Odyssey*. There's always a new translation, a new interpretation, another good reason to pick it up. In fact, *The Odyssey* was the very first ever Penguin Classic, translated by E. V. Rieu as the bombs fell on London during the Blitz. I take comfort from the vision of Rieu tuning out the bombs by immersing himself in the oldest story we have; perhaps I even feel a kinship. When I made the brash statement about Joyce that got me started on *The Odyssey*, something as small as my own age seemed like a large issue—that was June 2001, and only from the perspective of a few years later can we see how peaceful things were then. And just as it must have looked to Rieu, it now once again seems like we wish to shake our world to its roots. Huge armies mass for war; surprise attacks set cities ablaze. Among nations, within nations, within families, all is suspicion, all is uncertain. Like Rieu, for comfort in dark times I've tuned in to the oldest story we have, and I'll probably keep tuning in, enjoying new versions when I find them. Pop songs or box tops, movie plots or poems, I'm sure the *Odyssey* story will continue to enchant artists, and they'll continue to supply a steady stream of new takes on this old story.

Of course, enough is enough; you can take things too far. Derek Walcott wrote a poem called *Omeros,* a modern Caribbean treatment of the Homer stories, and from what little I've read that looks like fun. Greek poet Nikos Kazantzakis, on the other hand, wrote a sequel to *The Odyssey* detailing Odysseus's further adventures that goes on for 33,333 verses, longer than *The Odyssey* and *The Iliad* combined. Continuing the story with his own ideas is, of course, very much in the Odyssean tradition. But 33,333 verses? That sounds way too long, and way too difficult.

I swear I'll never read that.

Translations and Bibliography

BY THE TIME my affections for *The Odyssey* had passed the crush and fascination stages to arrive at full-fledged obsession, I had amassed an entire library of different translations, which I consulted to compare favorite passages or, since I have no ancient Greek, to worry out confusing spots. I kept mostly to the little blue one by Ennis Rees that June had bought me—apart from being a totem object, it was what one classics professor described as what he would expect if he asked an A+ student to translate on the fly: very faithful to the Greek, and rendered in poetic lines, so with it I felt very close to Homer himself. Just the same, as familiar as it became to me, those poetic line breaks sometimes slowed my eye; that's probably what kept me from greater reliance on the 1996 translation by Robert Fagles. Though universally praised and quite brilliant (Fagles calls Odysseus in the first line "the man of twists and turns," a wonderful rendering of a word variously translated as everything from "storm-tossed" to the pedestrian "versatile" of the Rees I carried), Fagles's translation retains poetic line breaks, which are just harder to read.

Speaking of poetry, when indulging my own A+ student tendencies, I commonly turned to the famous Alexander Pope translation that I found online, though it's hard to square your tweed-jacket *Masterpiece Theatre* fantasy with pop-ups about online porn and poker sites; so on those rainy afternoons when I repaired to armchair with cup of tea and *The Odyssey*, I usually dawdled over the Chapman translation. Though like Pope Chapman sticks to heroic couplets, Chapman adds marvelous marginalia: He describes "this inimitable and miraculous Poeme" as "the information or fashion of an absolute man," rather encouraging for someone like me, who saw things the same way. More, Chapman places short poems before each book giving the argument of what's to come: Thus, before Book IX, including the Cicones, the Lotus-eaters, and the Cyclops, Chapman succinctly writes, "The strangely fed / Lotophagi. / The Cicons fled. / The Cyclop's eye."

But when I just wanted to reread an episode so that I got it, so that it most smoothly made its way to my spirit, I turned always to two prose translations: The smooth, easy loops of Samuel Butler's 1900 translation go down easy, and the book includes a list of "Principal Personages of the Odyssey," which at times proved helpful. More, the three-page table of contents includes a tiny summary of each book, distilling the entire poem into a hugely convenient list; not only that, the Butler has the first map of *The Odyssey* I ever saw. And if it differed from my own, that's just part of the fun. Finally, the easiest-to-read version of the poem is probably the most widely known: the Penguin Classic, published in 1946, translated by E. V. Rieu. With an index, a glossary, a thorough introduction, and line numbers for each book, it formed the perfect companion to the stark text rendering of my Rees. Here's a list of the ones I used. My favorites are in **boldface type.**

Translations of *The Odyssey*

Butler, Samuel, trans. *The Odyssey of Homer.* Roslyn, N.Y: Walter J. Black, 1944.

Chapman, George, trans. *The Odyssey*. Princeton, N.J.: Princeton University Press, 1956.

Cook, Albert, trans. *The Odyssey: A Verse Translation, Backgrounds, Criticism.* New York: Norton, 1993.

Fagles, Robert, trans. *The Odyssey*. Introduction and notes by Bernard Knox. New York: Viking, 1996.

Fitzgerald, Robert, trans. *The Odyssey.* New York: Doubleday, 1961. Found in *Adventures in Reading.* Pegasus edition. Orlando: Harcourt Brace Jovanovich, 1989. Also in *Literature: Timeless Voices, Timeless Themes.* Gold level. Upper Saddle River, N.J.: Prentice Hall, 2000.

Palmer, George Herbert, trans. *The Odyssey.* Edited with an introduction and notes by Robert Squillace. New York: Barnes & Noble Classics, 2003.

Pope, Alexander, trans. *The Odyssey*. Project Gutenberg, Etext 3160, 2002
<http://www.gutenberg.org/etext/3160>.
Rees, Ennis, trans. *The Odyssey of Homer*. New York: Random House, 1960.
Rieu, E. V., trans. *The Odyssey*. London: Penguin, 1946.
Rouse, W. H. D., trans. *The Odyssey*. New York: New American Library, 1999.

Secondary Sources

THE REMAINDER OF THIS LISTING represents the portion of the vast sea of
literature surrounding *The Odyssey* that I encountered on my own journey. A reader with a different sensibility could easily start out in
another direction and create another list just as long without duplicat-
ing any of the titles. Just the same, this listing does provide the trail of
my own research, and thus may provide the source of ideas that struck
some readers as reasonable and worth pursuing further and other readers as sufficiently stupid to be worth researching themselves. In any
case, for readers just interested and looking for another place to go, I
have indicated books I found worthy, unusual, or nutty enough to be
worth exploring on their own merits by setting them in **boldface type.**

Classical Sources and Versions of Homeric Stories

Apollodorus. *The Library of Greek Mythology*. Trans. Robin Hard. Oxford:
Oxford University Press. 1997.
Apollonius of Rhodes. *The Voyage of Argo*. Trans. E. V. Rieu. London: Penguin,
1971.
Grant, Michael. *Readings in the Classical Historians*. New York: Scribners, 1992.
Herodotus. *The Histories*. Trans. Robin Waterfield. Oxford: Oxford University
Press, 1998.
Hesiod, Homeric Hymns, Epic Cycle, Homerica. Trans. Hugh G. Evelyn White.
Cambridge, Mass.: Harvard University Press, 2002.
Homer. *The Iliad*. Trans. Samuel Butler. Roslyn, N.Y.: Walter J. Black, 1942.
Horace. *Satires and Epistles of Horace*. Trans. Smith Palmer Bovie. Chicago:
University of Chicago Press, 1959.
Hyginus. *Fabulae: The Myths of Hyginus*. Trans. Mary Grant. Lawrence:
University of Kansas Press, 1960.
Ovid. *The Metamorphoses*. Trans. Horace Gregory. New York: Mentor, 1958.
Pausanias. *Guide to Greece*. Trans. Peter Levi. London: Penguin, 1971.

Plato. *The Republic of Plato*. Trans. Francis MacDonald Cornford. Oxford: Oxford University Press, 1945.

Polybius. *Histories*. Trans. Evelyn S. Shuckburgh. New York: Macmillan, 1889.

Quintus Smyrnaeus. *The Fall of Troy*. Trans. Arthur S. Way. Cambridge, Mass.: Harvard University Press, 1913.

Sandars, N. K., trans. *The Epic of Gilgamesh*. London: Penguin, 1972.

Sophocles. *The Complete Plays of Sophocles*. Trans. Sir Richard Claverhouse Jebb. New York: Bantam, 1982.

Strabo. *The Geography of Strabo*. Trans. Horace Leonard Jones. Cambridge, Mass.: Harvard University Press, 1989.

Tacitus. *The Agricola and the Germania*. Trans. Harold Mattingly. London: Penguin, 1979.

Thucydides. *The Complete Writings of Thucydides*. Trans. John H. Finley Jr. New York: Modern Library, 1951.

Virgil. *The Aeneid*. Trans. Patric Dickinson. New York: Mentor Books, 1961.

Modern Sources Regarding *The Odyssey* and Its Culture

Ahl, Frederick, and Hanna Roisman. *The Odyssey Re-Formed*. Ithaca, N.Y.: Cornell University Press, 1996.

Beye, Charles Rowan. *Odysseus: A Life*. New York: Hyperion, 2004.

Bloom, Harold, ed. *Odysseus/Ulysses*. New York: Chelsea House, 1991.

Boorstin, Daniel. *The Creators: A History of Heroes of the Imagination*. New York: Random House, 1992.

Brann, Eva. *Homeric Moments: Clues to Delight in Reading the Odyssey and the Iliad*. Philadelphia: Paul Dry Books, 2002.

Butler, Samuel. *The Authoress of the Odyssey*. Chicago: University of Chicago Press, 1967.

Cahill, Thomas. *Sailing the Wine-Dark Sea: Why the Greeks Matter*. New York: Doubleday, 2003.

Calvino, Italo. "The Odysseys Within the Odyssey." In *The Uses of Literature*. New York: Harcourt Brace Jovanovich, 1982.

———. "Why Read the Classics?" In *The Uses of Literature*. New York: Harcourt Brace Jovanovich, 1982.

Casson, Lionel. *Travel in the Ancient World*. Baltimore: Johns Hopkins University Press, 1994.

Clarke, Howard. *The Art of the Odyssey*. Englewood Cliffs, N.J.: Prentice Hall, 1967.

———. *Homer's Readers: A Historical Introduction to the Iliad and the Odyssey*. Newark: University of Delaware Press, 1980.

Clay, Jenny Strauss. *The Wrath of Athena: Gods and Men in the Odyssey*. Princeton, N.J.: Princeton University Press, 1983.

Dalby, Andrew. *Rediscovering Homer: Inside the Origins of the Epic*. New York: Norton, 2006.

Eliot, Alexander. *Greece*. New York: Time-Life Books, 1963.

Finley, M. I. *The World of Odysseus*. New York: New York Review Books, 2002.

Glenn, Justin. "The Polyphemus Folktale and Homer's Kyklopeia." *Transactions and Proceedings of the American Philological Association* 102 (1971): 133–181.

Grant, Michael. *The Ancient Mediterranean*. New York: Penguin, 1969.

Hughes, Bettany. *Helen of Troy: Goddess, Princess, Whore*. New York: Knopf, 2005.

Leed, Eric J. *The Mind of the Traveler: From Gilgamesh to Global Tourism*. New York: Basic Books, 1991.

Lord, Albert. *The Singer of Tales*. Cambridge, Mass.: Harvard University Press, 1960.

Luce, J. V. *Homer and the Heroic Age*. London: Thames & Hudson, 1975.

Malkin, Irad. *The Returns of Odysseus: Colonization and Ethnicity*. Berkeley: University of California Press, 1998.

Mondi, Robert. "The Homeric Cyclopes: Folktale, Tradition, and Theme." *Transactions of the American Philological Association* 113 (1983): 17–38.

Obregon, Mauricio. *Beyond the Edge of the Sea: Sailing with Jason and the Argonauts, Ulysses, the Vikings, and Other Explorers of the Ancient World*. New York: Random House, 2001.

Page, Denys. *Folktales in Homer's Odyssey*. Cambridge, Mass.: Harvard University Press, 1973.

Powell, Barry. *Homer and the Origin of the Greek Alphabet*. Cambridge, U.K.: Cambridge University Press, 1991.

Price, Roberto Salinas. *Homer's Blind Audience: An Essay on the Iliad's Geographical Prerequisites for the Site of Ilios*. San Antonio: Scylax, 1983.

Rhys, Brian. *Did Homer Live?* New York: E. P. Dutton, 1931.

Ruskin, John. *The Queen of the Air: Being a Study of the Greek Myths of Cloud and Storm*. New York: Caldwell, 1886.

Scott, John. *Homer and His Influence*. New York: Cooper Square, 1963.

Shay, Jonathan. *Achilles in Vietnam: Combat Trauma and the Undoing of Character*. New York: Scribner, 1994.

———. *Odysseus in America: Combat Trauma and the Trials of Homecoming*. New York: Scribner, 2002.

Snider, Denton J. *Homer's Iliad: A Commentary*. St. Louis: Sigma, 1987.

Stanford, W. B., and J. V. Luce. *The Quest for Ulysses*. New York: Praeger, 1974.

Stanford, W. B. *The Ulysses Theme: A Study in the Adaptability of a Traditional Hero*. Ann Arbor: University of Michigan Press, 1963.

Steiner, George, and Robert Fagles. *Homer: A Collection of Critical Essays*. Englewood Cliffs, N.J.: Prentice Hall, 1962.

Stewart, Desmond. *Turkey*. New York: Time-Life Books, 1969.

Strauss, Barry. *The Trojan War: A New History.* New York: Simon & Schuster, 2006.

Tracy, Stephen V. *The Story of the Odyssey.* Princeton, N.J.: Princeton University Press, 1990.

Regarding Homeric Geography and History

Bérard, Victor. *Dans le Sillage D'Ulysse.* Paris: Librairie Armand Colin, 1933.

————. *Ithaque et las Grece des Acheens.* Paris: Librairie Armand Colin, 1935.

————. *Introduction a L'Odysee.* Paris: Societe d'edition "Des Belles Lettres," 1924.

————. *Les Navigations d'Ulysse.* Paris: Librairie Armand Colin, 1935.

Bittlestone, Robert, with James Diggle and John Underhill. *Odysseus Unbound: The Search for Homer's Ithaca.* Cambridge, U.K.: Cambridge University Press, 2005.

Bradford, Ernle. *Ulysses Found.* New York: Harcourt, Brace & World, 1963.

Bunbury, Sir Edward Herbert. *A History of Ancient Geography Among the Greeks and Romans, from the Earliest Ages till the Fall of the Roman Empire.* **New York: Dover, 1959.**

Deuel, Leo. *Memoirs of Heinrich Schliemann: A Documentary Portrait Drawn from His Autobiographical Writings, Letters, and Excavation Reports.* **New York: Harper & Row, 1977.**

Lessing, Erich. *The Voyages of Ulysses: A Photographic Interpretation of Homer's Classic.* Basle: Herder Freiburg, 1965.

Ludwig, Emil. *On Mediterranean Shores.* Boston: Little, Brown, 1929.

Nathan, Fernand. *En Mediteranee dans le Sillage d'Ulysse.* Paris: Attiliao Gaudio, 1967.

Obregon, Mauricio. *Ulysses Airborne.* New York: Harper & Row, 1971.

Pillot, Gilbert. *The Secret Code of the Odyssey: Did the Greeks Sail the Atlantic?* **London: Abelard-Schuman, 1972.**

Roth, Hal. *We Followed Odysseus.* Port Washington, Wisc.: Seaworthy Publications, 1999.

Schildt, Goran. *In the Wake of Ulysses.* New York: Dodd, Mead, 1953.

Schliemann, Heinrich. *Ilios: The City and Country of the Trojans; the Results of Researches and Discoveries on the Site of Troy and Throughout the Troad in the Years 1871, 72, 73, 78, 79.* New York: B. Blom, 1968.

————. *Troy and Its Remains: A Narrative of Researches and Discoveries Made on the Site of Ilium, and in the Trojan Plain.* **New York: Arno Press, 1976.**

Severin, Tim. *The Ulysses Voyage.* New York: E. P. Dutton, 1987.

Thomson, J. Oliver. *History of Ancient Geography.* New York: Biblo & Tannen, 1965.

Tozer, Henry Fanshawe. *A History of Ancient Geography.* 1948. Reprint, New York: Biblo & Tannen, 1964.

Wilkens, Iman. *Where Troy Once Stood.* New York: St. Martin's, 1991.

Wolf, Armin, and Hans-Helmut Wolf. *Die wirkliche Reise des Odysseus.* Berlin: Langen Muller, 1983.

Wood, Michael. *In Search of the Trojan War.* New York: Facts on File, 1985.

Regarding Mythology

Campbell, Joseph. *The Hero with a Thousand Faces.* Princeton, N.J.: Princeton University Press, 1968.

————. *Myths to Live By.* New York: Bantam, 1972.

Hamilton, Edith. *Mythology.* New York: Warner Books, 1942.

Hendricks, Rhoda A. *Classical Gods and Heroes: Myths as Told by the Ancient Authors.* New York: William Morrow, 1974.

Hyde, Lewis. *Trickster Makes This World: Mischief, Myth, and Art.* New York: North Point Press, 1998.

Lefkowitz, Mary. *Greek Gods, Human Lives: What We Can Learn from Myths.* New Haven, Conn.: Yale University Press, 2003.

Modern Fictional or Poetic Treatments of Homeric Themes

Atwood, Margaret. *The Penelopiad.* Edinburgh: Canongate, 2005.

Barico, Alessandro. *An Iliad.* New York: Knopf, 2006.

Burton, Sir Richard, trans. *The Arabian Nights.* Adapted by Jack Zipes. New York: Signet, 1991.

Clarke, Lindsay. *The Return from Troy.* London: HarperCollins, 2005.

————. *The War at Troy.* New York: St. Martin's Press, 2004.

Cussler, Clive. *Trojan Odyssey.* London: Penguin, 2004.

Dante. *The Inferno.* Trans. Robert Pinsky. New York: Farrar, Straus & Giroux, 1994.

Gemmell, David. *Troy: Lord of the Silver Bow.* New York: Ballantine, 2005.

George, Margaret. *Helen of Troy.* New York: Viking, 2006.

Gluck, Louise. *Meadowlands.* HarperCollins, 1996.

Kazantzakis, Nikos. *The Odyssey: A Modern Sequel.* Trans. Simon Friar. New York: Simon & Schuster, 1985. *N.B.: This book not read.*

Keats, John. *Selected Poems and Letters.* Ed. Douglas Bush. Boston: Houghton Mifflin, 1959.

Koehler, Jeff. "The Lotus Eaters: The Lure of the Lost." In *Tin House* 5, no. 4 (Summer 2004).

Milligan, Peter, and Jamie Hewlett. *Tank Girl: The Odyssey.* London: Titan, 2002.

Plutarch. *The Lives of the Noble Grecians and Romans.* Trans. John Dryden. New York: Modern Library, 1961.

Shakespeare, William. *The Complete Works.* New York: Viking, 1977.

Spenser, Edmund. *Poetical Works.* Ed. J. C. Smith and E. de Selincourt. Oxford: Oxford University Press, 1975.

Tennyson, Alfred. *Selected Poems*. Ed. William C. DeVane. Northbrook, Ill.: AHM Publishing, 1957.

Walcott, Derek. *Omeros*. New York: Farrar, Straus & Giroux, 1992.

Regarding Joyce's *Ulysses*

Blamires, Harry. *The Bloomsday Book: A Guide through Joyce's Ulysses*. London: Methuen, 1966.

Hart, Clive, and Leo Knuth. *A Topographical Guide to James Joyce's Ulysses*. Colchester: A Wake Newslitter, 1975.

Joyce, James. *Ulysses*. Ed. Hans Walter Gabler. New York: Vintage, 1986.

McCarthy, Jack, with Danis Rose. *Joyce's Dublin: A Walking Guide to Ulysses*. New York: St. Martin's, 1986.

McCarthy, Joe. *Ireland*. New York: Time-Life Books, 1964.

Nicholson, Robert. *The Ulysses Guide: Tours through Joyce's Dublin*. Dublin: New Island, 2002.

Reference Books

Baldwin, Stanley. *The Odyssey: CliffsNotes*. New York: Wiley, 2000.

Baumgartner, Anne S. *A Comprehensive Dictionary of the Gods*. New York: Carol Communications, 1984.

Bently, Peter, ed. *The Dictionary of World Myth*. New York: Facts on File, 1995.

Fowler, Robert, ed. *Cambridge Companion to Homer*. Cambridge, U.K.: Cambridge University Press, 2004.

Graves, Robert. *The Greek Myths*. London: Penguin, 1960.

Harpur, James, and Jennifer Westwood. *The Atlas of Legendary Places*. New York: Weidenfeld & Nicholson, 1989.

Howatson, M. C., ed. *The Oxford Companion to Classical Literature*. Oxford: Oxford University Press, 1989.

Osborn, Kevin, and Dana L. Burgess. *The Complete Idiot's Guide to Classical Mythology*. 2nd ed. New York: Alpha, 2004.

Reid, Jane Davidson. *The Oxford Guide to Classical Mythology in the Arts, 1300–1990s*. New York: Oxford University Press, 1995.

Smith, William, ed. *Dictionary of Greek and Roman Geography*. London: Murray, 1873.

Smith, William, ed. *A Smaller Classical Dictionary*. New York: American Book Company, 1852.

TRANSLATIONS AND BIBLIOGRAPHY

Travel Guides Used in the Preparation of This Book

Greece

Ellingham, Mark, Marc Dubin, John Fisher, and Natania Jansz. *Greece: The Rough Guide.* London: Rough Guides, 2000.
Greek Survival Guide. London: Collins, 2003.

Italy

Green Guide: Italy. Watford, U.K.: Michelin Travel Publications, 2002.
Let's Go: Italy. New York: St. Martin's Press, 2004.
L'Inglese per chi Viaggia. Milan: DeAgostini, 2002.
Lonely Planet Phrasebooks: Italian. Victoria, Australia: Lonely Planet, 2003.
Michelin Tourist Guide: Rome. Clermont-Ferrand, France, 1997.
Time Out Guide: Rome. London: Penguin Books, 1996.

Tunisia

Morris, Peter, and Daniel Jacobs. *The Rough Guide to Tunisia.* London: Rough Guides, 2001.

Turkey, Corsica, and Malta

Blue Guide Turkey. 2nd ed. New York: Norton, 1995.
Lonely Planet: Mediterranean Europe. 5th ed. Victoria, Australia: Lonely Planet, 1999.

Acknowledgments

THERE ARE SO FEW oracles around these days, and they are so unpredictable, that when setting sail into territories unknown both geographically and intellectually, one turns for assistance to a wide variety of sources, from Athena herself on down to the people snoring next to me on overnight train journeys. To all I offer my deep gratitude, though, of course, I claim all errors within this book as mine alone.

Of the classics professors I spoke with, I thank above all Peter and Rebekah Smith of the University of North Carolina at Chapel Hill. They not only lent me books, translated for me, broke bread with me, and gently steered me, they also both read the book in manuscript form. Mark Sosower of North Carolina State University translated some Greek signage for me. Jonathan Burgess of the University of Toronto discussed Odyssean journeys ancient and modern, and I direct interested readers to his vastly helpful Web page: http://www.chass.utoronto.ca/~jburgess/rop/od.voyage.html.

On my own travels, Vasos Papagapitos of Travel Dynamics generously put me on the *Clelia II*, aboard which Carsten Stehr and the rest of the crew could not have been more helpful. Al Leonard, of the University of Arizona, lectured aboard ship as part of the tour program conducted by the Archaeological Institute of America and was most helpful to me afterward as well—as, of course, was the Learned Gentleman of Forceful Persuasion and the entire group of very friendly passengers, even the General. For great conversation I thank Al and

Bonnie Margulies, Al and Roma Connable, and the rest of the *Ulysses* bus tour group in Dublin, plus Dr. Gian Balsamo of the American University in Cairo, who discussed journeys to the underworld. Professor Klaus Freyberger, of the Istituto Archeologico Germanico di Roma, pointed me in the right direction during a dark time, and Narcy Calamatta became friend and tour guide in Malta. Dieuwke Becker and family kindly ferried me around Pylos. I met uncountable others: vastly helpful innkeepers, restaurateurs, ticket agents, booksellers, guides, captains, rental agents, and above all fellow travelers, to whom I can only send my gratitude and hopes that in their own travels they fare well. Jerry Sherk—mentor, counselor, and onetime all-pro defensive tackle for the Cleveland Browns—kindly taught me about the origin of our modern usage of *mentor*.

This book would never have come about if, after hearing my annoyed commentary on *All Things Considered*, Charlie Broschart had not convinced Matthew Bond to lead a *Ulysses* reading group, and if Matthew had not called me to join it. My gratitude goes to every member of that reading group but especially to Matthew, for both his keen understanding and his friendship.

The manuscript truly benefited from readings by Michael Singer, David Menconi, Ronnie Polaneczky, and my mom, Rachel Lesser, and especially from a vigorous edit by Neil Caudle. Sarah Hodges kindly provided a final read.

My agent, Michelle Tessler, supported this project from the moment she heard about it and has proven much more than mere business partner. Lucinda Bartley at Crown jumped into this book with fresh eyes and a clear heart when to do otherwise would have been easy, and her sensitive edit helped it reach its final form. Also at Crown, senior production editor Patricia Bozza and copy editor Jim Gullickson and designers Laura Duffy and Elina Nudelman expertly turned manuscript to book. Annik Lafarge originally acquired the book, and she's gone but not forgotten.

My wife, June, not only read the manuscript but put up with the considerable privations such an enterprise enforces on those around it; I can't imagine where I'd be without her. Our son, Louie, provides inspiration for, and inspires profound gratitude from, us both. Additional catering by Leigh Menconi.